AWAKENING EARTH

By Duane Elgin

Voluntary Simplicity (1981, revised 1993)
Awakening Earth
Contributor to:
    Beyond Ego: Transpersonal Dimensions in Psychology
    Changing Images of Man

AWAKENING EARTH

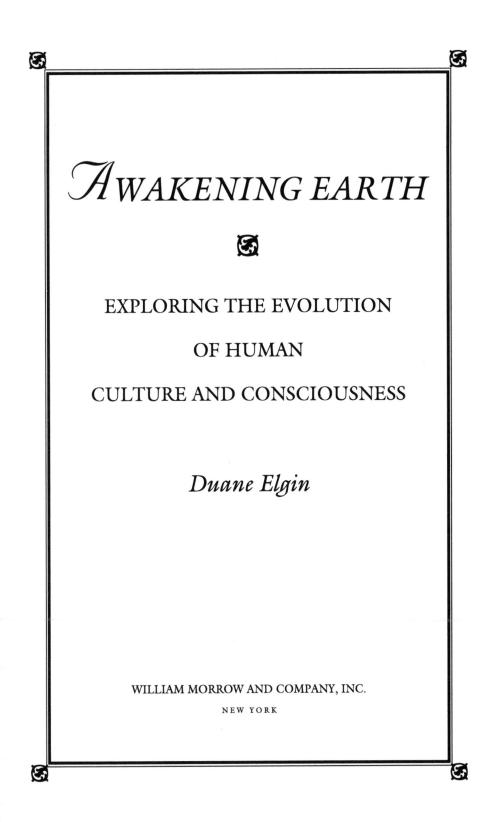

EXPLORING THE EVOLUTION

OF HUMAN

CULTURE AND CONSCIOUSNESS

Duane Elgin

WILLIAM MORROW AND COMPANY, INC.

NEW YORK

It is the policy of William Morrow and Company, Inc., and its imprints and affiliates, recognizing the importance of preserving what has been written, to print the books we publish on acid-free paper, and we exert our best efforts to that end.

Library of Congress Cataloging-in-Publication Data

Elgin, Duane.
   Awakening earth : exploring the dimensions of human evolution / by Duane Elgin.
        p.   cm.
   Includes bibliographical references (p.   ) and index.
   ISBN 0-688-11621-3
   1. Evolution.   2. Cosmology.   3. Philosophical anthropology.
   I. Title.
   B818.E54   1993
   128—dc20   93-10571
                                                    CIP

Printed in the United States of America

First Edition

1 2 3 4 5 6 7 8 9 10

BOOK DESIGN BY PATRICE FODERO

This book is dedicated to the citizens of the Earth
who invest their love and life energy
in building a sustainable, compassionate, and creative
planetary civilization.

$\mathcal{A}$CKNOWLEDGMENTS

For a dozen years I worked on this book whenever I could find time on evenings, weekends, and holidays. I anticipated another seven years would be needed to finish it when I received a grant from Mr. Laurance S. Rockefeller that enabled me to devote my full-time efforts to this work. I appreciate the support of Mr. Rockefeller enormously, as completing this "life project" has been one of the most challenging and satisfying experiences of my life. From the start I have appreciated Frances Vaughan for her loving encouragement and enthusiasm for seeing this book move into the world. Roxanne and Sidney Lanier provided unwavering encouragement and support which were vital in helping it reach completion. I want to thank Ann Niehaus for her loving support and patient listening as the book took form. Bill Croft was very generous in loaning me his Macintosh computer as well as generous with his time in keeping all the systems running. Bob Shuman was an enthusiastic editor, who supported this book all along its journey to publication. Alan AtKisson provided important feedback as this book was reaching completion, and to this task he brought the poetic ear of a musician, the discriminating intellect of a grammarian, and the compassionate consciousness of a world citizen. A number of other persons gave helpful feedback on this challenging manuscript; their responses were important for bringing greater clarity and perspective to this wide-ranging work. In particular I want to thank: Carolyn Anderson, Eleanor Anderson, Fr. Bruno Barnhart, Ted Becker, Sue Cliff, Georg Feuerstein, Bill Graves, Willis Harman, Peter and Trudy Johnson-Lenz, Bill Keepin, JoAnn McAllister, Pat Hopkins, Vicki Robin, Brian Swimme, and Drew Weeks. Hooshang Yashar developed many of the graphics with a commitment and patience that went beyond the call of duty. Finally I want to express my appreciation for other persons who have supported this work or touched my life and in important ways (perhaps unknowingly) have enriched this book: my parents and three sons (Cliff, Ben, and Matt); Sherry Anderson; Fr. Dan Berrigan; Bob Bushnell, Jr.; Joseph Campbell; Carolyn Corlett; Ram Dass; Scott Elrod; Foster Gamble; Joseph Goldstein; Jack Kornfield; Gary Lapid; Coleen LeDrew; Dana Meadows; Bill Moyers; Michael Murphy; Hal Puthoff; Marie Spengler; Russell Targ; Tarthang Tulku; Mary Thomas; Tom Thomas; Pearl Thorson; Sylvia Timbers; the U.V. Family; Roger Walsh; John White; and Ken Wilber.

—DUANE ELGIN
Mill Valley, California
May 3, 1993

CONTENTS

Part I: Stages of Development

Part II: Dimensional Cosmology

Part III: Appendices

$\mathcal{T}$HE CHALLENGE OF PLANETARY CIVILIZATION

We are rapidly approaching one of the great pivot points in the evolution of life on the Earth. The Earth's biosphere is being severely wounded—even crippled—by humanity. Yet through humanity, the Earth is awakening as a conscious global organism. These two facts are intimately related: pushed by the harsh reality of an injured Earth, the human family is being challenged to realize a new level of identity, responsibility, and purpose.

The human family confronts a future of great opportunity and great peril. On the one hand, a communications revolution is sweeping the planet, providing humanity with the tools needed to achieve a dramatic new level of understanding and reconciliation that in turn can support a future of sustainable global development. On the other hand, powerful countervailing trends are also at work—climate change, overpopulation, dwindling reserves of oil, the ruin of rain forests, soil erosion, ozone depletion, and many more. In the next few decades these driving trends will either devastate or transform the economic, cultural, and political fabric of the planet. It is bewildering to see how quickly economic progress has turned into ecological devastation. Yet, with a deteriorating biosphere already stretched past the limits of its ability to carry the burden of humanity, the views and values that have served us so well in the past must now be considered freshly.

If the Earth is to awaken in good health, then we need to stand back, look at the larger sweep of human evolution, and ask ourselves basic questions: Who are we? What are we doing here? What is the nature and purpose of human evolution? Where do we go from here as a species? Are we destined to wander blindly into the future, or are there major stages along the way that we can anticipate? Is the universe coldly indifferent to our struggles, sufferings, and joys—or is it compassionately noninterfering?

Although answers to these questions must be conjectural, there is a story of human evolution emerging from the enduring wisdom of the world's spiritual traditions as well as from new insights in science that suggest we are involved in a highly purposeful process of development. Just as there are recognizable stages in the movement of an individual from infancy to early adulthood, so, too, do there seem to be stages of learning that describe our maturation as a species. As told in this book, humanity's story has seven distinct chapters that describe our evolution from awakening hunter-gatherers to our initial maturity as a planetary-scale civilization. In my view *humanity is roughly halfway through seven stages of development that must be realized if we are to become a planetary civilization that is able both to maintain itself and to surpass itself into the distant future.* Describing these stages of development, and the cosmology that underlies them, are the two major objectives of this book.

Discovering the story of our evolutionary journey is vital. Confronted with a global crisis and lacking a vision of a sustainable future, we can lose confidence in ourselves, our leaders, and our institutions. A disoriented world civilization faced with dwindling resources, mounting pollution, and growing population is a recipe for ecological collapse, social anarchy, religious fanaticism, and authoritarian domination. We need to get our bearings for the journey ahead if we are to move swiftly toward our early adulthood as a planetary civilization.

SUSTAINABILITY—AND BEYOND

To be sustainable, a civilization must maintain the integrity of the physical, social, and spiritual foundations upon which it is established. To seek only to survive—to do no more than simply exist—is not a sufficient foundation for long-term sustainability. An insight from Simone de Beauvoir clarifies our challenge: "Life is occupied in both perpetuating itself and in surpassing itself; if all it does is maintain itself, then living is only not dying." *If we do no more than work for a sustainable future, then we are in danger of creating a world in which living is little more than "only not dying."* To engage our enthusiasm for evolution, we must look beyond sheer survival—we need a compelling sense of purpose and potential for living together as a world civilization.

If industrial societies are to turn away from materialism and commercialism as organizing values, then other values and purposes are needed that are at least as compelling. The survival and integrity of our biosphere, the quality of life for our children and friends, and the coevolution of culture and consciousness—these are life purposes that offer a powerful alternative to those of the industrial era. There is growing evidence that a substantial majority of the human family would support this shift in life orientation. For example, a Gallup poll for the first "Earth Summit" in 1992 surveyed people in twenty-two diverse nations around the planet and found that in all but three a majority is "increasingly worried about the global environment and gives its protection priority over economic growth."[1] For a majority of humans, representing a wide range of income levels, to place the well-being of the Earth ahead of their personal economic concerns shows that a dramatic shift in values and priorities is taking place around the world.

Although humanity is expressing growing concern for protecting the Earth's environment, we do not yet have a shared vision of how to build an advanced, global civilization while simultaneously restoring the health of the biosphere. We do not have a vision of the future that is sufficiently realistic, comprehensive, and compelling to be able to coalesce the enthusiasm of the human family into a process of sustainable and surpassing development. We have economic forecasts, but these are bloodless projections that do not inspire civilizations to reach new heights. We have projections for single issues—the prospects for the rain forests, AIDS, education, health care, and so on—but we don't have comprehensive visions of the whole planetary system that portray how humanity can live together successfully. We have technological forecasts—trends for computers, cars, air travel, nuclear technology, and so forth—but we have few integrative views that combine technology, psychology, spirituality, and sociology into persuasive scenarios of a diverse, creative, and sustainable future.

When we can collectively envision a sustainable and satisfying pathway into the future, then can we begin to construct that future consciously. We need to draw upon our collective wisdom and discover images of the future that awaken our enthusiasm for evolution and mobilize our social energies. By drawing upon the world's growing body of wisdom—in biology, anthropology, history, physics, systems theory, comparative religions, and so on—we can begin to discern the overall direction of human evolution that leads toward our maturity as a planetary civilization. With a clear vision of a positive future we can proceed with confidence on our evolutionary journey.

If humanity is successful in building an enduring civilization on the Earth, then it will come from the synergy of the collective experience and wisdom of the entire human family—the entire *species*. The world has become so interdependent that we must make it together, transcending differences of race, ethnicity, geography, religion, politics, and gender. It is the human *species* that is devastating the planet and it is the entire *species* that must learn to live together as a civilized and mutually supportive community. To focus on the development of civility among the human species is not to inflate unduly the importance of humanity within the ecosystem of life on Earth; rather it is to recognize how dangerous the human race is to the viability of the Earth's ecosystem. Humanity must begin consciously to develop a planetary-scale, *species-civilization* that is able to live in a harmonious relationship with the rest of the web of life.

A New Paradigm for Evolution

Two views of evolution—materialism and transcendentalism—are dominant in the world today; but a third view is emerging that integrates them both into a coevolutionary perspective. All three paradigms involve assumptions regarding not only our material and biological nature but also our consciousness and spiritual nature.

1. **Materialist View**—In this view, prominent in Western industrial societies, matter is considered the primary reality. Consciousness is secondary and is thought to emerge with high levels of complexity in the organization of brain matter. As the astronomer Carl Sagan writes, "My fundamental premise about the brain is that its workings—what we sometimes call 'mind'—are a consequence of its anatomy and physiology, and nothing more."[2] Philosopher Daniel Dennett compares human consciousness to a "virtual machine," a sort of computer software program that shapes the activities of the hardware system, the brain.[3] The materialistic paradigm views evolutionary progress in terms of material achievements in science, architecture, art, literature, and so on.

2. **Transcendentalist View**—In this view, prominent among many ancient Eastern religions and contemporary "new age" spiritual movements, consciousness is believed to be the primary reality and matter is secondary. The material world is seen as being constructed from consciousness, so undue attention to material things represents a distraction from, and a substitute for, the unfolding of consciousness. Evolutionary progress is a journey of transcendence that moves from matter to body to mind to soul to spirit.[4]

3. **Coevolutionary View**—In this emerging view, which integrates East and West, reality is seen as being comprised equally of matter and consciousness, which are in turn assumed to be continuously regenerated by the more fundamen-

tal reality—an infinitely deep Life-force that is called here the "Meta-universe." The evolutionary journey involves the synergistic development and refinement of both the material and the consciousness aspects of life.[5] With their coevolution we ultimately discover that we are identical with the vast and subtle Life-force from which everything continuously arises.

Each view of evolution has a dramatically different social expression. The **materialistic** paradigm emphasizes material growth and worldly expressions of significance, status, and power. The **transcendentalist** paradigm emphasizes rising above the material world with its seeming distractions and substitutions for the perfect peace of ultimate transcendence. The **coevolutionary** paradigm integrates the material and consciousness aspects of life into a mutually supportive spiral of development that can produce a sustainable, planetary civilization and a global "wisdom culture."

Basic to the coevolutionary paradigm is the idea that, moment by moment, the entire cosmos is being regenerated by an infinite field of Life-energy that is called here the **Meta-universe**. The Meta-universe is assumed to have been present before the Big Bang and is the generative ground out of which our universe (including the fabric of space-time) emerges in a flow of continuous creation. The Meta-universe thus infuses, underlies, and transcends our cosmos.* As a further note of definition, I will use the term *universe* to refer to the still-expanding system that emerged roughly fifteen billion years ago with the Big Bang. Although I will use the term *cosmos* to refer to the same system as the "universe," I often use that word to communicate an extra measure of appreciation for the aesthetic structure and purposeful harmony evident in the design of the universe.

We need to return to these basics of definition because the old approaches are no longer working *in isolation* from one another. For the past several thousand years the materialistic view has been dominant in the West and the transcendentalist view has been dominant in the East. Our time of planetary crisis demonstrates that both views

---

*An expanded description of the important concept of a Meta-universe is presented on pages 126–129 and 296–298.

have exhausted their evolutionary potential in isolation from each other. We need to move into a new era of coevolutionary development that integrates them into an organic whole. The West has pursued external, material growth without a balanced regard for the interior human potentials, and the result has too often been a life-denying and self-serving social order that is exhausting its vitality and sense of direction. The East has pursued the evolution of internal consciousness without a balanced regard for the exterior human potentials of material and social growth, and the result is that the development of consciousness has too often become a spiritual escape for the few, leaving many locked in a struggle for sheer survival. Where the West has concentrated on the finite and the momentary, the East has concentrated on the infinite and the eternal. The Eastern approach has been world-denying in its excessively transcendental orientation, while the Western approach has been world-destroying in its excessively materialistic orientation.

To achieve a balanced and sustainable way of living, each perspective requires the participation of the other.[6] Only if they are joined together can they reach beyond themselves to a new, unifying paradigm, involving neither the material passivity of the transcendentalist perspective nor the all-consuming worldly obsession of the materialist perspective. A coevolutionary perspective fosters entirely new dimensions of development. If the human family rises to this integrative challenge, we will embark on a breathtaking evolutionary journey—one that would not have been possible, and could not have been imagined, by either perspective working in isolation. The energy and creativity released by combining a balanced concern for the material and consciousness aspects of life are not simply additive, they are synergistic. In the partnership of the material and consciousness dimensions are the seeds of a new era of human growth that we have only scarcely begun to envision and explore. A coevolutionary perspective reveals an elevated pattern and purpose to human evolution that can guide us toward a future bursting with creative possibility.

KNOWING THAT WE KNOW, OR HUMANITY'S DOUBLE-WISDOM

We can get a clearer sense of direction for humanity's evolutionary journey by considering the scientific name we have given to ourselves as a species: *Homo sapiens sapiens.*[7] We are accustomed to the phrase *Homo sapiens,* but our full designation is *Homo **sapiens sapiens.*** To be "sapient" is to be wise or knowing. We humans describe ourselves as being more than *sapient* or wise, we are ***sapient sapient*** and have the unique potential of becoming "doubly wise" or "doubly knowing."[8] It has often been remarked that where animals "know," only humans "know that they know." *Our highest potential as a species is our ability to achieve full self-reflective consciousness or "knowing that we know."* As humanity develops its capacity for reflexive consciousness, it enables the universe to achieve self-referencing knowing of itself. Through humanity's awakening, the universe acquires the ability to look back and reflect upon itself—in wonder, awe, and appreciation.

Development of our capacity for reflective knowing is a complex and multifaceted process. We are moving through a series of stages, each of which draws out different aspects of this potential. As we develop our capacity for reflective knowing, we acquire new levels of mastery in our personal and social evolution—for example, an enhanced capacity for self-determination, reconciliation, cooperation, and creativity. With reflective knowing comes a double-registering of experience and the ability to assess the appropriateness of our actions against the guide of our own knowing. With reflective consciousness we become self-directing agents of our own evolution.

Reflective consciousness is basic to social as well as to personal evolution. For example, in a democracy when we are informed as individual citizens, then we "know." However, when we communicate among ourselves as citizens—publicly learning about and affirming our collective sentiments as an extended community—then we "know that we know." In our dangerous and difficult time of transition, it is not sufficient for civilizations to be wise—we must become doubly wise through social communication that clearly reveals our collective knowing to ourselves. To do this, we need to consciously use our mass media for vigorous public learning and dialogue regarding the critical choices for our future. Developing our capacity for reflective consciousness—both personally and socially—is a paramount evolutionary challenge.

STEPS TO OUR INITIAL MATURITY AS A PLANETARY CIVILIZATION

The following chapters focus on the stages of development involved in the unfolding of human culture and consciousness. But first it will be helpful to gain some perspective by summarizing the broad outlines of human history thus far. For roughly two million years our ancestors struggled in the twilight of self-recognition and self-discovery. Then, sometime during the rugged conditions of the last great ice age—roughly 35,000 years ago—physically modern humans broke free from the limited consciousness of the animal kingdom. With this initial awakening we entered an epoch of growth lasting nearly 25,000 years, during which time we developed sophisticated language, art, trading networks, musical instruments, and new tools of stone, wood, and bone. Then, roughly 10,000 years ago, we began another momentous transition by gradually shifting from the nomadic life of gathering and hunting to a settled life in small villages that relied upon a subsistence agriculture for survival. A peaceful and simple village life endured for thousands of years when, with surprising abruptness, the world's first large cities arose roughly 5,500 years ago. With the blossoming of agrarian-based civilizations, a new level of drive and dynamism entered the world. Humanity's evolutionary journey moved out of immersion within nature and began to take on a character that was uniquely human. Major civilizations emerged in Mesopotamia, India, China, and the Americas. For nearly 5,000 years these agrarian-based civilizations matured, generating the bulk of recorded human history. The next momentous leap forward began roughly 300 years ago, when a revolution in science and technology propelled a portion of humanity into the urban-industrial era. The gradual pace of urbanization and material development was transformed into an explosion of technological progress—moving forward with such ferocity and speed that it now threatens to devastate the entire biosphere of the planet.

If we stand back from these immensely complex historical dynamics, there seems to be a relatively simple process of development under way that involves three major phases in the evolution of culture and consciousness. The first phase lasts for several million years and is the time when our humanlike ancestors lived without any appreciable degree of self-recognition or reflective consciousness. The second phase began roughly 35,000 years ago when humanity became decisively self-aware and we moved into an era of rapid development. Since then we have been working through a series of developmental stages, increasing our capacity for reflective consciousness and building corresponding forms of civilization. Looking ahead, when we develop the full spectrum of capacities associated with reflective consciousness, we will then move into a third phase of "postreflective consciousness," or integral awareness with the wisdom essential for sustaining ourselves into the distant future. Figure 1 depicts these three major phases of evolution.

Humanity appears to be working its way through a relatively brief but critical phase of development. Millions of years were required to get to this transitional phase of evolution, and if we are successful in realizing its potentials, millions of years can follow. Hopefully the intermediate phase described in this book will be little more than a scratch on humanity's evolutionary calendar.

To fully coevolve our capacity for self-referencing consciousness along with a supportive planetary culture, I believe that humanity must work through seven major stages of development. Described simply, these are:

- **Era of Awakening Hunter-Gatherers**—Roughly 35,000 years ago humanity awakened with a distinct capacity for self-reflective consciousness. Nonetheless perceptions were extremely limited,

Figure 1: Three Major Phases of Human Evolution

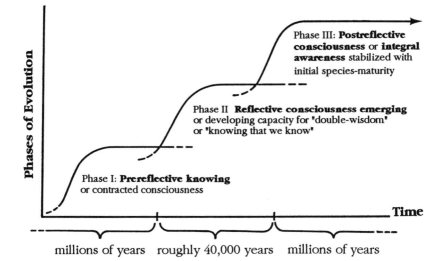

Phase III: **Postreflective consciousness** or **integral awareness** stabilized with initial species-maturity

Phase II **Reflective consciousness emerging** or developing capacity for "double-wisdom" or "knowing that we know"

Phase I: **Prereflective knowing** or contracted consciousness

Time

millions of years   roughly 40,000 years   millions of years

social organization was on a tribal scale, and life was centered around a gathering and hunting existence. Nature was viewed as intensely alive and filled with mysterious forces.

- **Era of Agrarian-Based Civilizations**—Roughly 10,000 years ago human perception expanded to include a new sense of time—a wheel of existence that embraced nature's seasons and cycles—and a farming consciousness emerged. With the development of systematic agriculture and a food surplus, the world's first great cities began to appear around 3,500 B.C. and developed all the basic arts of civilization (for example, writing, division of labor, a priestly class, religion, city-state governments, and massive architecture).

- **Scientific-Industrial Era**—By the 1700s in Europe nature's mystery and magic were giving way to impersonal science and the analyzing intellect. A progressing time sense coupled with a materialistic view of reality fostered an unprecedented emphasis on material progress. Technical innovation brought with it the rise of mass production, the extreme division of labor, the development of massive urban centers, and the rise of strong nation-states.

- **Communications and Reconciliation Era**—Given the pervasiveness of television, computers, and satellite systems around the planet, people in both agrarian and industrial societies are being swept up in the communications revolution. The opportunity for global communication provided by these new technologies is arriving just in time to allow the human family to enter into serious dialogue about how to cope with the intertwined system of problems that threaten our collective future. With communication we can discover a shared vision of a sustainable future. With reconciliation we can build the trust and sense of human community that will be essential for creating a future of mutually supportive development.

- **Bonding and Building Era**—After reconciliation comes building. In working together to translate the vision of a sustainable future into tangible reality, humanity will naturally develop a strong sense of community, compassion, and deep bonding. Cross-cultural learning and planetary celebrations will flourish. People will also feel a new depth of connection with nature and will work to restore the integrity of the global environment.

- **Surpassing Era**—With the sustainability of the planet assured, a new level of human creativity will be liberated. Planetary civilization will move beyond a concern for maintaining itself to a concern for surpassing itself. This will be an era of explosive growth as the creativity of billions of persons is set free. Given the creative tumult, the strong bonding achieved in the previous epoch will be essential to keep the world from swirling out of control and tearing itself apart. Humanity will learn to balance the drive for creative diversity with the need for sustainable unity.

- **Initial Maturity as a Planetary Civilization**—In reaching this stage, humanity will have acquired sufficient perspective, wisdom, creativity, and compassion necessary to sustain itself into the distant future. This stage represents both the completion of a long process of development and the foundation for a new beginning, perhaps to participate in a community of life of galactic scale.

In the briefest of terms, here is the story of humanity's evolution that is described in the following chapters: *In the three beginning stages of awakening, we separate ourselves from nature, develop our sense of autonomy as a species, and discover our abilities for rebuilding the world in accord with our designs. In the following three stages, we reintegrate ourselves with nature, explore our deep bonding with one another and with the cosmos, and develop our capacity to act in conscious harmony with the universe.* This is not a linear view of development; rather, it portrays a complex cycle of separation and return that leads to our initial maturity as a species.

Whether we are successful in filling out these evolutionary stages or whether we get off track and move into a dark age of stagnation and collapse will depend on the choices we now make freely. Our evolution is similar to a seven-stage rocket: Each of the booster stages must work properly if we are to be successful in launching a sustainable species-civilization. If any one of the stages fails, the evolutionary dynamic can veer off into stagnation or collapse. Figure 2 summarizes these dynamics of growth and portrays the optimal path for launching a planetary civilization.

Figure 2: Seven Major Stages for Launching a Mature Species-Civilization

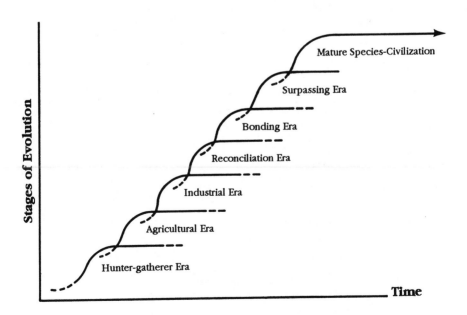

Arnold Toynbee spent a lifetime examining the emergence and decline of civilizations throughout history and described civilization as "a movement and not a condition, a voyage and not a harbour."[9] He also noted that the people and events that make good headlines tend to float on the surface of the stream of life, whereas it is the deeper changes, working below the surface of popular culture, that ultimately make history.[10] Consistent with Toynbee's insight, the seven stages of development described above are assumed to be the organizing paradigms that live beneath the surface of popular culture and whose potentials we are working to realize. While this approach bleaches out much of the complexity and richness found in the rise and fall of individual civilizations, it will reveal more clearly the step-by-step advance of culture and consciousness as we work to become a doubly-wise species-civilization. *At the core of our history as a species is the story of our movement through a series of perceptual paradigms as we work to achieve our initial maturity as a self-reflective and self-organizing planetary civilization.*

SACRED GEOMETRY AND THE STAGES OF DEVELOPMENT

At the heart of this book is a simple description of reality based upon fundamental principles of order and form—in other words, geometry. I believe that an invisible geometry permeates the universe and provides a structural foundation for all existence, both physical and perceptual: The same geometry that structures physical space also structures psychological or perceptual space. This geometry is the unseen organizing framework within which and through which all life evolves. As the underlying matrix for all existence and evolution, it seems appropriate to call this pervasive and supportive geometry sacred.

The concept of dimensions is fundamental to this book. To me a dimension is far more than a dry mathematical concept or simple, empty space. Dimensions are akin to the deep genetic code of the cosmos—they provide the organizing structure for material reality as it moves through countless billions of years of evolution. Nearly four hundred years ago the renowned mathematician and physicist Johannes Kepler made this penetrating observation: "Geometry existed before the Creation. It is co-eternal with the mind of God. . . . Geometry provided God with a model for the Creation. . . . Geometry is God Himself."[11] *There is no reality without dimensionality.* The miracle that anything exists at all depends upon dimensions to provide the context within which things—including the fabric of space and time—can become manifest. We exist within an invisible ocean of dimensional structure. An invisible organizing geometry provides not only a supportive architecture for our cosmos but also a nested series of learning environments within which and through which evolution unfolds.

Normally we view geometric dimensions as little more than lifeless mathematical concepts that have nothing to do with the richness of everyday life and the complexities of evolution. However, our universe appears to be a living organism of immensely intelligent design that is able to perform multiple functions simultaneously. *The same dimensional geometry that structures physical reality also structures our perceptions, creating the environments that both people and civilizations move through in a learning process.* Although the universe comes with no explicit "operating manual," we do not need one, as the fabric of reality has embedded within it the evolutionary insights that we seek.

While "dimensional evolution" can be viewed metaphorically, I believe each new stage in human civilization is accompanied by a literal change in dimensional perspective and experience. For example, the transition from a hunter-gatherer society to a farming society occurred because people shifted from seeing reality as a flat world of two dimensions to seeing reality as a depth world of three dimensions. In other words, by experiencing and then acting from a three-dimensional view of reality, we created the agricultural revolution. In a similar way, by experiencing and acting from a four-dimensional context we are making the transition from static, farming societies to dynamic, industrial societies. Whether viewed metaphorically or literally, if we can discern the broad outlines of the dimensional structure through which we are evolving, we can then make useful inferences about the basic evolutionary challenges and opportunities we will face in the future.

Each new dimension seems exquisitely designed to call forth new potentials from us. As we perceive the possibilities inherent in a new dimension, we begin to actualize them. Said another way, each new dimension provides a unique "opportunity space" or learning context for people and societies to fill out with their actions. The dimensional nature of reality is like a nested set of Chinese boxes: Each new dimension embodies an enlarged frame of reference within which are nested all previous dimensions.

The next eight chapters describe how each new dimension embodies a distinctive framework for perception that draws out characteristic patterns of creative expression. Dimensions are therefore invisible receptacles that enlarge the experienced scope of our lives by introducing entirely new domains of action and learning. With every added dimension, new capacities are revealed, new perspectives are introduced, and new goals become apparent that challenge our creativity. A dimension is a perceptual paradigm that structures our way of understanding, thinking, and acting. When we first enter a new perceptual paradigm (such as the agrarian era or the industrial era), we experience great freedom and creative opportunity. However, as we fulfill the potentials of a given paradigm, it eventually becomes a constricting framework whose partial nature leads to a crisis in human affairs. This crisis in turn leads to a breakthrough into the next more spacious perceptual context, and a new level of learning and creative expression is drawn out.

Freedom is fundamental to this cosmology. The sacred geometry that infuses the universe does not interfere with the choices we make, but instead maintains all that exists with unwavering equanimity. *Our future is not predetermined.* Within broad limits of human psychology and planetary ecology, we can fill out these stages of development in whatever way and with whatever timing we choose. Although the dimensional pattern does not determine how we will respond, it does create a series of powerful and resilient contexts within which—and through which—evolution unfolds. It is up to us to determine how we will fill out this sequence of evolutionary environments. Just as individuals choose their unique pathway to adulthood, so, too, will the human family choose its unique pathway to maturity.

While the immense problems faced by humanity make the short-term future look bleak and distressing, I am confident in our long-run evolutionary capacity as a species. Humanity does have the ability to communicate its way through these challenging times and to build a future of mutually supportive development. It is heartening to see that we have already begun the process of building a shared consciousness among the human family regarding our responsibility toward the rest of life on the Earth. With environmental "Earth Days," the "Earth Summit," and global TV events such as "Live Aid for Africa," humanity has begun to establish a collective consciousness and species-memory. A global culture is now being born. We have already begun to create the first glimmerings of a conscious, planetary civilization. The Earth is awakening.

ABOUT THE REST OF THIS BOOK

The remainder of this book will explore the critical, transitional phase in the evolutionary life cycle of humanity—the phase that extends from where humans first awaken at a tribal scale to where we first establish ourselves as a planetary-scale civilization that is able to endure into the distant future. To facilitate the reader's journey, this book is divided into two major sections. The first section consists of nine chapters that present the story of human evolution from our initial awakening to our initial maturity as a planetary civilization. To make this story more readable, descriptions of the underlying theory of "dimensional evolution" have been kept to a minimum. The core concepts and cosmology that provide the underpinnings for this theory of the coevolution of culture and consciousness are presented in the second section.

Incontrovertible, scientific "proof" does not exist to validate the cosmology that underlies this book. This theory extends beyond the dimensional boundaries of most current science and consequently cannot be proven by that science alone.[12] Nonetheless this theory is not arbitrary—it draws upon knowledge from a wide range of disciplines and is based upon a straightforward logic that is described at length in the last four chapters of the book. This evolutionary pattern is also highly congruent with Western psychology and the perennial wisdom of the world's spiritual traditions; and these correlations are described in the first appendix. Although the details of this book are the product of twenty years of broad-ranging research, the organizing pattern was a gift from the universe that emerged as the culmination of half a year of self-directed meditation. The meditative origins of this cosmology are described in the second appendix.

To know where we are going, it is useful to know from where we have come. We begin this story of human evolution by reaching into the distant past and describing stages of perceptual and cultural development through which much of humanity has already progressed. In seeing how human perceptions have already gone through three major transformations—each time radically changing our understanding of nature, the cosmos, and ourselves—we can more readily anticipate the changes that will accompany future evolutionary transformations. (If an historical perspective is not of interest, the reader can jump directly to the modern era and the challenge of global reconciliation—Chapters 4 and 5.) We turn, then, to the phase of humanity's evolution that leads from our initial awakening as a species to our initial maturity as a planetary-scale civilization.

PART I

STAGES OF DEVELOPMENT

CONTRACTED CONSCIOUSNESS
AND THE ARCHAIC ERA

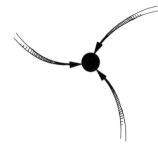

The **first dimension** is the stage of embedded or *contracted consciousness*. It is symbolized by a black hole that allows nothing to escape, not even light. Analogously, in this stage the light of reflective knowing is drawn inward by the gravitational pull of deep unconsciousness. A prereflective consciousness was characteristic of our earliest human ancestors, who were largely running on automatic—relying primarily on instinct and habit. Their way of life remained virtually unchanged over thousands of generations. Some degree of reflective consciousness must have begun to awaken more than a million years ago when *Homo erectus* migrated out of Africa and, to cope with the harsh ice-age climate, learned to make warm clothing, construct shelters, and control the use of fire. Nonetheless it is only with the evidence of burials, dating from roughly 60,000 years ago, that we find a clear recognition of death and, presumably, conscious reflection on the "self" that lives.

CONTRACTED CONSCIOUSNESS AND THE ARCHAIC ERA

Because our everyday experience of life seems so natural and we take it so much for granted, it is nearly impossible to imagine the perceptual experience of our early ancestors who, several million years ago, struggled for survival. Nonetheless we can conduct an experiment in our imagination—an experiment in unlearning—to give us a taste of the life experience of our early human predecessors. We begin our journey by setting aside modern consciousness and squeezing ourselves into the barely awakening reflective consciousness of our distant relatives. To accomplish this challenging feat of forgetting, imagine doing the following:

- Take all of the chairs, tables, beds, couches, lamps, and other furniture out of your house.
- Get rid of all of your kitchen utensils and appliances. From now on, you'll be doing your cooking directly over a fire, forgoing even the use of clay pots. Each day eat only the berries and roots you gather—and the animals you hunt down.

- Abandon all of your fabric clothes. Sew a set of animal skins onto your body for wearing throughout the winter months. In the summer you may simply choose to do without.

- Get rid of your bathroom, toilet paper, shower, soap, shampoo, toothpaste, and toothbrush. Become accustomed to strong bodily smells as a permeating fact of life.

- Say good-bye to your apartment or house. Use a skin-covered tent as the primary shelter for the several families with whom you live. Then move away from the city or suburbs and into the country-side. Get used to tribal-scale living—for the rest of your life, roughly twenty-five close relatives will comprise your primary community. Once or twice a year you may attend gatherings with several hundred persons where you may trade a few stone tools, hunt as a community, and find a mate.

- Eliminate your television set, radio, newspaper, books, and maga-zines. Charadelike stories told about the animals, plants, and the two dozen people around you is now your news and entertain-ment.

- Forget the vast majority of your language—pare your vocabulary down to a few dozen basic nouns and a handful of verbs. Learn to use facial expressions and bodily gestures to convey much of your meaning.

- Drastically shrink the scope of your world. Forget any concept of "the Earth" or "the cosmos"—the distance you can walk within several days is your entire arena of knowledge and concern.

- Because you move regularly, get rid of any possessions that weigh you down or slow you down. Take with you only what you can easily carry.

- If you are injured or sick or you have a toothache, just ignore the pain. There are no doctors, no dentists, no antibiotics, no aspirin, and no anesthetics.

- Subtract thirty to forty years from your life expectancy. If you live to be forty, you are a fortunate elder. Expect at least half of your children to die before the age of six.

- Forget all that you know about gardening. Obtain most of your food through the efforts of women, who forage for wild nuts, berries, and fruits. A much smaller proportion of food comes from men, who hunt for animals.

- Forget all of the animals that you have domesticated—dogs, cats, cows, goats, sheep, and horses. You are alone in the world.

- Except for brief moments of insight, disregard your ability to stand back and observe yourself. Everything that happens is up close and immediate.

- Forget most of your ability to think things through. You have not yet developed the ability to analyze and plan beyond the most rudimentary level.

- Drop all expectations of material progress or improving your standard of living. Technologically you have no more than a few stone tools—and these you manufacture on the spot as you need them.

- Put aside any sophisticated emotions, such as romantic love. You do not have a sufficiently distinct sense of yourself and others to support such feelings.

- Ignore yourself except for your bodily impulses and instincts. When you are hungry, look for food; when you are sexually aroused, look for sexual gratification.

- Exclude an extended past or future from your awareness. All that is significant is happening *now*. Do not plan ahead beyond the next day or two. Forget your knowledge of the regular migration of animals, birds, and fish. Also forget your knowledge of the cycles of nature. Each new season and each new moon is a miracle.

- Exclude art from your life. You have no shell necklaces, no carvings, and no painting to express your aesthetic sentiments. Also forget music. There are only the sounds of nature, the occasional human voice—and silence.

- Omit all you know about science and a lawful universe. Everything that happens is the result of invisible and unknown forces.

- Don't dwell on death. Your experience of loss and grief lasts only for a few hours and then passes into the forgetfulness of present-centered demands. You live a largely unexamined existence and feel only a vague sense of anything—or anyone—that is absent.

- Don't worry about the meaning of life. In fact don't think about "meaning," because it is not a meaningful concept. Existence is an unquestioned fact to be taken for granted.

Only when we have done all of this—and have contracted our reflective consciousness to a virtual point—can we begin to approximate the life experience of the archaic hunter-gatherer. Of course we cannot truly forget all these aspects of life, but this experiment reveals how much learning and development we have already realized and now take for granted. For all the shortcomings and problems of our era, it is clear that humanity has already traveled an enormous evolutionary distance toward the goal of becoming a consciously self-referencing and self-organizing species—a species that is sufficiently self-aware to choose consciously what we want to become.

THE DAWN OF REFLECTIVE CONSCIOUSNESS

The origins of reflective consciousness are so ancient that we can only speculate on when our capacity for double-wisdom truly began to emerge. Research shows that chimpanzees (our closest animal relative, with whom we share 98 percent of our genes) can hold grudges, nurse resentments, form strong family ties, and experience grief over the loss of a loved one.[1] Research also indicates that chimps have the ability to learn simple mathematical skills and to recognize themselves in a mirror.[2] Because our earliest human ancestors, *Australopithecus africanus*—the "southern ape of Africa" who lived roughly three million years ago—had larger brains than chimps, it seems likely that they had a capacity for self-recognition that was at least comparable to modern-day chimpanzees. If so, the dawn of reflective consciousness extends back more than three million years!

Given that *Australopithecus africanus* had some capacity for self-recognition (as well as deliberate communication, a limited ability to look ahead and plan for a hunt, some ability for mental abstraction in order to build and use stone tools, and some degree of differentiation of self from the environment), it seems plausible that the potential for a modern human consciousness was a latent waiting to unfold to its contemporary level of complexity. In short, the seed potentials for the full awakening of reflective consciousness have existed within the human organism for millions of years. These abilities were not recently added to our biogenetic repertoire; rather, we arrived as protohumans with these potentials built in—they had only to be activated for them to unfold. If this is true of our past, then it is likely to be true of our future: We are already preengineered for successful evolution to the highest levels of reflective consciousness (a view of evolution that assumes that a high degree of design-intelligence is embodied throughout the processes and structures of the universe).

The capacity for self-recognition emerged and stabilized ever so gradually over these millions of years, and it was not until about 35,000 years ago that a critical threshold in consciousness was reached. The capacity for fleeting self-recognition characteristic of the first stage should not be equated with the stabilized "I-sense" that emerged in later stages and that enabled individuals to reflect upon themselves and to act with some degree of conscious deliberation. There is an enormous psychic and evolutionary distance between the capacity for momentary self-recognition and a steady mirroring capacity that we can consciously bring to bear in organizing our lives. Before exploring the millions of years of historical evolution leading up to biologically modern humans, it is useful to consider the perceptual geometry of the first dimension with its highly contracted consciousness.

THE FIRST DIMENSION: CONTRACTED CONSCIOUSNESS

Self-reflective consciousness requires some degree of separation between consciousness and the self. There must be some distance or space between knowing and the object of knowing, between observer and observed. In most animals there is knowing, but there is not the ability to stand apart from the knowing process. When there is no separation between observer and observed, self-referencing consciousness remains contracted into a single point. With knowing so compressed, there is not the perceptual distance to stand back from, to reflect on, and be conscious of one's existence for more than a brief moment at a time. The first dimension, then, corresponds to the life experience of our earliest human ancestors. Except for brief moments of intense, primal knowing, there was only a vague recognition of a distinct self that was separate from the rest of nature. Most of the time our earliest ancestors were running on automatic, with their faculties for sensing, feeling, and thinking working in accord with biological givens and unquestioned social habits.

In the first dimension, existence was monotonous, muted, and nearly invisible to itself. With almost no ability to stand back from immediate existence and see the self as an independent entity that could operate on nature, the ability to build tools and to achieve mastery over the natural environment was extremely limited. With a highly restricted capacity for self-perception, only biological ties provided a strong source of kinship and social connection. A restricted, tribal clan probably marked the limits of one's sense of personal empathy and affiliation. Because feelings such as love, guilt, and hope require some degree of double-knowing, which enables us to acknowledge to ourselves that this is what we are experiencing, the range of emotions of our early ancestors must have been severely limited.

OUR ANCIENT ANCESTORS

It seems plausible that, more than three million years ago, *Australopithecus africanus* had already begun the long journey from the dim ember of animal awareness to the steady candle-flame of consciousness characteristic of the initial emergence of reflective knowing in the second dimension. Although there is great uncertainty about the course of evolution, it seems likely that *Australopithecus africanus* evolved into the first being to whom we have given the designation *homo;* hence, the first "human" was *Homo habilis* ("the handy human"). *Homo habilis* lived in Africa from roughly 2.5 million years ago until roughly 1.5 million years ago, walked upright, and had roughly the same level of manual dexterity as do modern people. They made the earliest known stone tools by simply flaking off one side of a cobblestone to form a jagged cutting edge (interestingly, similar tools are made by the contemporary "stone-age" Tasaday tribe in the Philippines).³ On the other hand, their brain was only approximately half the size of that of modern humans, and their larynx was not well developed for supporting speech. (The physical evolution of the human brain over a more than 3-million-year period is shown below.)

Figure 3: Evolution from Early Human Ancestors to the Modern Era

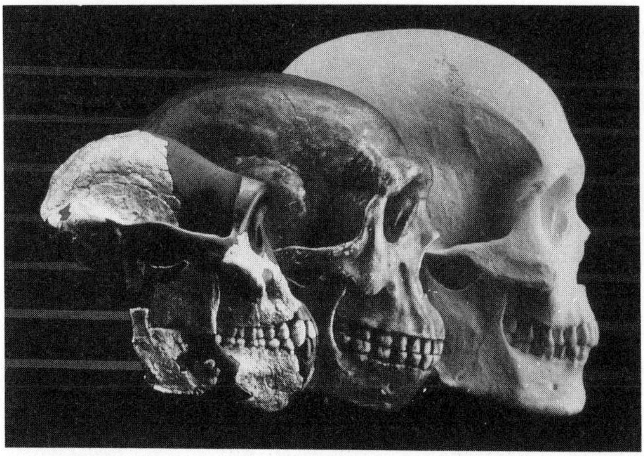

The brain capacity of the three-million-year-old *Australopithecus afarensis* (*far left*) was 400 cubic centimeters whereas *Homo erectus* (which emerged roughly 1.5 million years ago) had an average brain volume of 850 cc., and modern *Homo sapiens* (which arose some 100,000 years ago) has a brain that averages nearly 1,400 cc.

By 1.5 million years ago *Homo habilis* had evolved into *Homo erectus* ("the upright human"). While our *Homo erectus* ancestors had heavy bones and thick muscles, seen from a distance, they would have appeared to be humans, not apes. Only up close would physical differences be clearly evident: jutting brows, a low forehead, and a massive jaw distinguished *erectus* from modern humans. These early ancestors had crude but effective stone tools, and a sense of kinship and family. It was *Homo erectus* that first made the journey from the tropics of Africa into the cooler climates of Europe and Asia. In coping with the ice ages *Homo erectus* learned to develop warm clothing, build tents for shelters, and hunt with a new level of proficiency. Surviving the harsh climates of the ice ages surely placed a premium on intelligence, inventiveness, and social cooperation. By 500,000 years ago *Homo erectus* knew how to control the use of fire, although it would not be until much later that humans would master the art of starting fires. With a brain roughly three-quarters the size of modern humans' and a more developed larynx, *Homo erectus* ancestors were probably capable of a significant degree of communication—perhaps using a mixture of a few words, hand gestures, and facial expressions—which enabled them to hunt cooperatively.

All these developments suggest that a growing degree of reflective consciousness was emerging. Hunting strategies, family interactions, and community migration would have been greatly facilitated by even a rudimentary ability for speech. Still it was not until the emergence of anatomically modern hunter-gatherers, roughly 35,000 years ago, that speech could match contemporary levels of speed and facility. Given anatomical differences, it is estimated that *Homo erectus* communicated much more slowly than modern humans—perhaps with only one-tenth the speed and with a far more limited range of sounds. Nonverbal communication (through gestures and facial expressions) must have played an important role in enabling *Homo erectus* humans to express their meanings and feelings visually.

Although primitive stone tools enabled *Homo erectus* to hunt a wide range of animals, the gathering of plants was probably the primary source of food. The division of labor between the sexes was relatively unique to humans: In general, it is thought that men were responsible for hunting larger animals and protecting against predators, whereas women were responsible for gathering berries, fruits, nuts, roots, and smaller animals (which could comprise as much as three quarters of the average diet). This division of roles was amplified by the need to care for the young, who were born with an undeveloped brain and required considerable attention during the first few years of life. With infants dependent upon the mother, a pattern of mutual dependency emerged: men depended upon women to raise children and gather foods, while women depended on men to go hunting and provide protection from predators. Infants, in turn, depended upon their mothers and the strength of the overall family structure for their security. Tied together into a web of mutual interdependence essential to the survival of all, a distinctive social fabric based upon family and clan was probably emerging more than a million years ago. Because women gathered a majority of food, as well as prepared the food and cared for the infants, it is clear that their role was not secondary to that of men.[4] Cooperation between the sexes and caring for others were traits basic to human survival as well as to the evolution of the species.

With the control of fire, the development of rudimentary communication, and the growing dependence of children, *Homo erectus* began to develop temporary homes or encampments. These encampments—estimated to be composed of twenty to fifty persons and perhaps a dozen families—nurtured our earliest experience of community.

The sharing of food strengthened bonds among people, promoted an ethic of reciprocity, and expanded the sense of kinship to the scale of the community. Extensive food sharing appears to be relatively unique to humans. Richard Leakey, the noted paleoanthropologist, reports that chimpanzees (our closest genetic relatives) are highly social, and yet they almost never share their food with the entire band.[5] Leakey goes on to say that when our earliest ancestors switched from individual feeding to extensive food sharing at a home base, it marked a profound shift in the way of life. When food is extensively shared, it increases feelings of mutual interdependence and mutual regard among people, and this would further bind together the family and clan. Accompanying food sharing was growing cooperation in both gathering and hunting. As Leakey concludes, "The food-sharing hypothesis is a very strong candidate for explaining what set early hominids on the road to modern man."[6]

Hints of an awakening reflective consciousness in early humans are also revealed in the first glimmerings of artistic sensibility. Although we have no cave paintings, carved ivory, necklaces, or other art that demonstrates an artistic consciousness among *Homo erectus,* their design of stone tools shows an appreciation for symmetry and balance that exceeds the requirements of functionality, and this provides the first tangible evidence of an aesthetic sense.[7]

A popular misconception is that early humans were highly aggressive. While archaic humans were meat eaters and skilled hunters, it appears that cooperation rather than aggression was the foundation

for society. Given a relatively mobile existence and lack of possessions, and given the importance of food sharing for the clan's survival,
it seems unlikely that greed provided much incentive for aggression.
Humanity's potential for violence probably did not blossom until the
rise of settled societies with clearly defined territories, numerous
possessions, strong social organizations, and a possessive consciousness that came from seeing others with substantial material advantages.

Perceptually *Homo erectus* continued to live in the faint dawning
of an awakening reflective consciousness. On one hand, to sustain a
family structure, gather and share food, and hunt successfully, men
and women had to be able to plan ahead, communicate basic ideas,
and coordinate their actions. On the other hand, their primitive tools
show a monotonous sameness over an immense span of time—for
roughly ten thousand generations there was no evidence of newness
or invention![8] A reflective consciousness was present, but it was almost entirely collapsed upon itself—a budding flower making only
the smallest opening to the sun.

The origin of anatomically modern humans is a subject of considerable controversy.[9] On the one hand, some geneticists think that
physically modern humans arose in Africa relatively recently (roughly
200,000 years ago) and then spread around the world, replacing all
other early human groups. On the other hand, some anthropologists
think there is no single geographic origin for modern humans; instead they theorize that archaic humans originated in Africa perhaps a
million years ago and then gradually developed their modern physical
characteristics in many separate regions around the world. Whatever
the origin of physically modern humans, the transition from *Homo
erectus* to early *Homo sapiens* (the "wise human") marks the close of
the first dimension (and a largely contracted consciousness) and the
opening of the second dimension (and the initial awakening of a reflective consciousness).

The ancestor that seems to best characterize the transition from
the first to the second perceptual stage is the Neanderthal. *Neanderthal* is a term now used to describe the earliest *Homo sapiens,* who
lived from roughly 200,000 years ago until approximately 35,000
years ago, when they suddenly (in evolutionary time) became extinct.

They had a brain capacity at least equal to that of contemporary humans, although their skulls were not yet of modern anatomical form (they had distinct brow ridges, a lower forehead, a more receding chin, and larger teeth). Nonetheless, in the words of paleoanthropologist Richard Leakey, Neanderthals led a "complex, thoughtful, and sensitive existence."[10]

It is significant that Neanderthals are the first human ancestors known to bury their dead. Their burials date from roughly 60,000 B.C. and show evidence of a belief in a life beyond this world. Not only are individuals found with flowers and medicinal plants, there are also burials with other goods—stone tools and apparently food—presumably so that the person could make the journey into the afterlife realm.[11] Another striking example of a distinctly human consciousness comes from the burial of an older man, roughly forty years of age, who was found with an undeveloped arm that had been deformed at birth. A society governed by the ruthless law of the jungle would not have allowed a crippled individual to survive. That this crippled and aged individual did survive indicates the presence of a caring community and a sense of kinship. With Neanderthals, then, we have the first direct evidence of social compassion.

The burial practices of Neanderthals are significant in revealing the emergence of a reflective consciousness. Although other animals grieve for a fellow creature at the time of death, humans are the only beings that consciously anticipate the prospect of death and then imagine a life that extends beyond. The ability to anticipate death and to experience awe over its prospect is what Joseph Campbell called a second mind. He said this second mind needs to be reconciled with our "first mind," that of our animal innocence.[12] There is no evidence of the "second mind" with its anticipation of the awesome reality of death until relatively recently in human evolution (again, approximately 60,000 B.C.). Despite the awakening of an aesthetic consciousness expressed through the symmetry of stone tools of *Homo erectus,* there is no evidence of a death consciousness demonstrated through deliberate burials until Neanderthals. If we assume that it is only with a distinct consciousness of death that humanity begins to reflect intensely on the nature of life, then the decisive awakening of reflective consciousness began in the Neanderthal period.[13] In becoming conscious of the mystery of death, humanity was thrown back upon itself and was challenged to explore the deep mystery of the "self" that lives and dies.

A growing capacity for reflective consciousness by Neanderthals was also surely driven by the need to invent ways to survive in the harsh climate of the north. The invention of shelters, the design of clothing, the use of fire for warmth and protection—all these required some ability to stand back from a challenging situation and observe how it could be improved. Although Neanderthals demonstrated a range of behaviors and skills that indicate their awakening, we should not overestimate their level of reflective consciousness. They did not understand, for example, how to make bone needles for sewing clothes; they did not know how to weave baskets or construct pottery; nor did they leave any paintings. No examples of portable art have been found (for example, carvings from bone or ivory, or necklaces made of seashells or the teeth of animals) that would suggest the differentiated sense of self that accompanies the use of bodily ornamentation. Indeed, fewer than a dozen objects that bear even the simplest markings have thus far been discovered in Neanderthal sites.[14] Finally, there is no evidence that Neanderthals understood and took advantage of seasonal migrations of fish and animals. For example, although the highly predictable migrations of reindeer became very important to modern hunter-gatherers, these were apparently not exploited by Neanderthals.[15]

There is still no agreement why Neanderthals disappeared so rapidly. Were they so limited in speech and reflective consciousness that they could not compete effectively for food with their successors, the Cro-Magnons? (The term *Cro-Magnon* was taken from the place in France where the first anatomically modern humans were found. The term has since been expanded to refer generally to the first modern humans around the world—the preagricultural hunter-gatherers.) Were Neanderthals killed off by Cro-Magnons in a process of genocide? Did they die off naturally as a result of greater vulnerability to disease and an inability to compete for food? Were they absorbed by Cro-Magnons through interbreeding? Whatever the process, by roughly 35,000 years ago, Neanderthals had become extinct and the world was inhabited exclusively by Cro-Magnons. With the emergence of physically modern humans, a decisive step was made into reflective consciousness—and the Earth has not rested since.

A DEBT OF GRATITUDE

The modern human journey began in earnest roughly 35,000 years ago with Cro-Magnon humans. At this time the glacially slow development of human culture and consciousness suddenly achieved a critical mass and began its take-off into the sustained development that leads directly to the modern era. Humanity had finally broken free from its contracted consciousness and moved into the world with a dramatic burst of creative energy.

In looking back at the nearly three million years involved in the initial awakening of reflective consciousness, we can honor an ancient lineage. An immensity of time and effort has brought us to where we are now. We owe an enormous debt of gratitude to our archaic ancestors, whose efforts enabled us to mount an agrarian revolution, then an industrial revolution, and now a communications revolution. We stand on the perceptual foundations developed by our predecessors from the deep past. In the same way that we are invisibly supported by their monumental efforts to awaken and advance, future generations will stand on the civilizational foundations that we build at this critical juncture in the evolution of life on Earth.

SURFACE CONSCIOUSNESS AND THE ERA OF AWAKENING HUNTER-GATHERERS

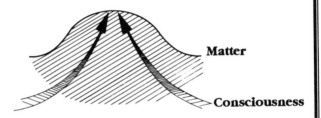

The **second dimension** is the stage of *surface consciousness.*
Early hunter-gatherers experienced the world as immediate
and up close. Judging from archaeological evidence, such as
increasingly sophisticated stone tools, cave art, Venus figurines, and elaborate burials, the decisive awakening of
hunter-gatherers began roughly 35,000 years ago. A two-
dimensional consciousness enabled humans to take the first
"step back" in order to observe themselves and the simple
fact of material existence. Because life was experienced with
such directness and closeness, the world seemed governed
by magical and mysterious forces. Social organization was on
a tribal scale, and people's sense of identity came from affiliation with the tribe and a sense of intimate connection with
nature. This stage continued until the transition to the agricultural era, roughly 10,000 years ago.

SURFACE CONSCIOUSNESS AND THE ERA OF AWAKENING HUNTER-GATHERERS

Fossil records leave only indirect evidence of the perceptions and behaviors of our ancestors. We can make educated guesses, but we cannot know with certainty how human consciousness and culture evolved. What is clear from archaeological evidence is that humanity was finally able to break free from the cocoon of contracted consciousness approximately 35,000 years ago. After dozing for more than three million years in a faint dawn of conscious awareness, we humans finally awakened into the stark sunlight of life and discovered the simple fact that we were here—the "flat fact" of our existence. What a remarkable transition this must have been as individual awakenings were shared with others through simple gestures of mutual recognition. Although still shaking loose the ancient slumber, early humans used the power of reflective consciousness to achieve an unprecedented scale of social cooperation and creativity. The first awakening of the capacity for "knowing that we know" expanded the human character and brought into the world new feelings of mystery and awe, laughter and tears, love and fear.

There is of course no recorded history of these transitional times, so we will never know the heroic struggles and accomplishments of the countless women and men who worked to awaken humanity to the possibilities of this stage. However accomplished, this is the time when humanity reached a critical mass in our capacity for self-recognition. We began in earnest our developmental journey toward full self-referencing knowing.

Physically these ancestors were modern humans. Dressed in contemporary clothes, a Cro-Magnon could walk down a city street today and blend into the crowd unnoticed. Unlike Neanderthal predecessors, who had heavy bones, thick muscles, massive jaws, and brow-ridged skulls, Cro-Magnons had much lighter bone structures and were missing the characteristic brow ridges. And they were gracefully slender compared with their heavy-boned and stocky Neanderthal predecessors.[1] In fact if a Cro-Magnon child were raised in a modern society and given a good education, there is every reason to believe that she or he could fully adapt to modern conditions.

Among other accomplishments, Cro-Magnons were the first humans to create art, bake pottery, make music, and undertake great migrations into North and South America. They also created new tools and developed expanded trading networks and social relationships. These outward changes signal a profound inner change in consciousness. Overall Cro-Magnons were intelligent, sophisticated, and complex people with a rich culture and a mythical sensibility. Their emergence with a modern body type roughly 100,000 years ago and their decisive cultural presence by approximately 35,000 years ago marks the point when the imperceptibly slow development of human consciousness finally ignited and launched a process of growth that leads directly to the current era. The spark of consciousness struck during the time of *Australopithecus africanus* grew into a glowing ember under the care of *Homo erectus,* and then burst into the flame of reflective consciousness with Cro-Magnon humans.

THE SECOND DIMENSION: SURFACE CONSCIOUSNESS

The great divide separating archaic humans from awakening hunters and gatherers is the opening of a two-dimensional view of reality. The architecture of the human psyche blossomed as the second dimension created a context with sufficient mental space to enable our ancestors to stand back and to acknowledge the simple fact of existence.[2] Still, this was a "thin" and compacted consciousness as the reflective capacity was turned back upon the bare fact of physical existence and little more. The world was experienced as up close and very immediate—a magical place filled with unknown and uncontrollable forces, unexpected miracles, and strange happenings. Nature was known as a living field, an animated and vital presence without clear edges or boundaries between the natural and the supernatural. Daily life was an interwoven mixture of unseen forces and unexplained events, for people had neither the concepts nor the perceptual framework to describe rationally how the world worked.

The classic 1946 study by Henri Frankfort et al., *The Intellectual Adventure of Ancient Man,* describes how for modern humans in a scientific age the surrounding world is seen primarily as an "It," whereas for early humans it was seen as a "Thou."[3] Where contemporary humans see a world filled with separate and lifeless things, the awakening hunter-gatherer saw a world of living and interconnected beings. Again, according to Frankfort, for early humans every thing, every place, and every event was filled with life, including "the thunderclap, the sudden shadow, the eerie and unknown clearing in the woods, the stone which suddenly hurts him when he stumbles while on a hunting trip."[4] The sacred nature of life was not contemplated with intellectual detachment; it was experienced as an immediate reality, engaging every faculty simultaneously. Thoughts, feelings, and sensations coalesced at each moment into an experience that was direct, unique, and largely inarticulate.

For early humans space was not seen as the empty, neutral, and lifeless container of modern science; instead space was personal, and each space had a characteristic feeling tone and identity. Space vibrated with energy, uniquely alive at each location and in each specific situation. Instead of a neutral context, space was a numinous field of living energy that could be either familiar or alien, friendly or hostile.[5]

Time, like space, was not objectified by our ancestors. Few were able to stand back far enough from their experience to see time "happening." With two dimensions the experience of life was so immediate and so up close that early humans did not have the perceptual depth to stand back and characterize the unfolding of existence as "time." Without an objectified sense of time—without being able to name it or describe its workings—there was little sense of the future; instead, most things happened in the simple, passing present.[6] Every recurring season and flow must have been a unique miracle: the return of springtime after a long winter, the annual migration of animals, the waxing and waning of the moon—all were mysterious wonders. For most people time was sensed as disconnected "snapshots" of existence—as a series of episodic pulses or momentary gestalts barely tied together. There was not a secure sense of faith in the predictable cycles of return in nature. As humans had only a vague rational understanding of the forces causing seasonal cycles, the use of ceremony and magic would have seemed critical for assuring the rebirth of spring and a bountiful supply of plants and animals for food. Because a two-dimensional perceptual geometry does not support forward-looking behavior, early humans were probably like many modern-day hunter-gatherers: seldom saving for the future and trusting in nature and their skills to provide for the present.

THE TWO-DIMENSIONAL SELF

The two-dimensional sense of self was a compressed mixture of instincts, bodily sensations, emotions, and barely formed concepts. For most people life was largely unexamined and taken for granted. Despite an emerging reflective capacity, there was generally only diffuse attention given to one's self. Most of the time people were running on automatic, responding through habitual patterns to familiar drives for meeting basic needs for security and survival.

People also saw themselves as inseparable from their immediate family or tribal group, which in turn was immersed within and inseparable from the living presence of nature. An Indian from the west coast of North America described colorfully how he did not feel himself to be an individual who could exist apart from the network of family and tribe. He asked rhetorically, "What is a man?," and replied, "A man is nothing. Without his family he is of less importance than a bug crossing the trail, of less importance than spit or dung."[7]

Accompanying this intense connection with family and tribe was a limited reflective consciousness and language to objectify reality. Most thinking was oriented toward specific goals and concrete projects—organizing a hunting venture, cooperating to harvest seasonal nuts and berries. Abstract reasoning—the type of thinking that enables us to make sophisticated comparisons and conduct mental experiments—was almost entirely undeveloped.

THE TWO-DIMENSIONAL SOCIETY

Awakening hunter-gatherers lived in small groups. Best estimates are that the typical size of hunter-gatherer groupings were on the order of two or three dozen persons, or roughly six family groups—an optimal size for social cooperation.[8] Judging from the social organization of modern hunter-gatherers, the family was probably the basic social unit around which the larger group or tribe was organized. A household unit is both flexible and efficient; depending on the available food supply, the size of the tribal group can be expanded or contracted by adding or subtracting family units.[9]

Like contemporary hunter-gatherers, our ancestors probably participated in large gatherings once or twice a year, perhaps involving roughly twenty bands, or five hundred people.[10] These gatherings gave people an opportunity to socialize, look for a prospective mate, exchange tools and art objects, and perhaps engage in the large-scale hunting of migrating herds.

The "flatness" of perception in two dimensions is consistent with the nonhierarchical or flat social structure that characterizes hunter-gatherer societies. Although there was differentiation of labor based upon sex, everyone shared relatively equal status. Because most tasks were simple and repetitive, there was little basis for status differences, and this fostered an equalitarian social structure. Competitiveness and status seeking were probably seen as vices rather than virtues. As in many contemporary hunter-gatherer societies, the greatest recognition and honor probably went to those who showed the most skill in maintaining the community and who shared most generously with others. Nonetheless Cro-Magnon burials do show evidence of status differences emerging, as some persons were buried with ivory beads, valuable spears, rings, and other items. Elaborate burials for a few individuals coupled with increasing use of body ornaments indicate that differences in social position were growing despite a general emphasis on social equality.

A vital ingredient of culture during this period was the feminine principle or archetype that was the ruling spirit or mythos of cultural life. While the masculine archetype tends to be action oriented, goal directed, competitive, and aggressive, the feminine archetype tends to be relationship oriented, nature connected, receptive, and nurturing. Joseph Campbell writes that "in the neolithic village stage . . . the focal figure of all mythology and worship was the bountiful goddess Earth, as the mother and nourisher of life and receiver of the dead for rebirth."[11] The powerful role of the feminine archetype is expressed in the great quantities of the so-called "Venus figurines" that were produced during a time of increasing cold and advancing glaciers, between 20,000 and 30,000 years ago.[12] Most striking is the fact that so many appear to have been crafted according to an accepted convention or design—most are only a few inches high, with exaggerated breasts, wide hips, tapering legs, and a head without facial features. Because these figures have been found across a wide band stretching from the Atlantic coast of France and Spain across Asia to the borders of China, it has been suggested that they are evidence of a widely shared Earth Goddess mythology.[13] Because there is growing evidence of trade networks across this same region, it is possible these figurines symbolized the emergence of a shared mythical-spiritual consciousness that served to connect people with nature and with one another.

ARCHAIC SPIRITUALITY: SHAMANS AND CEREMONIES

The natural and supernatural were intimately connected for early hunter-gatherers. Where contemporary humans might see a rainstorm and say it was caused by changing wind currents and air temperatures, an early hunter-gatherer might attribute the storm to a god, or to a shaman's intervention, or see it as an omen of good or ill. In a two-dimensional worldview there was not the spaciousness to stand back and see causal relationships among events separated in time. Every thing, every place, and every situation was infused with a mysterious presence that worked in unseen ways, with a magical logic. Each situation, place, and thing was understood as having a unique life, will, and personality of its own. Even common objects were seen as alive with their own intelligence and power. In his book about native American Indians *The Ohlone Way*, Malcolm Margolin describes how for tribal peoples everything demanded a personal relationship: "people, animals, plants, bows, arrows, cradles, pestles, baskets, springs, trails, boats, trees, feathers, natural objects and manufactured objects as well. Everything was alive, everything had character, power, and magic and consequently everything had to be dealt with properly."[14] Our ancestors invented innumerable rites and rituals to acknowledge and gain favor with the powers of nature, and with important objects and places. The relationship to this infusing intelligence and power was so close, so strong, and so intimate that "nature" was barely recognized or named as a separate aspect of life.

With nature seen as alive with forces, each event or being or place was seen as unique, unprecedented, and with an individual character that could only be known through a direct encounter—not by comparison with other things and experiences.[15] In the immediacy of two dimensions, various types of experiences blended together, so there were no sharp distinctions between the worlds of dreams, altered states of consciousness, and "ordinary" reality; nor was there a clear division between the realm of the living and the realm of the spirits.[16] Here is how the American Indian Ishi—a man from a Stone Age culture who stumbled into the twenty-first century in 1911 as the last survivor of his tribe—approached life: "He lived at ease with the supernatural and the mystical which were pervasive in all aspects of life. He felt no need to differentiate mystical truth from directly evidential or 'material' truth, or the supernatural from the natural: one was as manifest as the other within his system of values and perceptions and beliefs."[17]

Because people did not understand how nature worked and saw the world as governed by unseen forces, it was vital to learn how to control these forces—and this brings in the role of the shaman. The shaman was the man or woman able to reach behind the veil of the visible world and engage the Life-force behind all things in order to serve the community—healing the sick, assuring a good hunt, preserving the ceremonies and rituals of the groups, and much more.[18] The shaman was a very powerful person in a community where life was filled with unknown, mysterious, and magical events and where superstitions and taboos flourished. For nearly every aspect of life, from birth to death, it was important to call upon the assistance of favorable life-energies. Understandably, then, a special role was given to those individuals who claimed they could journey into the realm of hidden forces and affect them beneficially. Although people viewed the spirit world as blending into a seamless whole with everyday reality, still, for purposes of healing and other important rituals, one needed a shaman to facilitate the connection between the life-energy of the community and the subtle spiritual realm.

Collective rituals of drumming, chanting, and trance dancing were important for giving persons a direct experience of union with the Life-force behind manifest existence. By dancing or drumming or chanting together, a community acknowledged its collective participation in a process that would take them into the world of spirits. The scholar of Hindu culture Heinrich Zimmer says that "dance induces trance, ecstasy, the experience of the divine, the realization of one's own secret nature, and, finally, merging into the divine essence."[19] From the native American culture comes this description of the power of trance dancing for the Ohlone Indians of California:

> The dance went on for hours, sometimes for a whole day or even longer. The dancers stamped and stamped. They stamped out all sense of time and space, stamped out all thoughts of village life, even stamped out their own inner voices. Dancing for hour after hour they stamped out the ordinary world, danced themselves past the gates of common perception into the realm of the spirit world, danced themselves toward the profound understanding of the universe that only a people can feel who have transcended the ordinary human condition and who find themselves moving in total synchronization with everything around them.[20]

The ceremonies of the awakening hunter-gatherers involved sympathetic magic and ritual sacrifice to influence the powerful forces and spirits that animated material events.[21] In the early conception of causality as magical reciprocity, you got something by giving something. If something precious were sacrificed—an animal, a finger from one's own hand, or even another human being—then something equally precious might be given in return.

THE SEASONS OF A PERCEPTUAL PARADIGM

The unfolding of a perceptual paradigm moves through an organic cycle similar to the change of seasons. First, a new dimensional stage sprouts into an exuberant **springtime** of growth. Second, there is a season of blossoming, where the potentials of a given stage reach their fullest expression and flowering in a **summertime** of development. The third stage is an **autumn** of initial decline, during which time the potentials of the paradigm are harvested by the person or civilization. Finally, the perceptual paradigm reveals its limitations and moves into a bleak **winter** and crisis to await the transition into the next dimensional perspective.

The seasons of growth for the unfolding of the second perceptual paradigm span the period from roughly 35,000 B.C. to 3500 B.C. Given the scarcity of archaeological evidence, we have no more than an impressionistic understanding of the evolution of culture and consciousness during those thirty thousand years. How wonderful it would be to look back through a magical videocamera to see the customs, songs, games, ethics, and attitudes of our ancestors. Still, we can make a number of conjectures about their way of life from the tools, art, and encampments that remain.

Spring (35,000 B.C. to 15,000 B.C.)

Roughly 35,000 years ago physically modern humans were living in a world still in the grip of the ice ages. Mile-deep glaciers covered much of what are now England, Russia, Eastern Europe, and large portions of North America. It would be another 25,000 years before the ice would fully recede to produce what we now assume is our "normal" warm climate. These massive sheets of ice captured enough of the Earth's water to cause ocean levels to drop as much as several hundred feet—creating land bridges between what is now England and Europe and between Russia and Alaska (the latter land bridge enabled early humans to migrate into North and South America).

After roughly three million years, the capacity for reflective consciousness was anchored within the human family, sparking an explosion of innovation in both stone tools and cave art. We can only speculate on the reasons for this profound change. Certainly the intense demands of living through the ice ages must have been a catalyst to get people reflecting on more effective ways of surviving. In contrast to the myth of cave-dwelling ancestors, most Cro-Magnons are thought to have lived in dwellings constructed from animal skins, bone, and wood. To endure in the harsh climate of northern and eastern Europe, people were pushed to improve their use of fire, to improve their design of clothing and shelters, and to acquire a keen understanding of the location and availability of food. To adapt to the changing seasons would also place a premium on reflective consciousness (or the ability of a person or group to stand back and view a situation with greater objectivity, creativity, and flexibility).

The springtime of humanity's first stage of reflective consciousness was marked by a dramatic increase in artistic activity. Ornaments appear suddenly and in large quantities in sites dating back perhaps 35,000 years.[22] The presence of jewelry and ornaments (for example, necklaces made from seashells or from the teeth of bears and lions) indicate that, early on, people devoted considerable time and energy to decorating their bodies. It also shows an awakening self-recognition being expressed through an aesthetic consciousness. We can only speculate on the purpose of these ornaments: To identify the clan to which they belonged? To attract a mate? To express their unique identity for the sheer fun of it? Whatever their role, body ornaments provide some of the clearest evidence of an awakening human consciousness.

Cave art also appears for the first time in this period. For approximately fifteen thousand years (roughly 35,000 B.C. to 20,000 B.C.) cave art is fairly crude, consisting of roughly drawn animals, abstract signs (groups of dots, grids, zigzags), and vulvas. The full blossoming of cave art would not come for thousands of years—until roughly 15,000 B.C. Still, any level of artistry represents an historic first step in the objective representation of experience and the tangible anchoring of an awakening consciousness. Although early paleoanthropologists assumed cave art was primarily a vehicle for sympathetic hunting magic, there is a growing consensus that it probably provided a shamanistic context for important rites and rituals, such as the initiation of adolescents into adulthood.

Compared with Neanderthals, Cro-Magnon tools show striking advances in their number, diversity, and sophistication of design. Cro-Magnons were masters at creating stone tools that were as sharp and functional as many of the metal tools that we have today (except that they were brittle). These tools could be used for chopping wood, cutting meat, scraping a hide, spearing a fish, or sewing a coat of fur. The emergence of particular tools is instructive: A bone flute has been found that dates from roughly 32,000 B.C.—the first evidence of musical instruments. The sewing needle was invented in roughly 23,000 B.C. Often made from ivory or antler, the needle spread rapidly throughout the world. An understanding of the principle of the lever was expressed in the invention of a "spear thrower" in roughly 17,000 B.C. (this is a short throwing arm made of wood or antler that connects with the end of the spear and greatly increases its power and range). Overall, the combination of cave art, portable art, music, and new technologies all indicate that a distinct, new level of consciousness and culture was emerging.

Summer (15,000 B.C. to 8000 B.C.)

The full blossoming of this era is strikingly evident in its cave art. The golden age of Cro-Magnon cave art occurred during the final five thousand years of the ice ages, from about fifteen thousand to ten thousand years ago. In this period we find roughly 80 percent of all the known art of the Upper Paleolithic—and what a magnificent and impressive heritage it represents.[23] In this ancient art we find an economy of expression and a natural exuberance equal to that of a Western Picasso combined with that of an Eastern Zen master skilled in calligraphy. One mysterious aspect of cave art is the contrast between the sophisticated artistry in painting animals and the nearly complete absence of human images, or their primitive rendering as little more than crude stick figures. Because these were skilled artists, it is not clear whether this indicates a lack of self-reflective consciousness regarding human existence or a strict taboo against representing the human face and form.

There is strong evidence of expanding social connections during these millennia. The discovery of seashells, ivory, and specialized rock hundreds of miles from their place of origin indicates that an extensive trading network existed during the last part of the ice age. Rather than economic exchanges, these are thought to have been social exchanges intended to cement ties and relationships among groups so as to create mutual obligations and therefore a source of aid in difficult times. By the late ice age many tribes were no longer isolated but were trading stories, food, tools, shells, and ornaments and had a sense of connection and community that could extend for hundreds of miles.

Autumn/Winter (8000 B.C. to 3500 B.C.)

It is no accident that the hunter-gatherer way of life came to a close after the ice ages ended. When the glaciers retreated, the climate became warmer and more humid, the winters were shorter and less severe, and grasslands were replaced by forests. In this transformed world a new way of life began taking root: the awakening gatherers and hunters were in the process of becoming settled farmers and were on the verge of discovering the potentials of a whole new dimension of perception and action. A change as momentous as the first awakening of reflective consciousness was taking place with the Agricultural Revolution. If there is one change that symbolizes the shift into the autumn or even winter of growth of the second dimension, it is the end of the age of cave art that had lasted for 25,000 years. By 8000 B.C. we no longer find evidence of cave art and its vibrant renderings of animals.

Another indication of the autumn of the second dimension can be seen in the transformation of the Earth Goddess figurines. When they first appeared around 26,000 B.C., they lacked any facial features; however, twenty thousand years later, by roughly 6000 B.C., we find special care being given to creating their faces (see Figure 4).[24] Particularly striking are the eyes, which were often made of inlaid stone. This dramatic increase in the accuracy of human representation began around 8000 B.C. and corresponds with the widespread development of agriculture.[25] The shift from faceless and eyeless goddesses to a figurine with clear facial characteristics and strong eyes suggests that a new self-awareness was awakening within humanity to accompany the shift to a more settled, agrarian way of life.

Although the beginnings of the agricultural era are often placed around 8000 B.C., there is evidence of primitive hoe cultivation along the Nile as early as 13,000 B.C. Richard Leakey believes that people of the ice age probably exerted more control over their food resources than was previously thought. He suggests that the Agricultural Revolution may have occurred by simply placing greater emphasis on an

Figure 4 : The Growing Realism of Facial Representation Between 25000 B.C. and 6000 B.C., Suggesting an Expanding Capacity for Self-Reflective Consciousness

Earth Mother of Willendorf,
Austria, circa 25000 B.C.

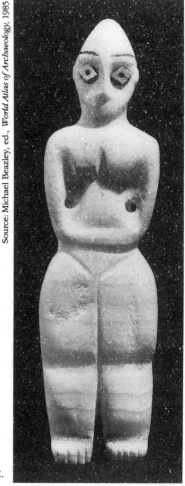

Goddess Statuette from
Tell Sawwan, Iraq, 6000 B.C.

everyday activity with which people were already familiar, rather than through the introduction of totally novel techniques.[26] In Leakey's view Cro-Magnons had preadapted over a period of thousands of years by systematically collecting food and establishing semisettled villages. Although its impact was revolutionary, the emergence of settled villages and an agricultural economy was an adaptation that occurred over millennia.

In the period between 9000 B.C. and 7000 B.C. we find dramatic evidence of a new pattern of settlement in Mesopotamia—a "village." With sweeping changes in the economic basis of life, human settlements changed from circular compounds (a tribal form of equalitarian organization) to rectangular grids (a village form of organization). The traditional settlement for hunter-gatherers was a tribal-scale society of several dozen persons with a group of huts placed in a circle. A circular pattern mirrors an open, equalitarian, and sharing society. However, as the population expands beyond a few dozen persons, a circular compound grows to an unworkable size. By shifting from a circular compound to a rectangular-village form of settlement, it was easy to expand along streets and thereby to include a population of hundreds. However, a rectangular settlement pattern implies the breakdown of the inward-oriented tribal society and economy where all is visibly open and shared. Instead in a village society the basic economic and social unit tends to be the extended family with an enclosed house and place of food storage.[27]

The spiritual transition from a hunter-gatherer way of life to an agrarian existence is symbolized in the shift from a feminine, Earth-oriented spirituality to a masculine, sky-oriented spirituality. In terms of longevity, it is important to acknowledge that a feminine-based, Earth-oriented spirituality persisted for more than twenty thousand years (from at least 25,000 B.C. until nearly 3500 B.C., when the first large-scale civilizations emerged)! By comparison, the masculine-based, sky-oriented spirituality has endured only one fifth as long—from roughly 3500 B.C. to nearly A.D. 2000, a "mere" five thousand years or so.[28]

It is not clear if the feminine/Earth-oriented archetype developed unbroken. Some see a direct line of development from the paleolithic Venus figurines (perhaps representing a clan mother society) through to the vegetation-oriented fertility goddess that supported the emergence of a more settled, agrarian way of life. Others see the lineage of the feminine Earth Goddess as more fragmented and view the continuity of its heritage as more uncertain.[29] In either case the change from an Earth to a sky orientation symbolizes a profound shift in perception that corresponds to the shift from the second to the third dimension.

The shift from an Earth to a sky orientation symbolizes a huge expansion in perceptual consciousness—a vast increase in the depth of reality that is consciously seen and recognized. With this added perceptual depth, humanity was given a way to stand back from the Earth and begin to develop the spaciousness of perception needed for imagining, and then building, the world's first city-state civilizations.

A long and complex time of transition extends from the emergence of an agrarian way of life, around 9000 B.C., to the rise of the highly organized city-states, around 3500 B.C. During these millennia we see both the fulfillment of the second dimension and the opening of the third dimension.[30] This six-thousand-year period includes the fullest expression of the feminine/Earth Goddess mythos from the paleolithic era, and it then shades into an awakening masculine/Sky God orientation to empower a rising agrarian revolution. As both the autumn and the winter of the second dimension and the springtime of the third dimension, this was a complex period of transition between two views of reality and ways of life (see Figure 5).

Figure 5: Transition from Second to Third Stage

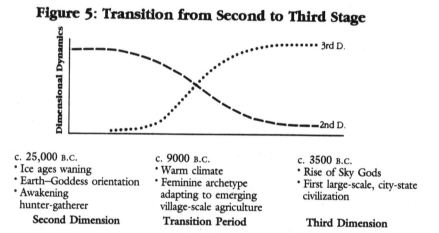

c. 25,000 B.C.	c. 9000 B.C.	c. 3500 B.C.
• Ice ages waning	• Warm climate	• Rise of Sky Gods
• Earth–Goddess orientation	• Feminine archetype	• First large-scale, city-state
• Awakening	adapting to emerging	civilization
hunter-gatherer	village-scale agriculture	
Second Dimension	**Transition Period**	**Third Dimension**

An Earth Goddess spirituality did not collapse with the flowering of villages and farming but apparently made a successful transition into the beginnings of the agricultural era. Since farming is an Earth-oriented activity, it seems a natural and direct adaptation to apply Earth Goddess symbols in the context of a simple, agrarian society. More pointedly, the earliest farmers were probably women. The domestication of both plants and animals in southeastern Asia (the cradle of earliest agriculture) was apparently accomplished by women rather than men. The earliest farmed plants were probably similar to yams and bananas (which are propagated by cuttings), and the earliest domesticated animals were household animals, such as dogs, pigs, chickens, and llamas. Carl Sauer writes in his book *Agricultural Origins and Dispersals* that, "in this culture, the women had domain over the tilled land and the homes. Women were cooks and cultivators, domestics and domesticators. These societies were largely developed and organized by their women."[31]

When the gradual changes toward small-scale farming reached a critical mass, they produced a food surplus sufficient to support the needs of an urban minority. With the rise of the more complex city-states, a whole new level of consciousness and cultural organization were required to hold them together. Earth Goddess symbols were then replaced by the more expansive symbols of depth consciousness represented by the Sky Gods.

The shift to a depth consciousness symbolized by the Sky Gods had both functional and dysfunctional aspects. On the one hand, it opened a new perceptual domain for humanity that made possible enormous advances in civilization. Depth consciousness provided a previously unknown, psychic distance from which to stand back and look consciously at the Earth and see its potential for being farmed. It also enabled humans to look more consciously at human society and see its potential for being organized into large-scale structures. On the other hand, the shift from the feminine Earth Goddess orientation to the masculine Sky God orientation was dysfunctional to the extent that the feminine side of life was not integrated into the emerging masculine culture but instead was repressed.[32]

The feminine archetype's appreciation for the fertility of nature and the reverence for life's regenerative powers were deemphasized by the male, priestly class, who saw in the lawful movements of the heavens a more systematic and orderly foundation for living. While the priestly premise worked for a number of centuries, catastrophe will result if humanity does not soon reconnect with and reintegrate the wisdom of the Earth Goddess into the process of advancing civilization. The environmental devastation of the planet is due, largely, to humanity's lack of conscious appreciation for the limits of the regenerative powers of nature. Our slowness to respond to mounting environmental tragedies vividly shows our great need to recover the feminine archetype with its feelings of intimate connection with the biosphere.

SUMMARY

The awakening of humanity has been explored through the perceptual lens of a two-dimensional view of reality, and the results correspond well with the descriptions found in archaeology and paleoanthropology. With the awakening of the initial stage of reflective consciousness in Cro-Magnon times, the development of "double-wisdom" began in earnest, and a process of maturation was launched that is continuing today. No longer would humans live within the dim consciousness of the first dimension; instead they would be able to see the stark reality of the bare fact of their physical existence in the world. Now the human journey begins in earnest.

DEPTH CONSCIOUSNESS AND THE ERA OF AGRARIAN-BASED CIVILIZATIONS

The **third dimension** is the stage of *depth consciousness* and includes most of recorded human history. In this epoch humans were able to stand back far enough from their prior immersion within nature to recognize regular cycles and seasons (the wheel of time), and begin deliberate farming. With the development of a productive agriculture, the first agrarian-based civilizations emerged in roughly 3500 B.C. in Mesopotamia (and soon after in Egypt, India, and China). With depth consciousness the domain of the sacred shifts from the Earth to the heavens—and religion shifts from an Earth Goddess spirituality to a Sky God spirituality. All of the basic arts of civilization blossomed at this time, including writing, organized government and religion, massive architecture, division of labor, mathematics, and astronomy. Still, most individuals lived as impoverished peasants with no expectation of material progress.

⊛

DEPTH CONSCIOUSNESS AND THE ERA OF AGRARIAN-BASED CIVILIZATIONS

It is hard to overstate the importance of the invention of agriculture. Many would agree with Richard Leakey, who calls it, "without exaggeration, the most significant event in the history of mankind."[1] To understand this revolutionary development, we will explore the underlying perceptual transformation generated by the emergence of a "depth consciousness."

The agrarian revolution began at least twelve thousand years ago, marked by the shift from gathering and hunting into a settled existence. This shift radically changed the nomadic way of life that had been the norm for our ancestors for several million years. Once small-scale villages and subsistence agriculture became established, it then took roughly seven thousand years (from approximately 10,000 B.C. to 3500 B.C.) before large-scale, city-state civilizations emerged. A critical mass of development was reached around 3500 B.C., when quite suddenly there arose the first large-scale, agrarian-based civilizations in history. Beginning in ancient Mesopotamia, all of the basic arts of high civilization were rapidly developed: writing, mathematics, astronomy, irrigation, organized government, a priestly class and organized religion, armies, massive architecture, metal technology, the wheel, pottery, weaving, and much more. For the next five thousand years (from 3,500 B.C. until the Middle Ages around A.D. 1500), humanity would be occupied with one overriding challenge—realizing the potentials of depth consciousness and agrarian-based civilization.

The churning of society should not be equated with evolutionary advance. The social turbulence during this stage was immense, with empires rising and falling through innumerable invasions, migrations, and wars. Most of the activity was a struggle to conquer land and people and usually ended where it had begun—with a new division of power over land and/or people but without any fundamental change in human perception and behavior.[2] I will attempt to look beneath the churning of history and seek out the deeper currents in the evolution of human consciousness and society. There is an advantage to taking a paradigmatic view of history: It bleaches out the "sound and the fury" of countless wars, conquests, territorial divisions, and rulers and enables us to see more clearly the process of evolutionary change. The disadvantage to this approach is that because the era of agrarian-based civilizations covers the bulk of recorded human history, it is utterly impossible to do justice to the immense range and diversity of experience embraced by this epoch. Therefore the historical descriptions presented here are intended to do no more than illustrate the dynamics of dimensional evolution.

TRANSFORMATION: THE BIRTH OF AGRICULTURE

The shift to farming was a gradual and natural transformation. With the end of the ice ages a warmer climate increased the availability of wild wheat and other grasses as a source of food, and people adapted by shifting their diet accordingly. To discover how difficult it would be for a family to survive on the harvest of wild grain, an archaeologist used a nine-thousand-year-old flint sickle to see how efficiently he could cut grain. The results were surprising—he found that a family could probably harvest enough wild wheat and barley in the space of only three or four weeks to feed themselves for a year![3] This experiment suggests that a settled small-village way of life could have been established long before systematic farming got under way. By combining the gathering of wild cereals with seasonal hunting, a gradual transition to a settled way of life could have been readily accomplished. People apparently made small, incremental improvements in food raising that over time accumulated into a thorough revolution in living. Probably over thousands of years people learned to weed wild fields of wheat to increase their yield, to plant seeds around the margins of wild fields to extend the size of the crop, and to protect the fields from grazing animals. From such modest beginnings came one of the most fundamental transformations the world has ever known. The surplus of food that farming produced made possible the eventual rise of large-scale, urban civilizations.

Agriculture seems to have originated in several major areas of the world independently. Joseph Campbell describes the agrarian revolution beginning first in southeastern Asia (in roughly 11,000 B.C.) with the domestication of plants such as bananas and yams and household animals such as dogs, chickens, and pigs. Agriculture emerged sometime thereafter (roughly 9000 B.C.) in southwestern Asia with the farming of grains (wheat and barley) and the herding of animals (sheep, goats, and cattle). The transition to agriculture is estimated to have occurred in the New World of Central and South America beginning in roughly 7000 B.C.[4]

The small-village way of life based on rudimentary agriculture had great stability. The transition from the earliest successful farming to the rise of city-states took roughly seven thousand years—an immense span of time.[5] Where we now consider one generation to be a significant block of time and a century an enormous span, these small, agrarian-based villages endured for fifty or more centuries without any appreciable change. These millennia of stability were important for establishing a way of life that, in turn, provided the foundation for the eventual rise of the world's first "high" civilizations.

These transitional times were a relatively peaceful period in human history—a lull before the storm of sustained civilizational development. Some suggest that the influence of a feminine consciousness and Earth Goddess spirituality were responsible for the absence of organized conflict during these millennia. There is sometimes the further suggestion that had the masculine consciousness and patriarchal spirituality not become so dominant, human civilizations could have continued to develop peacefully over the last five thousand years. Although the patriarchal herding cultures were more aggressive than the matriarchal planting cultures, placing the burden of peaceful or violent evolution primarily on the shoulders of either a masculine or feminine consciousness seems misdirected.

In her book *The Mismeasure of Woman* Carol Tavris says the view that "men compete, women cooperate; men destroy nature, women live in balance with nature" is simplistic and unproductive.[6] In my view a more important factor in the rise of conflict was a radically changing social psychology as people moved from small, equalitarian villages to large, hierarchical city-states. Another important factor was that in the period of small-village life there was a natural abundance of land and food and relatively few people to compete for resources and therefore little need for warfare. At the same time a simple, village way of life required relatively few possessions, so there was little to protect. Finally, in an equalitarian society there was not the strong social hierarchy and centralized control that is essential for organizing an army.

Over the millennia each of these factors changed. With a more settled way of life population grew and put increasing pressure on available resources. With development came more elaborate homes, tools, and possessions to protect and defend. With increasing specialization there emerged a social hierarchy and the understanding of how to organize large-scale armies that could either attack or defend. It is these material, social, and psychological factors, more than the dominance of either the masculine or the feminine archetype, that created the conditions for large-scale social conflict.

Although the origins of large-scale civilizations are still shrouded in mystery, Joseph Campbell suggests they may have emerged from the interaction of the more aggressive, male-oriented hunting and pastoralist cultures with the more peaceful, female-oriented planting cultures.[7] From the synergy of their interaction may have emerged a worldview that was completely new—no longer tied to either the realm of animals or to that of plants, but founded upon a recognition of the mathematical orderliness of the heavens. Whatever the origins, patriarchal, male-oriented societies arose in a number of areas of the world and gained power over planting cultures. The labors of the agriculturalists were then used to support the building of celestially based civilizations that were governed by a male-dominated priestly class.

Current estimates are that the world's first "high" civilizations coalesced around 3500 B.C. in Sumer (in what is now Iraq), in Egypt around 2800 B.C., in India around 2500 B.C., in China around 1500 B.C., and in Mexico around 1200 B.C. These earliest civilizations had a number of characteristics in common:

- Each civilization had several cities bustling with life and trade. Although only a small fraction of the overall population lived in them, these cities were vital to the character, culture, religion, and governance of the civilization.
- All of the early civilizations developed some form of writing, mathematics, and astronomy.
- Civilizations were organized around a Sky God spirituality with a powerful priestly class. A patriarchal religion worked in concert with a strong, centralized government.
- There was a clear division of labor among merchants, rulers, warriors, and artisans.
- Each civilization developed well-organized armies capable of large-scale warfare.
- Sophisticated communication networks were developed to support trade and governance.

With a half dozen or more large-scale, agrarian-based and celestially oriented civilizations blossoming around the world at roughly the same time, major changes were occurring in the culture and in the consciousness of humanity.

The Third Dimension:
Depth Consciousness

When our perceptual framework expanded from two to three dimensions, a new depth and spaciousness was added to our experience of the world. Our minds were able to encompass new vistas, the knowledge of which thoroughly transformed every aspect of our existence—our view of self, society, nature, space, time, and religion. A clear indication of the shift from the surface consciousness of two dimensions to the depth consciousness of three dimensions was the shift from an Earth Goddess orientation to a Sky God, or heaven-centered, orientation. Joseph Campbell explains that from the time of the earliest city-states supported by a priestly class (ca. 4000 B.C.) to the end of the Middle Ages "every known high civilization—except, for a time, the Greco-Roman—took its spiritual instruction from these priestly watchers of the sky."[8] The shift from an Earth to a sky orientation represents a profound transformation of perception and a momentous opening of a new chapter in human history.

Campbell describes the emergence of high civilizations in the ancient world as a "highly conscious creation . . . of a new order of humanity, which had never before appeared in the history of mankind; namely, the professional, full-time, initiated, strictly regimented temple priest."[9] The authority of the priest came, in turn, from observing the sky or heavens. Unlike the Earth Goddess spirituality, which focused on the local plant and animal kingdom, the priestly class focused on the heavens and stars for their insights and authority. The organization of everyday life was based on the idea that worldly order should mirror the heavenly order.[10] Campbell writes, "As in heaven, so on Earth. To the priestly knowers of that cosmic order an absolute, divinely directed moral authority was attributed."[11] The earliest city-states, then, were an Earthly expression of a cosmic order that was discerned by the priestly class. As Campbell further writes, "It can be said without exaggeration that all the high civilizations of the world are to be thought of as the limbs of one great tree, whose root is in heaven."[12] Ancient astronomy, says Campbell, "led to the realization, altogether new to the world, of a cosmos mathematically ordered; and with this awareness, the focus of mythic concern radically shifted from the earlier animal and plant messengers to the night sky and its mathematics."[13]

Despite the power of this new perceptual paradigm, it was far from the modern view of the cosmos. For example, the early Sumerians viewed the Earth as a flat disk that was enclosed by a solid surface, to which were affixed the points of light that we know as stars.[14] Despite its limitations, the shift from an Earth orientation to a sky orientation transformed humanity. Instead of looking to local plants and animals as the embodiment of mystery and the sacred, the immensity of the sky was now the primary source of reverence and awe, authority and power. This enlarged frame of reference, in turn, made it possible to "stand back" and view humanity's relationship to the Earth with more distance and objectivity.

An excellent illustration of the role of Sky Gods in the cosmology of the agrarian-based civilizations can be found in the book *The Intellectual Adventure of Ancient Man*. Thorkild Jacobson describes the central place of the sky in the Mesopotamian civilization, which gave birth to the first large-scale city-states: "Anu, the highest of the gods, was god of the sky, and his name was the everyday word for 'sky.' The dominant role which the sky plays—even in a merely spatial sense—in the composition of the visible universe, and the eminent position which it occupies, high above all other things, may well explain why Anu should rank as the most important force in the cosmos."[15] Jacobson describes the power of the sky in ancient cosmology: "The vast sky encircling one on all sides may be felt as a presence at once overwhelming and awesome, forcing one to his knees merely by its sheer being."[16] The sky inspires a feeling of majesty and greatness—and a realization of one's own cosmic proportion, even insignificance. Attention to the sky emphasizes the vast distance between one's self and the power that sustains this overarching presence.

Seeing a powerful presence and lawful order in the heavens fostered a new sense of detachment and separation from the Earth. With an expanded psychic distance or perceptual space from which to stand back and look consciously at the Earth, humanity saw more clearly the potential for farming the Earth, for domesticating plants and animals, and for organizing human affairs into urban and social structures of unprecedented scale.[17] Humanity now had the perceptual tools to begin to transform the material and social environment.

Organizing society around sky-oriented laws that were interpreted by a priestly class served a vital social function. The first city-states contained tens of thousands of inhabitants and were confronted with the challenge of how to organize the activities of a large community with an unprecedented degree of social differentiation. Instead of the equalitarian social structure of the small-scale villages, city-state society was broken up into distinctly different social classes: priests, kings, merchants, soldiers, peasants, artisans, and others. The diverse activities of these classes were brought into an orderly relationship through the overarching power of the priests, whose authority was derived from the heavens themselves. The orderly movement of the stars gave a model for creating order here on Earth—in setting the time for planting and harvesting, in the scheduling of important events and ceremonies, and in the structuring of society.[18] We now take our capacity for large-scale social organization for granted; but at the time, the ability to organize city-states (and then the earliest nation-states) represented a trailblazing transformation in human affairs.

In seeing the world with more depth, the perception of time was also transformed. Whereas in the flat, up-close world of two dimensions time was barely observed, in the in-depth world of three dimensions, time's ebbs and flows are clearly recognized. With depth consciousness, people can work with the seasons, cycles, and rhythms of nature. In practical terms a farming-based society has a future orientation of sufficient depth to know when to plant, cultivate, and harvest crops.

Time in the third dimension is in "dynamic stasis"—moving around in circles, going from spring to summer to winter and back to spring, but it is not "going anywhere." Like the movement of the stars, time seems forever circular and repetitious. Although this time sense was empowering to the extent that it enabled an agrarian-based society to emerge, it did not support the perception that life itself was "going somewhere" or that it would substantially improve materially.

Despite the rise of city-states, the vast majority of persons were still peasant farmers, who felt that while the fortunes of individuals and families might rise or fall, the circumstances of the whole community would not fundamentally change.[19] Improving the lot of everyone was not in the scheme of circular time. There is no "progress." Even the Greeks, revered for their rationalism, viewed nature as "one great organism" involved in "ever-recurrent cycles."[20] A broadly shared sense of temporal progression (and thus material progress) would not emerge until the birth of the Industrial Revolution thousands of years later.

Although humanity was awakening in the agrarian era, people did not perceive the world in the same manner we now take for granted. For example, the world's first high civilization in Sumer did not have an historical consciousness. Despite their ability to build a large city-state civilization and invent tools that are basic to a modern way of life (the wheel, a calendar, and mathematics), they wrote no history. The respected authority on Mesopotamian civilization, Samuel Kramer, explains that the early Sumerians "possessed neither the essential intellectual tools of definition and generalization nor the evolutionary approach fundamental to historical evaluation and interpretation."[21] Events were seen as being planned and brought about by powerful gods. The early scribes did not yet have the perceptual capacity to stand back, dispassionately examine, and then record the unfolding flow of events. Kramer says that the Sumerians were "intellectually immobilized by this sterile and static attitude" toward history.

Some suggest that Christianity, with its apocalyptic vision of the Second Coming of Christ, transformed cyclical time into linear time. Although Christianity did develop a forward-looking time sense, it was anticipating a profound discontinuity in time. Instead of fostering a belief in progress in this world, the early Christians were expecting the end of history. This view of time anticipated a dramatic break from the present to a different time altogether, when the current world would end and be transformed into the new kingdom of God. The Christian view of time did not promote a linear view of progress and perfection in the here and now; rather it looked forward to a new order that would miraculously descend and sweep away the past. Although this apocalyptic view of time helped awaken an historical consciousness, it was different from the scientific view of temporal and material progress that was to provide the underpinning for the Industrial Revolution. Progress for scientists was material and worldly, whereas for Christians it was nonmaterial and otherworldly. Where Christianity looked beyond the present to the abrupt end of ordinary material existence, science looked at everyday life and saw an upward-bending curve of material progress. Ancient Christianity saw the end of time and life in the material world; the scientific mind-set would see the promise of great progress in the here and now.

THE DAWN OF EMOTION AND THE ''SOCIAL EGO''

With the blossoming of the third dimension the sense of "self" expands and acquires a new depth that is primarily emotional in nature. Where the individual in a two-dimensional perceptual frame is largely governed by instinct and bodily impulse, the person in a three-dimensional frame is largely governed by emotions and social expectations. This does not mean that the capacity for rational thought was absent; rather, it means that in a preliterate and prerational society, feeling-based communications were the dominant currency of the culture.

In the era of agrarian-based civilizations, the flow of feelings were largely a given and not subjected to systematic mental scrutiny. Symbols of family and society (such as a flag or coat of arms) would have great power to focus allegiance as much of life's meaning was found through a sense of social belonging and shared commitments. More rational communication and analysis was a capacity that would not broadly emerge until the fourth dimension and the scientific-industrial era. Therefore, most persons were not highly articulate in describing their emotional experience. Communication was more a matter of direct assertion of feelings without benefit of reflective inspection of those feelings.

The blossoming of emotion was essential for the cohesiveness of city-state civilization. With tens of thousands of persons brought together with an unprecedented diversity of work roles and status differences, a new kind of "social glue" was required to hold the complex social structure together—and that glue was the bonding force of emotion. Where blood ties and kinship held together the small-village society in the second dimension, it was the power of emotional bonds and fellowship that held together the civilizations in the third dimension. Emotions were the bridging force that linked together disparate individuals and occupations into a cohesive whole. In his book *Human Evolution* anthropologist Bernard Campbell writes that "the expression of emotions is the basis of social life; it creates and maintains both bond and structure in society."[22] Rather than a loosely knit collection of persons, city-states were bonded into tight communities with strong feelings of allegiance. Drawing again from the work of Samuel Kramer, we learn that in ancient Sumer, "the inhabitants of a city were known as its 'sons' and were considered a closely related, integrated unit. Normally, they took pride in their city, god, and ruler and were ever ready to take up arms in their behalf."[23]

An emotionally bonded society still left ample room for conflicts and competition. For example, the ancient Sumerians had a reputation for being ambitious, competitive, and aggressive. They had a strong drive to achieve superiority over others and their enthusiasm for prestige and victory deeply influenced their view of life and their education, politics, and economics.[24]

Overall, the added depth of three dimensions created enough perceptual space to enable people to see themselves as separate from nature, separate from other city-state communities, and separate from other classes within one's community. Seeing the self as increasingly distinct promoted a sense of personal autonomy and empowerment. People saw they could farm nature, tame animals, build houses and monuments, and undertake activities that were uniquely different from the workings of the natural environment. As people acquired confidence in their ability to plan, organize, and control their future, the "magical" qualities of nature were diminished commensurately.

An expanded time sense pushed humans to develop their ability for mental abstraction and to develop new words and concepts to orient the imagination. It also brought a more poignant awareness of the seasons of an individual's life and the inevitability of death, intensifying people's recognition of impermanence and mortality.

The experience of self was further expanded by the dramatic change in material circumstances. With a settled existence there were far more things for people to possess compared with the days of a mobile, hunter-gatherer way of life. Even a simple farmer could own land, housing, animals, farm tools, and personal adornments. In turn the very act of possessing things affirmed a person's unique identity as the one who was doing the possessing. In being able to possess objects "out there," a reciprocal awareness was fostered "in here," and individuals acquired a growing sense of self-possession. With possessions came material possessiveness and a material basis for defining oneself ("I am the person who owns . . .").

With the rise of large-scale cities the cooperative and sharing manner of the small-village way of life was replaced with competition and possessiveness. Social differentiation developed rapidly as people sought to possess things—land, housing, tools, jewelry, positions, and titles—for their exclusive use and that of their heirs. People also sought to possess (and oppress) other people, for it is during this epoch that we see the rise of slavery and the oppression of women.

Although society was becoming increasingly divided into rich and poor classes, the vast majority of people were poor peasants who did not expect their material situation ever to improve markedly. Feelings of unquestioned duty and unchanging destiny dominated society, as most people lived out the social roles into which they had been born.

OF PEASANTS, CITIZENS, AND CIVILIZATIONS

To understand the mind-set of civilization in the third dimension, it is important to appreciate the great extent to which it remained connected with nature and agriculture. Although the urban minority had a powerful influence on culture, the overall society continued to be organized around and oriented toward farming. Much of the raw material used in urban manufacturing was produced on the surrounding farms, and much of the trade in the cities was in agricultural products.[25] City dwellers also worshiped gods personifying natural powers and participated in rites that marked the major seasons of the year. Urbanization, then, did not erase the city dweller's strong sense of connection with the land and nature.[26]

On this agrarian foundation were constructed the first large cities, with tens of thousands of persons. No longer were communities small, isolated, relatively self-sufficient, and homogeneous; they were large, interconnected, interdependent, and heterogeneous. No longer could people rely primarily on personal relationships with a small tribe known intimately; they had to rely increasingly on more impersonal transactions with persons in specialized occupations (potters, wheelmakers, jewelers, moneylenders, butchers, tailors). Instead of obtaining food directly through sharing, it was purchased by haggling over prices. Less and less could people live a simple existence, "running on automatic." Instead they had to become increasingly reflective and intentional in their lives and interactions with others.[27]

Unlike industrial-based civilizations, which rest on the labor of a large and relatively affluent middle class, the agrarian-based civilizations rested on the labor of a large and impoverished peasant class. To understand the distinctive nature of agrarian-based civilizations, we must therefore understand the nature of peasant society. In his overview of humankind's rise to civilization, anthropologist Peter Farb describes how an impoverished peasant class has been the basis for civilizations for at least five thousand years: "Institutionalized poverty, generation after generation, became the peasants' way of life; it was on the foundation of that poverty that Sumer, Babylon, Egypt, Greece, Rome and other empires were erected."[28] The lack of expectation of material progress by peasant society is described simply and poignantly by a woman in her thirties from a poor village in contemporary China. When asked what she wanted from life, she replied, "Enough to eat and drink, and that things not get worse."[29]

From ancient to modern times, peasants have not only been physically trapped inside a subsistence way of life but also mentally trapped inside a cocoon of customs, superstitions, and limited expectations. A masterful account of peasant cultures is provided by Richard Critchfield, who lived with peasants around the world.[30] Critchfield describes peasants as present-oriented, fatalistic, bound by tradition and custom, and family-centered. Most peasant villagers have an intense love of their land and feel a personal bond with the soil. Their mental universe does not extend much beyond the village, so their outlook on life is quite narrow. They tend to be fatalistic, believing that life is predestined and difficult to change. Most peasants tend to believe in supernatural forces, and they often rely on faith healing, protective magic, and personal gods directly concerned with their welfare. Displays of wealth and social status are strongly censured by the rest of the community, since there is the feeling that the advance of the few can take place only at the expense of the many. Overall, the way of life and attitudes of the peasant majority in agrarian civilizations were very different from those of the middle-class majority of industrial civilizations.

Compared with an industrial economy, the range of occupations in an agrarian-based civilization were quite narrow. People were often expected to pursue the same craft or trade as their family and were limited by rigid customs, illiteracy, superstition, and poverty. While agrarian-based civilization represented a dramatic change from the hunter-gatherer and small-village way of life, it also contained many primitive elements—a lack of social mobility, arranged marriages, the oppression of women, restricted access to formal education, and rule by political and spiritual elites.[31] A great distance still needed to be traveled to develop social forms that would support the full expression of our human potentials.

In the hunter-gatherer stage there was such a high degree of equality among people that a natural democracy existed. This form of democracy persisted through the transitional period of small villages and then into the early stages of city-state development in Mesopotamia. In ancient Sumer political power initially rested in the hands of free citizens, who met in an assembly consisting of an upper house of elders and a lower house of free men.[32] This early form of democratic government did not last, however. As struggles between city-states became more violent, and as barbaric invasions increased, the kings that had been temporarily appointed by the assembly of free citizens achieved hereditary status. Early expressions of democracy devolved into a long era of kings and ruling elites, and it would not be until the urban-industrial revolution that democracy would reemerge forcefully.

A distinctive feature of society in the agrarian era is the shift to male domination. Where the two-dimensional society was small-scale, equalitarian, and oriented toward the feminine archetype, the three-dimensional society was large-scale, socially differentiated, and oriented toward the masculine archetype. Almost universally the father and the oldest male were recognized as the head of the family, and kinship was traced through the father's side of the family. In almost every area of life the males generally outranked women, from voting rights to property rights to divorce rights.

The feminine archetype—with its more receptive, equalitarian, and unitive orientation—was well suited for the hunter-gatherer and small-village way of life characteristic of the second dimension. However, to accomplish the unprecedented task of separating humanity from semiconscious immersion within nature and developing large-scale civilizations, it seemed to require the more active, aggressive, and separative orientation of the masculine archetype. In turn, as the masculine principle came to dominance, a new level of hierarchy, competition, and striving was brought into human affairs. The masculine archetype came to influence nearly every aspect of life—from the gender of gods, priests, and rulers to that of the heads of households. Although some measure of gender balance can be found in the strong emphasis on community, family relationships, and emotional bonding, the third dimension seems largely dominated by the masculine archetype. To point out the functional role of the masculine archetype is not to approve of the oppression of women over the thousands of years when the agrarian-based civilizations were developing; rather it is to see that the emergence of the masculine archetype appears to have been a temporary response to the perceptual needs for building early civilizations.

Feminine mythology apparently played an important role in bringing the masculine archetype into civilizational dominance. According to legend, the revered goddess of ancient Sumer, Inanna, used trickery to acquire from a male god the "gifts of civilization" that she then brought to her city—one of the first in the world. Among the many civilizing gifts brought to Sumer by the goddess Inanna were the rights, privileges, and trappings of priesthood and kingship; the arts of warfare and statesmanship; and the arts of prostitution, sacred and profane, of the temple and tavern. Ironically some of the attributes of the patriarchal era that most offend the modern consciousness of sexual equality were the very "gifts of civilization" brought by the goddess Inanna. Although some suggest that a male priesthood developed this mythology to justify the oppression of women, it seems equally plausible that the rise to dominance of the masculine archetype was essential for the development of city-state civilizations.[33]

The masculine archetype brought the action-oriented and self-starting energy needed for humanity to differentiate itself from nature and to undertake the enormous task of building city-state civilizations. Equality between gender archetypes was apparently beyond the perceptual capacities and psychological maturity of humanity at this stage of development. An immense amount of learning—embracing two stages of perceptual development—would be required before a level of consciousness and culture could emerge where gender equality would be viewed as both natural and functional. Only after realizing the potentials of the masculine archetype would civilization return to reclaim the lost aspects of the feminine. In his book *The Passion of the Western Mind* Richard Tarnas writes that while the evolution of the Western mind has been founded on the repression of the feminine archetype, *"the deepest passion of the Western mind has been to reunite with the ground of its being.* The driving impulse of the West's masculine consciousness has been its dialectical quest not only to realize itself, but also, finally, to recover its connection with the whole, to come to terms with the great feminine principle in life: to differentiate itself from but then rediscover and reunite with the feminine, with the mystery of life, of nature, of soul."[34] Early civilizations had a great distance to travel, however, before they would begin to realize the goal of archetypal integration described by Tarnas.

Like the oppression of women, the development of large-scale warfare seemed an inevitable result of the partial consciousness and great powers unleashed by the opening of the third dimension. The same centralized authority and hierarchy that could organize a city-state could also organize an army. With the building of city-states there was much to protect—fertile fields and herds, homes and buildings, extensive tools and personal possessions. In the words of anthropologist Peter Farb, "War and domination were built into the ancient city as inescapably as the very mudbricks and stone that went into the physical structures themselves."[35] Humanity was leaving behind the peaceful, equalitarian, and small-scale village societies that characterized the millennia prior to the transition to city-states.[36] Henceforth peace would not be an unconscious given; instead it would depend upon conscious choice.

Andrew Bard Schmookler, in his book *The Parable of the Tribes*, describes how no one civilization could impose peace upon everyone else, but any one civilization could impose upon all the rest the necessity for power seeking and warfare.[37] Because the civilizations that survived were those that were most effective in their exercise of power, it created a vicious circle in which civilizations felt it necessary to become power-oriented to defend themselves against other power-oriented societies. Peace was a condition that had to be consciously chosen by all civilizations that impinged upon one another. And for peace to become a conscious choice of entire nations, a level of maturity was required that exceeded that of the agrarian era or even the industrial era. Humanity could eventually choose to live in peace, but only after learning and relearning the painful lessons of conflict and war.

THE RISE OF THE SKY GODS

In the agrarian era, spiritual attention shifted from the immediacy of a nature-oriented Earth Goddess in two dimensions to the remoteness of heaven-oriented Sky Gods in three dimensions. Nonetheless the Earth-oriented religion of the second dimension probably continued to be important to the village dwellers and peasants, whose labors were vital to the agrarian-based civilizations. Sky-oriented religions were probably much more important to the city dwellers, who experienced the depth consciousness characteristic of these first, large-scale civilizations.

The differences in spirituality between the second and third dimensions are reflected in the psychic and psychological distance between humanity and the divine implied by each perspective:

- **Hunter-gatherer spirituality and the role of shamans**—For ancient hunter-gatherers there was virtually no perceptual distance between the individual and the spiritual forces in the world. People felt the immediate presence of mysterious and invisible forces in their lives. Religious institutions were not required, as people participated directly in the supernatural. The shaman's role was to participate with individuals and the community in this supernatural process through trances, magic, divination, and other means in order to cure sickness, bring rainfall, ensure success in conflict, and meet personal needs.

- **Agrarian-based spirituality and the role of priests**—In the depth world of three dimensions there was a new distance between the individual and the spiritual realm—a new dualism between heaven and Earth, between the individual and the transcendent gods.[38] The Sky Gods represented the awesome and remote powers of heaven, and the priest was the intermediary that bridged the distance between the individual and the divine. Where the shaman worked to facilitate the direct experience of healing and the enlivening of spiritual forces, the priest tended to work indirectly through rituals and prayers that were institutionalized in the authority of the church and state.

With the emergence of Sky Gods, the distance between the realm of humanity and the realm of the gods increased, and the process of institutionalized worship (which implicitly acknowledges this separation) took on greater importance. Religious institutions and the priestly class acquired great power and authority as divine intermediaries in a world still assumed to be interpenetrated by supernatural forces that could be influenced by prayer and faith.

The perceptual geometry of the third dimension is consistent with a transcendental spirituality. Because the material world was not seen as going anywhere (except through endless rounds of repetition), and because the spiritual realm was seen as transcendent or apart from this world, it was only natural for people to imagine that the role of religion was to enable them to get off the worldly wheel of death and rebirth. Many of the great religions that emerged in this stage (Buddhism, Hinduism, and Taoism) were explicitly concerned with getting beyond the material world and moving into transcendent spiritual realms. Most of these wisdom traditions did not encourage material and social change but rather worked for deep change in the inner psyche and soul, so that a person would not be reborn into this world of strife and pain.

THE SEASONS OF THE THIRD DIMENSION

The period from roughly 10,000 B.C. to 3500 B.C. was a time of gradual transition from a nomadic, tribal, gathering and hunting way of life to a settled, small-village way of life that relied upon the domestication of plants and animals. We could view this period as the springtime of the agrarian revolution, or as the autumn and winter of the second dimension (with the decline of the hunter-gatherer way of life). More fundamentally these millennia represent a time of complex transition between two dominant views of reality and ways of life. For that reason I'll reserve the designation of "springtime" of the third dimension for the period when agrarian-based civilizations emerged most decisively—roughly 3500 B.C.

The emergence of a new kind of geometric art just before the rise of the city-state civilizations (ca. 4500–3500 B.C.) provides intriguing evidence that a shift in human consciousness was under way at this time. Joseph Campbell describes this dramatic change in aesthetic consciousness by saying that "with the appearance in the world of well-established, strongly developing settled villages, there breaks into view an abundance of the most gracefully and consciously organized circular compositions of geometrical and abstract motifs on the pottery.''[39] The abrupt appearance of these well-composed, abstract geometric designs in the centuries just preceding the development of large-scale civilizations suggests that a new aesthetic consciousness—and a new objectivity in human perception—was emerging rapidly.

Spring (3500 B.C. to 600 B.C.)

During this period the earliest high civilizations of the world burst into existence. The first civilization to emerge was apparently that of Mesopotamia (in roughly 3500 B.C. in the delta region formed by the Tigris and Euphrates rivers), followed by Egypt (roughly 2800 B.C. along the Nile), then India (roughly 2500 B.C. in the Indus Valley), and China (roughly 1500 B.C. along the Yellow River). Civilization emerged in the Americas in the region of Mexico in approximately 1200 B.C. with the Olmec Empire (although there is evidence that an advanced civilization may have developed in South America in what is now Ecuador as early as 3000 B.C.). All of these societies developed the constellation of activities we now associate with "civilization"—writing, astronomy, massive architecture, a division of labor, a professional priesthood, and centralized government. Because many of these civilizations were isolated from one another (particularly India, China, and the Americas) and because, despite their independence, they all developed at roughly the same time with similar attributes, it suggests that when a critical threshold is reached in the coevolution of culture and consciousness, civilization will inevitably arise.

The ancient civilizations developed over a period of roughly three thousand years and then, around 600 B.C., the pace of change began to accelerate around the world. Internal decay and repeated barbarian invasions transformed the cultures of the Indus River, Mesopotamia, and Nile Valley. Despite her relative isolation, even China was going through a major metamorphosis. Throughout the world, social change was accelerated by the invention of the horse-drawn chariot, iron-age technology, and new weapons of war.

Summer to Autumn (600 B.C. to A.D. 1500)

Around 600 B.C. the world entered what many historians have called the Classical Age. New civilizations were flourishing in Greece,

Persia, Rome, China, and India. Each made great contributions to philosophy, religion, art, science, and government. A number of the world's great religions were also founded at this time.

Not all civilizations developed at the same pace or in the same direction. For example, by A.D. 500 the western or European portion of the Roman Empire had collapsed and fallen into a dark age, while the eastern portion (called Byzantium and located in Mediterranean Asia) continued to keep the spark of learning and culture alive for another thousand years. During this thousand-year period the most significant contributions to civilization came from Byzantium, the Moslem-oriented cultures, and Asian sources such as China and India.[40] In the Americas the Mayan Empire reached its height around A.D. 800 and then went into decline. With the coming of the Crusades, around 1100, Europe renewed its contacts with the prospering civilizations of Byzantium and was awakened from the stagnation of the Dark Ages. Europe also acquired technologies such as the compass that would enable oceangoing explorers to launch a new era of trade and discovery.

Transition (A.D. 1500 to 1800)

By the 1400s the Crusades and other explorations helped spark a Renaissance in the arts and sciences of Europe. A religious reformation also swept through Europe at this time, affirming the role of the individual and bringing into question every aspect of established Christian doctrine. By the mid-1700s the combined impact of the Renaissance and Reformation brought Western civilization to the brink of the Industrial Revolution. During this same period the vigor of the Asian and African civilizations diminished, shifting the leadership for advancing civilization back to the West. Voyages by Europeans to the Americas (particularly the Spanish) resulted in massive destruction to the ancient civilizations in the region now known as Central America. Dominance shifted to the militarily powerful nations of England, Europe, and North America, and their economic growth, in turn, was propelled forward by economic advantages gained through slavery and the ability to exploit the natural resources of weaker nations.

SUMMARY

The story of agrarian-based civilizations comprises the bulk of recorded human history. During these millennia humanity experienced enormous social turbulence—the rise and fall of empires, the growth and decline of institutional religions, and shifts in cultural dominance between different areas of the world. Yet underlying this ferment was the stability of the perceptual geometry of the third dimension with its more expansive and yet circular view of reality, identity, and society. This perceptual paradigm supported the unfolding of an immensely complex and rich epoch marked by tremendous social upheaval, much of which should not be equated with true social evolution since, when wars of conquest were over, little more had changed than a redistribution of power over land and people.

It was not until the transitional period in Europe (from approximately A.D. 1500 to 1700) that the world would see, not another eddy in the surface currents of history, but a sea change in culture and consciousness. A number of powerful revolutions blossomed in Europe that continue to reverberate around the world: a scientific revolution challenged the belief in the supernatural and the authority of the church; a religious reformation questioned the role and function of religious institutions; a renaissance brought a new perspective into the arts; an industrial revolution brought unprecedented material progress; an urban revolution brought masses of people together in new ways, breaking apart the feudal pattern of living; and a democratic revolution fostered a new level of citizen empowerment and involvement. These powerful revolutions were expressions of the opening of a new perceptual paradigm, and they mark a dramatic break with the era of agrarian-based civilization.

DYNAMIC CONSCIOUSNESS AND THE SCIENTIFIC-INDUSTRIAL ERA

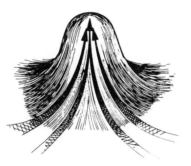

The **fourth dimension** is the stage of *dynamic consciousness* and is an epoch of explosive material growth driven by revolutions in science and technology. The wheel of time opens into a progressing spiral, and people perceive the potential for broad material progress. Material development becomes a primary measure of success as the mystery of nature gives way to science and an analyzing intellect. People strongly identify themselves with their intellect and, in this predominantly materialistic and existential reality, people feel relatively unique and alone. A new sense of personal autonomy and freedom fosters greater citizenship in government, entrepreneurship in economics, and self-authority in spiritual matters. This era is also characterized by massive urbanization and the development of an affluent middle class.

$\mathcal{D}$YNAMIC CONSCIOUSNESS
AND THE
SCIENTIFIC-INDUSTRIAL ERA

The scientific-industrial revolution marks the beginning of the modern era of development. After thousands of years of subservience to nature, humanity reached a critical mass of knowledge and power that enabled entire civilizations to stand apart from, and seemingly achieve dominion over, nature. Because we now see the many problems generated by the scientific-industrial era, it is difficult to appreciate the enormous promise it held when viewed from its springtime of growth just a few hundred years ago. For the masses of people the agrarian era represented an unbroken cycle of poverty, disease, and drudgery. People saw that, with practical inventions, their bleak way of living could be improved dramatically. With ingenuity and entrepreneurship, great material advances were possible in the here and now.

As with other epochs, it is impossible to state with precision when the fourth dimension opened. In Europe a renaissance of thought got under way in the 1400s. Small currents merged into a flood of industrial activity in England and Europe by the late 1700s. By the late

1900s this revolution was generating at least as many problems as it was intended to solve (toxic wastes, the greenhouse effect, rain-forest destruction, nuclear proliferation, alienation, crime, and so on) and its autumn of growth had arrived. Within a scant three hundred years an entire perceptual epoch had emerged, blossomed, and begun to disintegrate—a remarkable acceleration in the pace of civilizational evolution.

The phrase *scientific-industrial era* is no more than a shorthand description for a sweeping change in culture and consciousness that, in the experience of Europe and the United States, involved the intertwined impact of at least seven distinct revolutions:

- The **scientific revolution** transformed our way of looking at the world and our approach to knowledge. Scientists assume we live in a universe governed by natural laws that can be discovered through reason and rigorous testing of hypotheses. The scientific method proved so powerful that it challenged the supremacy of supernatural explanations and undermined the authority of the church.

- The **religious reformation** questioned whether the churches were essential intermediaries between people and the divine. By challenging the role of religious institutions, the reformation undermined the divine right of kings and helped create a secular foundation for government.

- The **Renaissance** was expressed in a new attitude of skepticism, self-criticism, individual empowerment, and a rebirth of interest in Greek and Roman thought, which had been submerged during the Dark Ages. It was also expressed in a new worldliness and appreciation of human beings as ordinary people with strengths and weaknesses.

- A second **Agricultural Revolution** was made possible by improvements in technologies for planting, cultivating, transporting, and storing food. These innovations greatly increased agricultural productivity and made it possible for a steadily increasing proportion of the population to live and work in an urban environment.

- The **Industrial Revolution** brought unprecedented material progress as human and animal energy were replaced by the artificial power of coal, natural gas, gasoline, and electricity. With the steam engine came mechanization of fields and factories and the mass production of food and goods. New economic structures emerged as money was substituted for barter and trade barriers were reduced. Economic integration fostered political and social integration.

- An **urban revolution** accompanied the Industrial Revolution and brought an unprecedented proportion of the population together in cities of immense scale and complexity. Gradually the impoverished peasant class developed into a more affluent middle class.

- A **democratic revolution** emerged as an expression of the new degree of citizen freedom and empowerment. Based on a growing belief in the integrity and ability of the individual, the rights of kings were progressively limited and democratic rights expanded.

The combined impact of these powerful revolutions constituted a new perceptual paradigm that emerged first in Europe and the United States and that eventually radiated out to transform the world.

EXPERIENCING DIMENSIONALITY

Before describing the perceptual paradigm of the fourth dimension, it is important to distinguish between our ability to *think dimensionally* and our ability to *experience dimensionally*. We are multidimensional beings who are able to directly experience, and then learn from, the multidimensional nature of reality.[1] *We can experience directly many more dimensions than we can grasp conceptually.*

The invisible geometry that upholds our existence is present everywhere. Dimensions are not simply mathematical abstractions; they are the pervasive matrix of our very existence, as intimate and close as the air we breathe. Because the dimensional nature of reality is so close, so subtle, and so intimate, it is easy to overlook. Yet because we live within and move through a vast range of dimensions, it is only natural that we can directly know and experience the multidimensional nature of reality. We can experience far more than three dimensions, even if we cannot conceptualize the nature of those further dimensions. For example, to experience and then realize the potentials of the agrarian revolution and third dimension did not require people to understand the physics of three-dimensional space and time. Instead it required people directly to appreciate the cyclical and in-depth nature of reality and then work to actualize the potentials inherent within that felt experience. Likewise, to appreciate and live out of the fourth dimension does not require people to understand the mathematics of relativity theory; rather, it requires that people develop their intuitive grasp of the dynamic and relativistic nature of self and material reality—essentially, an existential and materialistic understanding of ourselves and the world—and then to actualize the potentials awakened by this expanded frame of reference.

THE FOURTH DIMENSION: DYNAMIC CONSCIOUSNESS

As with other dimensional epochs, the pattern of perception characteristic of the fourth stage did not open up in one fell swoop but emerged gradually over centuries. This new perspective was first expressed by artists and then later spread to religion, economics, politics, and physics.

The opening of the fourth dimension brought a new degree of spaciousness and dynamism into people's experience of life. The world was no longer seen as locked into unchanging cycles that were not going anywhere; instead, there was a new "roominess" within which people could live and move.* An important expression of the expanded spaciousness of this epoch is found in the development of

---

*It appears that the spatial aspects of dimensions are perceived long before the temporal aspects. For example, in the earliest Buddhist teachings the experience of space was basic to meditation instructions, and it was not until a thousand years later (in the tenth century A.D.) that Buddhist thinkers realized the profound mystery and experience hidden within conventional notions of "time."[2]

an accurate three-dimensional perspective in art—a perception that, remarkably, did not arrive in the world until roughly the 1300s during the Renaissance in Europe, the time of initial transition to the scientific-industrial era. Although the pioneering Florentine artist Giotto is credited with being the first person to fully conceive of a flat canvas in three-dimensional terms (where things closer are larger and things farther away are proportionately smaller and disappear into a vanishing point on the horizon), it was not until the early 1500s that Leonardo da Vinci brought perspective forcefully into the world of art and popularized it.[3]

Despite the fact that we now take perspectivity for granted, it was almost entirely absent from human consciousness until this time. Cultural historian Jean Gebser writes, "There is no evidence of an awareness of qualitative and objectified space in early antiquity or in the epoch preceding the Renaissance."[4] Surprisingly, then, an understanding of perspectivity is a perceptual capacity of recent origins. As Gebser explains, "Crucial to perspectivity is the 'vanishing point' at the horizon of one's field of vision. Yet that vanishing point is only the opposite to the point of origin, which is the eye of the spatially conscious subject."[5] *To see how we see* requires that we stand back from immersion in the process of seeing and look at both the scene and the seer simultaneously so as to put them into accurate relationship. Three-dimensional depth perspective, then, requires a new step back in consciousness: A person must move, in their consciousness, from inside the three-dimensional reference frame to outside of it in order to see the relationship between the observer and the scene.[6] *We began to see things in an accurate three-dimensional perspective only when our experienced context for looking at the world began to expand into four dimensions.*

Although Eastern artists did not develop an objectified perspectivity, they made their unique contribution to our way of seeing. In his book *Art and Physics* Leonard Shlain explains that "instead of establishing a point of view somewhere off and in front of the canvas, as in the West, the central point was *within,* inside the landscape. . . . The Chinese landscape painter assumed that the beholder, along with the artist himself, was *in* the landscape, not looking at it from the outside."[7] Although Eastern artists did not develop the science of three-dimensional perspectivity, they did express a sophisticated appreciation of the aliveness and generative power of space—a view that the West is only beginning to accept as quantum theory describes particles suddenly coming into existence from out of seemingly empty space. The intuitions of both Western and Eastern artists were far in advance of the formalisms of science. It would take physics nearly four hundred years to catch up with and begin to explain the transformation in perceptual experience portrayed by artists in the East and West.

The ability to stand back from immersion within a three-dimensional world was a decisive step in the evolution of humanity's perceptual paradigm. With disidentification from the unvarying spatial framework of three dimensions, people were liberated perceptually and began to look with fresh and critical eyes at those institutions that embodied confining norms and absolutist values—primarily the church and state. Ultimately, in a four-dimensional reality, each point occupies a unique and distinct place in the fabric of space-time. All is relative. There is no favored position. Because each person and place has its valid status and standing in a relativistic universe, the cosmological basis for absolute authority is profoundly undermined. Each person's point of view is valid and distinct. Each person is a legitimate source of authority for their unique point of view and perspective.

Because each person is viewed as having a singular place in the universe, the new perceptual framework supports the rise of a new level of individualism—and this transformed religion, science, culture, and economic life. In religion the church could no longer claim that it occupied a favored position in the universe, and this fostered greater freedom in belief and worship. In science there was greater freedom from superstition and religious dogma and the ability to more openly explore the nature of the universe. In culture, there was greater freedom for intellectual inquiry and creative expression. In economic affairs there was greater opportunity for persons to work freely as entrepreneurs and to market their skills to the highest bidder as free agents.

The new perceptual geometry fostered a new sense of time as well. In the three-dimensional framework, time was seen as a wheel moving around and around in endlessly repetitive cycles, not going anywhere. With the new spaciousness provided by four dimensions, time was no longer compressed into a flat wheel and locked into endless cycles but could move outward. Time opened into an evolving spiral of development that could progress without apparent limit (see Figure 6).

Figure 6: Time as an Open and Progressing Spiral

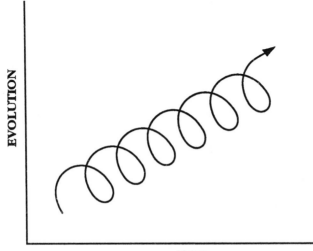

Because reality was seen as material and time as progressing, a powerful perceptual foundation was established that enabled people to visualize the potential for material progression or progress. Indeed the drive to material development is the most basic expression of the time experience of the fourth dimension. An expectation of perpetual novelty and innovation became widespread in popular consciousness. Along with the ability to imagine material progress came a new facility for practical invention and projecting plans into the future. No longer was progress something to be achieved by the few at the expense of the many; now it was possible for everyone to advance. (Although this new perception of progress emerged initially in a Western European context, it is rapidly becoming a global norm as the communications revolution diffuses the psychology of materialism and rising expectations.)

One particular aspect of the changing sense of time had a profound impact on physics—namely, the shift from the notion of a "cosmic now" in three dimensions to the "relativity of simultaneity" in four dimensions. With four dimensions the universe was no longer viewed as having a single time that applies throughout; instead every point in space-time was seen as unique. Time for any point could only be defined relative to some other point because there was assumed to be no discernible, underlying time that could integrate these relative times into a cosmic whole. (While relativity theory does not prohibit the possible existence of a cosmic now in higher dimensions, it assumes there is no "place" or accessible frame of reference from which to stand back from the relativity of space-time in order to verify the existence of a grand-scale simultaneity.)

The perceptual paradigm of the fourth stage had a powerful impact upon religion. Because this mechanistic view of reality was so effective in describing how nature worked, it undermined explanations that relied on supernatural forces. If the material universe obeys natural laws and science enables these laws to be discovered, then the universe is a lawful place, and people no longer need to fear that some capricious and wrathful God will intervene arbitrarily in their lives. If the universe runs in accord with objective laws and mathematically describable principles, then it seems improbable that an unpredictable and fickle deity will intrude into worldly affairs. In the scientific view it is through the power of the intellect, rather than the power of prayer, that we can discover the laws of the universe and become masters of our own fate. The more we can learn about the master machine that is our universe, the more power and control we can acquire and, in turn, the more comfort and convenience we can add to our lives.

With science describing the universe as a masterfully constructed machine, the aliveness infusing nature so characteristic of earlier dimensional epochs was replaced with a view that the cosmos is composed largely of empty space, dead matter, and autonomous human beings. Humanity now stood isolated at the pinnacle of evolution in a nearly lifeless universe. With human beings occupying such a unique and elevated position, it seemed appropriate for people to use their power to exploit nature to serve their own well-being. Predictably, then, the great power of the intellect was used to exploit the seemingly diminished aliveness of nature on behalf of those most intensely alive—human beings.

THE SEPARATED SELF

The perceptual geometry of the fourth stage has produced the most differentiated and encapsulated beings that the world will ever know. The self of the scientific-industrial era is assumed to be locked inside a biological body that is cut off from direct experience of other people and the rest of the universe. Having experienced this extreme separation—as both psychological alienation and as technological empowerment—humanity can begin the long journey to reconnect with the Life-force that animates our cosmos. Despite the anxiety generated by being so far removed from the nurturing Life-force, this is a highly purposeful stage of development. In this era we acquire our most distinct and empowered sense of "self" as biological-material beings, communities, and nations. Once we know ourselves as separate and unique, we can then begin to reclaim our subtle connection with all of existence.

The perceptual geometry of the fourth dimension naturally fosters an existential sense of self. To reiterate, in a four-dimensional reference frame there is no special status to any position or any place—all is relative. If no place has a favored position, then no person or institution can claim special knowledge or privilege; each person's point of view becomes equally legitimate and valid. No longer are people subservient to the authoritarian views of a church or state or culture; instead they see themselves as empowered individuals who are capable of acting in their own self-interest, economically, politically, socially, and spiritually.

The rise of the autonomous individual in the context of industrialized society was a revolutionary social invention. Even the early Greek city-states, despite their professed concern for the individual citizen, did not foster the degree of autonomy found in the industrial era. Joseph Campbell writes that in early Greece "the individual derived his importance from his relation to the state; he was viewed as a citizen who depends on the state and who can contribute to its welfare. But it is the state that is omnipotent."[8]

What most distinguishes individuals in the scientific-industrial era is their use of the intellect as a potent tool for discovering the laws underlying the universe and for mastering nature. Given the powerful role of the intellect, people naturally tend to equate their identity with their thinking process. The ability to reflect consciously on the thinking process itself has not yet emerged decisively. Instead consciousness is assumed to be a by-product of bioelectrical activity in the brain and without any independent status. In not thinking consciousness can provide a bridge beyond the apparent fact of our physical separateness, we don't subject our self-experience to rigorous scrutiny, and a self-reinforcing and self-fulfilling process of identity formation develops. The self of the fourth dimension, then, is a thought thinking about itself—a self-referencing mental loop. Were it not for the penetrating reality of death, the encapsulated thinking ego could continue indefinitely as a thought system continually reconfirming its own existence.

When we think we are material beings, it is only natural that we search for satisfaction of our wants through material sources. We substitute temporary pleasures for the deeper satisfaction of genuine union with the Meta-universe. Instead of discovering eternity at the core of our being, we project our search outward into the substitute "immortality projects" of acquiring a house and car, building a business, establishing a social reputation, and acquiring other expressions of power and prominence.[9] The urge to possession is driven by more than the desire for these things; it is an unconscious drive to overcome death by using our tangible acquisitions to demonstrate the significance of our lives. In not recognizing the artesian well of eternity forever bubbling up from within the core of our being, the search for that which has lasting value becomes misdirected.

After attaining the unprecedented autonomy and material power of the scientific-industrial era, gnawing issues remain: Why do we have this freedom and this power? What is the purpose of life? Is our ability to possess and consume the primary measure of meaning and worth? These questions cannot be answered satisfactorily within the perceptual paradigm of the fourth dimension. Nonetheless, despite its limitations, the fourth stage represents an important epoch, as it enables humanity to develop an unprecedented degree of personal autonomy and capacity for self-determining behavior. In developing our existential identity, we plant the seeds for our further transformations. After fulfilling the potentials of this stage, we find diminishing satisfaction from a consumerist approach to life, alienation from our core sense of self, separation from the natural environment, and loss of an enduring sense of community. In short, after completing this stage, we are fully ready to begin our journey of reunion with the universe.

URBAN-INDUSTRIAL SOCIETY

The most striking evidence of social change in the industrial era is the massive shift of people from a rural to an urban setting. When this era began in Europe and the United States in the late 1700s, more than 90 percent of the population lived and worked on farms. By its conclusion two hundred years later in the late 1900s, more than 95 percent of the population lived and worked in cities and suburbs. In these bare statistics is the story of an extraordinary social, political, and economic transformation.

Prior to the Industrial Revolution the amount of surplus food from farming was marginal, supporting only a fraction of the population in an urban lifestyle. But improved plows, the mechanical tractor and reaper, and other technological advances created a huge increase in agricultural productivity, and food surpluses soared. For the first time in history it was possible for a majority of the population to move from the farms to the cities and engage in manufacturing and related activities. This opened the floodgates to a sweeping pattern of changes—a middle class emerged to replace the peasant class, a belief in material progress replaced the expectation of scarcity, free markets replaced feudal control, and a psychology of self-determination replaced a spirit of subservience.

For thousands of years most people had lived as peasant farmers, subservient to the absolute power of church and state, and with very little control over their destiny. Industrialization, however, set in motion a dramatic change in class structure. The center of gravity in industrial society shifted from impoverished peasants to a relatively well-to-do economic middle class, thereby transforming politics, religion, and business. Although these changes required centuries to accomplish and were accompanied by enormous abuses, still the fact and direction of change was clear. The Industrial Revolution brought a much more affluent, educated, and empowered middle class to the center of civilization.

Material affluence was gained at considerable social cost. The urbanizing and industrializing process tore individuals from their traditional communities and extended families and made them autonomous workers—cogs in the great machine of industry. Instead of small-scale, emotionally bonded communities nurtured by many generations of families and relationships, people moved into impersonal cities with few ties to an extended family. As cities grew ever more massive, they became primarily economic engines to power the mega-machine of industrial civilization. These human-created environments were divorced from contact with nature's wildness as well as its rhythms and cycles. Cities were not organized to serve a feeling of community and sense of beauty; rather they were oriented to serve economic efficiency. Urban environments concretized the paradigm of the industrial era and mirrored back to their inhabitants only human-generated patterns and perceptions—the straight edges of rectangular buildings and grids for traffic, the impersonal corporations and factories, and the overwhelming mass of humanity that crowds out a diverse ecology of plants and animals.

Basic to an urban-industrial society is the existence of psychologically autonomous individuals who have the self-confidence and self-authority to enter into economic contracts. This respect and trust for individuals in economic affairs spills over into social relations and strengthens the foundation for democracy and self-government. While a free-market economy liberated people from centuries of oppression by a landed aristocracy, it also transformed the primary purpose of life into the pursuit of material gain. Free-market principles promoted a narrow expression of personal freedom, fostered un-precedented competition, and produced a mass marketplace of alie-nating scale and complexity. Overall, the development of an autonomous sense of self in a materialistic world has been purchased by rewarding some of the most antisocial impulses of humanity—raw greed, unbridled competition, and the drive to acquire unlimited money and power.

The flowering of democratic forms of governance was a natural expression of the perceptual paradigm of the fourth dimension. The rise of science undermined those who made supernatural claims to political power or rule by divine right. At the same time a relativistic universe is a democratic universe: just as every spatial position has equal validity in the physical universe, so, too, does each person have equal validity in the social universe. Further, in a paradigm where the wheel of time opens to reveal a spiral of worldly progression or prog-ress, it encourages the perception that both material conditions and social institutions can evolve and progress. Finally, success with tech-nological invention tended to foster a corresponding faith in a capac-ity for social invention. People felt empowered to invent new forms of government (for example, the United States with its complex pattern of checks and balances, which ensures that no single branch of gov-ernment can exercise absolute control).

Another characteristic of the scientific-industrial era is how strongly it embodies the masculine archetype. Until the Industrial Revolution no civilization had pursued the goal of material progress so relentlessly, or worked so intently to organize and shape nature according to its will, or had been so driven by the competitive and aggressive urges of its citizens. While these masculine qualities may be viewed by some with disfavor, they were nonetheless vital to social evolution. It seems unlikely that humankind could have advanced from agrarian-based civilizations to industrial-based civilizations by relying primarily upon the ancient feminine archetype of the Earth Goddess (the second dimension or stage). To extract ourselves from immersion within nature, we needed the empowerment, separation, and action-orientation characteristic of the male archetype. Balance will return as we move into the epochs of global reconciliation and bonding (the fifth and sixth dimensions) where we will need the nature-connected and relationship-oriented qualities of the feminine archetype.

SCIENCE AND SPIRITUALITY

Like every other facet of life, spirituality in the industrial era was dominated by themes of secularism, individualism, relativism, and expectations of worldly progress. We have already noted how the scientific-industrial paradigm empowered the individual at the expense of the institutional churches. Joseph Campbell summarized it this way: "In the broadest view of the history of world mythology, the chief creative development in the period of the waning Middle Ages and approaching Reformation was the rise of the principle of individual conscience over ecclesiastical authority."[10]

The cosmology of the fourth dimension had a revolutionary impact on our view of spirituality. From a scientific perspective, once our cosmos came into existence with the Big Bang, nothing more was assumed to be required to keep it going—the cosmos was "just here" and continued to exist of its own accord. The Earth and all of its creatures were assumed to be made from debris left over from the Big Bang. Particles of matter floating through vast reaches of empty and lifeless space coalesced into a planet, which now provides a platform on which life has arisen and evolved. Consciousness was not assumed to be present until beings developed a very high level of biological complexity and social organization. Humans were ultimately isolated—constructed entirely from matter and encapsulated by their skin.

Because the cosmos was viewed as a gigantic machine that functioned in accord with lawful processes, there was no need for participation by a divine Life-force. The way to know God was by knowing the nature of the cosmos that "he" created; and the way to know the cosmos was through the power of science and the analyzing intellect. We can call this form of spirituality *Scientific Humanism* on the premise that science is the tool for knowing God and humanity is at the pinnacle of God's creation.

In the universe of Scientific Humanism, little true mystery remains—mostly just unanswered scientific questions. Matter is dead, and space is simple emptiness, so the universe is almost entirely lifeless except for a few, special islands of life, such as Earth. The overall universe is assumed to be indifferent to human endeavors and without an organizing consciousness of its own. Because the universe is assumed to have no apparent purpose and no particular concern for the human agenda, our strategy in life should be to get by as best we can, recognizing that ultimately the meaning and purpose we create upon our little island of existence is dwarfed by an immensity of indifference. Overall, this is a bleak and intimidating cosmology whose logic produces a profound alienation from the divine Life-force.

In the perceptual paradigm of the fourth dimension, science replaces religion as the primary source of explanation. A theology that "God is dead" (or, perhaps more accurately, a theology that "God is no longer directly involved") emerges during this era. An unknown and seemingly unknowable Life-force seems to have set this extraordinary machine-cosmos into motion and then to have stood back and allowed "natural laws" to take their course.

The scientific view of reality places humanity at the pinnacle of evolution. Because no other advanced life-forms are known, and because the universe itself seems to be a relatively lifeless entity, humans are assumed to be the most evolved beings in existence. With humanity at the cutting edge of conscious evolution, it may seem appropriate for the most intensely living to use this largely lifeless material reality to further their own evolutionary ends. The outcome of this worldview is summarized by the Zen scholar D. T. Suzuki: "Man is against God, Nature is against God, and Man and Nature are against each other."[11]

The cosmology of the fourth dimension bleeds the mystery from nature and replaces it with rational laws and machinelike processes. Because the "grand machine" of the universe can be understood through the analyzing intellect, there is the assumption that, in time, all questions about the cosmos will vanish before the dissecting power of science. Awe is replaced with agnosticism. In assuming we are material beings that are cut off from meaningful connection with the larger universe and in further assuming that we can only rely upon our intellect and physical senses to acquire useful information, the role and value of intuition, prayer, dreams, and other subjective sources of knowing are discounted and even denied.

The materialistic and intellectual orientation of the fourth stage is a double-edged sword. On the one hand, it promotes unprecedented economic growth and scientific understanding. On the other hand, the rational orientation negates the validity of many subjective or "spiritual" experiences. Although this era is often called the Age of Enlightenment, ironically it has diminished our access to enlightening experiences.[12] The four-dimensional frame of reference:

- Is profoundly relativistic and denies the existence of a grand-scale simultaneity of time or a cosmic now, thereby negating the experience of "cosmic consciousness"

- Views the individual as entirely encapsulated within a biological body and thus cut off from direct experience of a divine Life-force

- Considers consciousness to be a product of biochemical processes and neurological complexity, thereby negating consciousness as an infusing presence in the cosmos

The biologically based, materialistic cosmology of the fourth stage reduced enlightening experiences to an "altered state of consciousness"—an experience of biological well-being that occurs when there is harmonious functioning between the body and the brain. The language of materialism—altered *states* of consciousness—indicates that this perceptual paradigm approaches reality by taking static mental snapshots of a world that is forever moving. Yet these mental snapshots are secondhand representations of reality and are not themselves the real thing, because the universe being "mentally photographed" is never at rest. The pervasive dynamism of reality is invisible to a materialistic and intellectual view, which sees a stable world of concrete objects.[13]

THE SEASONS OF
THE FOURTH DIMENSION

With each successive dimensional epoch, we have seen a dramatic reduction in the amount of time required to move through it. The industrial era conforms to that pattern. A skeletal overview of the major seasons of growth involved in the unfolding of the scientific-industrial paradigm is described below.

Transition from the Agrarian Era (A.D. 1500 to 1800)

There is evidence that the scientific-industrial revolution began to emerge in Europe as early as A.D. 1200; however, it did not become a dominant force in England and Europe until four hundred years later in the mid-1600s. The experience of England provides a useful way to summarize and illustrate the industrializing process. In 1200 England was still dominated by the feudal system. By the 1400s it was a seafaring nation with a mixture of commercial and feudal characteristics. By the 1600s England was rapidly becoming more of a commercial and capitalist society than a feudal society, and by the 1700s commercial economics and capitalists had gained national influence.[14] Although the vast majority of persons still lived on farms, by the 1700s a mechanized sector was developing rapidly in the expanding cities, where the basic labor was paid labor and the ruling class was the capitalist class.[15] As this example illustrates, the Industrial Revolution was actually a gradual transformation that, in the case of England (generally regarded as the pioneer for the industrial era), spanned five centuries.

An interesting example of the new level of reflective consciousness in Europe that emerged with the Renaissance is provided by Morris Berman in his book *Coming to Our Senses*. Berman describes how after the 1600s there was a distinct rise of self-consciousness in table manners. In etiquette books there was "a preoccupation with how one will appear to an external observer—a preoccupation that requires taking a position on yourself as a 'specimen,' an object of contemplation."[16] The upper and middle classes "came to be detached observers of their own behavior, in contrast to the more spontaneous and 'blurry' behavior of the Middle Ages."[17]

The scientific-industrial worldview that burst forth in the period between the fifteenth and seventeenth centuries is summarized elegantly by Richard Tarnas, who writes that, "the West saw the emergence of a newly self-conscious and autonomous human being—curious about the world, confident in his own judgments, skeptical of orthodoxies, rebellious against authority, responsible for his own beliefs and actions . . . conscious of his distinctness from nature, aware of his artistic powers as individual creator, assured of his intellectual capacity to comprehend and control nature, and altogether less dependent on an omnipotent God."[18]

Spring (1750 to 1900)

The 1700s were a time of decisive breakthrough in science with stunning advances in chemistry, astronomy, physics, and biology. Nonetheless, it is the revolution in technology represented by James Watt's first commercially successful steam engine in 1765 that, for many, marks the takeoff period for industrial development. The steam engine was used to power locomotives and boats as well as factories. With this invention, mass production—and mass urbanization—proceeded in earnest, particularly in England, Europe, and the United States. Many other technological innovations converged to further advance the Industrial Revolution; for example, the McCormick reaper, developed in the mid-1800s, helped to further revolutionize agriculture with mass harvesting techniques. With new technologies increasing agricultural efficiency, the proportion of the population living in cities and working in factories increased steadily, and a peasant class was being transformed into a middle class.

Summer (1900 to 1970)

The full blossoming of industrial activity did not occur until the early 1900s (again, initially in the United States and Western Europe). The gasoline-powered automobile, airplanes, widespread use of electricity, light bulbs, telephones, and many other key innovations emerged in the early 1900s. The pace of invention accelerated dramatically during the two world wars, which put a premium on new technologies of transportation, communication, and destruction. Early in this century Einstein developed the theory of relativity and brought our intellectual understanding of space and time into harmony with the felt experience of the past several centuries. By the 1960s industrial societies in the West had radio, television, the nuclear bomb, jet engines, suburban cultures, and "future shock." The pace of material and social change was accelerating exponentially.

Autumn and Transition (1970 to 2000)

Placing a man on the moon in 1969 seems to symbolize the fullest blossoming of the scientific-industrial era. Not only was this a stunning technological achievement, it also symbolized the opening of a new era of reflective consciousness. Humanity was now able to stand back and see the Earth as a living biosphere hanging in deep space. Simultaneously the problems of environmental pollution and resource depletion were becoming a widespread public concern, and this was symbolized by the first "Earth Day" in 1970. Finally, 1972 marks the beginning of the global debate over the issue of "limits to growth." Consequently, 1970 seems a useful demarcation for the beginnings of the autumn of growth for the industrial era and for the transition into a new dimensional perspective.

By the early 1990s we can see a number of forces at work that promise to generate fundamental changes in how we see ourselves, the universe, and nature. Once again, these represent far more than surface turbulence—they foreshadow deep changes in our perceptions of reality, identity, and society that have already begun to create a new culture and consciousness:

- Television, satellites, and computers are merging into an integrated, multimedia system and creating a central nervous system for the planet that is transforming virtually every aspect of life. The **global communications** revolution is just getting under way, but it is already having a profound impact on world politics and is awakening a new consciousness among the people of the Earth.

- A global shift toward **democratic forms of government** and greater citizen participation in decision making indicates that a new level of conscious self-determination is emerging.

- A global **environmental movement** is emerging that is deeply concerned with the health of the Earth's ecology. This movement also has a strong concern for other life-forms and future generations as well as **sustainable development** at a global scale.

- A so-called **Gaian perspective** has emerged that views the Earth as a self-regulating system that works through complex feedback mechanisms to maintain itself within fairly close parameters of climate and chemistry. Extrapolating from the wisdom of natural systems, humanity can begin to see its need to become a consciously self-regulating and self-governing global community.

- A **feminist movement** is challenging the masculine orientation that has dominated the scientific-industrial era. The new feminine consciousness is fostering a renewed concern for relationships, a reverence for nature, and an appreciation for community.

- There is widespread interest in a **new physics** that is seeking to unify the fragmented and materialistic view of the universe that underlies the industrial-era paradigm. Unification in physics has its parallels in a concern for whole-systems thinking in biology, ecology, psychology, and elsewhere.

- There is growing interest in humanity's diverse spiritual traditions. Wisdom that has developed slowly over thousands of years in isolated spiritual traditions is now suddenly available to people around the world. A new **global spirituality** is emerging that respects the common wisdom at the heart of all the world's religious traditions.

- Research into biofeedback, the healing power of the psyche, parapsychology, and so forth indicates that **consciousness** is a phenomenon whose potentials transcend those recognized by the scientific paradigm of the industrial era. Consciousness research will in turn foster a coevolutionary view of reality.

The blossoming of these and other developments indicates that a new perceptual paradigm is coalescing, particularly in Western industrial cultures. A significant fraction of humanity is making the transition from a mentalistic and materialistic view of reality to one that includes a transpersonal dimension and a coevolutionary view of culture and consciousness. A new springtime of growth in the dimensional evolution of the planet is already beginning to emerge.

SUMMARY

The perceptual paradigm of the scientific-industrial era generated an epoch of unprecedented social dynamism, moral relativism, intellectual absolutism, nation-state egotism, and technological giantism. Both humans and the rest of life on the planet have paid a very high price for the learning realized during this era. Although people in industrialized societies are more intellectually sophisticated and psychologically differentiated, they are also more isolated—feeling separated from the divine Life-force, nature, and other persons. The life and mystery of the cosmos have been bleached out by analytical science, leaving us adrift in a universe that seems indifferent to our struggles. Feelings of companionship and community have been stripped away as many live nearly alone in vast urban regions of alienating scale and complexity. Unprecedented economic and political freedom have been won, but at great cost when life seems to have little meaning or sense of purpose beyond ever more consumption. The perceptual paradigm of the scientific-industrial era has immense drive but virtually no sense of direction beyond sheer accumulation. It is a dynamic with no moral anchor or guiding ethic—an economic engine with no idea where it is going beyond its drive to acquire material things and material power.

The perceptual paradigm of the industrial era will take humanity as far from our connection with the divine Life-force as we will ever experience. Feeling alone and disconnected from the universe, this is an era of both alienation and empowerment for humanity. In seeing the fragility of our planet's ecosystems and the damage we have already done, our attention must shift to discovering how the human family can live sustainably on the Earth.

REFLECTIVE CONSCIOUSNESS AND THE ERA OF COMMUNICATION AND RECONCILIATION

The **fifth dimension** will be the stage where the observing capacity is turned back upon the self and, with a witnessing or *reflective consciousness,* people will be able to approach life with a new measure of detachment. This will be an epoch of profound stress and challenge as humanity must cope with an intertwined pattern of critical problems generated by the scientific-industrial era, including resource depletion, climate change, pollution, and overpopulation. A more detached perspective will support the process of local-to-global communication that can lead to reconciliation around a shared vision of a sustainable future. New multimedia systems that integrate television, satellites, and computers will provide the "social brain" for world civilization to know its own mind and communicate its way through this stressful stage.

$\mathcal{R}$EFLECTIVE CONSCIOUSNESS AND THE ERA OF COMMUNICATION AND RECONCILIATION

On entering the fifth stage we move into the unknown. Caught within a rapidly closing circle of problems, the human family is challenged to reconcile its many differences and actively cooperate in building a sustainable future. Humanity has never had to work together to preserve a habitable planet, so we should not be surprised that this is unfamiliar territory. We are pioneers in a new dimension of perception and action.

Global reconciliation requires global communication. It seems no accident that the same generation of technology that brought humanity tools of mass destruction also brought counterbalancing tools of mass communication. We are caught up in a worldwide race between communication and catastrophe. We need no miraculous new technologies in order to win this race. Humanity is, if anything, already overendowed with tools of mass communication that can rapidly transform our drift toward calamity into an exciting and purposeful process of reconciliation around a pathway of sustainable development.

No one can predict which pathway we will choose during the second half of our journey of civilizational awakening. If humanity remains divided against itself and pitted against nature, our future is bleak. Whether we realize our potentials for integration into a synergistic planetary civilization is a matter of our own choosing. It has taken nearly forty thousand years for us humans to pull ourselves free from absorption in nature and stand apart in our uniqueness. Now our hard-won separation threatens our survival. We have reached a pivotal time in our species evolution when we must make a momentous turn to reconnect with the natural world from which we struggled so mightily to escape and to heal the separations that divide us as a human family.

A BITTERSWEET EPOCH

The era of reflective consciousness and planetary reconciliation will likely be a bittersweet epoch—one that will initially bring a bitter spring and summer in the form of unprecedented suffering for all of life on Earth. Later it may bring a sweet autumn of harvest if humanity is successful in achieving authentic global reconciliation around a shared vision of a sustainable future.

We will learn many lessons in the coming epoch—primarily those that concern our capacity for psychological, cultural, and spiritual reconciliation as a global family. Before we achieve reconciliation in that now-distant autumn, we will first have to learn how to live together cooperatively on this planet. We will have to discover how to actively listen to one another as a diverse, global culture. We will have to develop a deep and genuine capacity for mutual understanding and mutual appreciation. These changes will not occur without a profound transformation in how we see one another as a human family. Fortunately this transformation in consciousness is already in progress and appears to be gaining momentum roughly in proportion to the pace with which the world moves into the full blossoming of the communications era.

Powered by a communications revolution, a significant threshold in species awareness and evolution is already being crossed: We are beginning to know ourselves as an entire human family. A few hours of species-awakening occurred in 1969, when people around the world paused to watch the moon landing. A few more hours occurred with the "Live Aid" television broadcast in 1985 to raise famine-relief funds for Africa—a program that was seen by roughly two billion persons around the planet. For many people much of the significance of these two events came from knowing that many other people around the Earth were sharing in this same experience all at the same moment.

The ability collectively to witness our own knowing represents a powerful evolutionary advance because it enables us to take charge of our social development with a new level of clarity and intentionality. When we can see our actions in the mirror of reflective knowing, we can become self-directing agents of our own evolution. Our knowing becomes undeniably self-evident, and this promotes accountability, responsibility, and follow-through in personal and social action.

We are acquiring the capacity for reflective consciousness at the civilizational scale just in time. The problems generated by our semi-conscious material evolution are becoming so severe that a witnessing consciousness is crucial if we are to avoid either feudal stagnation or biospheric collapse.

PLANETARY COMPRESSION AND TRANSFORMATION

A painful reality seems to lie at the heart of the evolutionary process: We seem to grow only through the push of dire necessity. If that is so, then the formidable challenges we face in the decades ahead seem designed to provide the crises needed to awaken the capacity for reflective consciousness so that we can employ this capacity to secure our long-term survival as a species. Although each stage of development has been immensely demanding, the coming stage may be the most painful and difficult humanity will ever face. Massive famine, civil unrest, and ecological devastation may be necessary to motivate humanity to genuinely unite in a shared effort to live together cooperatively on the planet. If so, we will not choose a path of sustainability without first looking directly into the abyss of a new dark age of planetary feudalism that reaches into an endless future of suffering and sorrow. Only after humanity comes face-to-face with its destructive potentials and divided past will we begin to build a unified future.

We are moving into a time of steel-gripped necessity—a time of intense, planetary compression. Within a generation the world will become a superheated pressure cooker in which the human family is crushed by the combined and unrelenting forces of an expanding world population, a dramatically destabilized global climate, dwindling supplies of nonrenewable energy, and mounting environmental pollution. The circle has closed, and there is nowhere to escape. These forces are so unyielding, and the stresses they will place on our world are so extreme, that human civilization will either descend into chaos or ascend in a spiraling process of profound transformation. On the one hand, if humanity is unwilling to work for the advance of all, then the world will collapse into resource wars, and misery, poverty, and calamity will descend on the planet. On the other hand, unprecedented suffering may awaken humanity by burning through the unconscious denial, greed, and fear that now divide us. A new human alloy may emerge from the furnace of these superheated decades. Fiery compression may fuse the human family together with a new sense of identity that is strong enough to support the building of a sustainable global civilization.

It seems only natural that humanity would reach, and then extend beyond, its limits to growth. Because nearly every organism will work to exploit its ecological niche to the fullest extent, overshoot and collapse is a common occurrence in natural systems. Since we have never before had such powerful access to the entire planet as our "ecological niche," we have no experience in exercising restraint as a species and caring for the overall biosphere. We learn through experience, and we have never encountered this situation before; so we should not be surprised if a great tragedy is necessary to awaken the evolutionary intelligence of humanity. Great compassion will be needed to cope with the immense suffering that will result from the combination of our technological powers and our limited experience.

The suffering of the coming era will not be without value or purpose. The immense hardship of these transitional times will liberate humanity from its narrow concerns and restricted sense of community and will generate instead a strong sense of species-identity. Despite all our good intentions, without this coming era of collective distress and adversity, the human family is unlikely to awaken to its global identity and evolutionary responsibility. It is the immense suffering of millions—even billions—of precious human beings coupled with the widespread destruction of many other life-forms that will burn through our complacency and isolation. Needless suffering is the psychological and psychic fire that can awaken our compassion and fuse individuals, communities, and nations into a cohesive and consciously organized global civilization.

GLOBAL RECONCILIATION: A MULTIPLE CHALLENGE

A world divided against itself is a recipe for global collapse. Reflective consciousness provides the vehicle for getting beyond a competitive stalemate and for reconciling the polarities that divide the world and keep it from working as an integrated system. Reconciliation does not mean that past injustices and grievances are erased; rather, by being publicly acknowledged and accepted, they no longer stand in the way of our collective progress. When injustices are mutually acknowledged, it releases both parties from the need to continue the process of blaming and feeling resentful; instead they can focus on cooperative actions for building a sustainable future. Humanity needs to bring a spirit of reconciliation to many areas:

- **Economic reconciliation**—Enormous disparities exist between the rich and the poor. Reconciliation requires narrowing these differences and establishing a world minimum standard for economic well-being that supports people in realizing their potentials. Economic reconciliation also suggests that wealthier people and nations would begin to voluntarily simplify their participation in the material side of life and to shift increasing amounts of energy into psychological, cultural, and spiritual growth while at the same time assisting developing nations.

- **Ecological reconciliation**—Living in sacred harmony with the Earth's biosphere is essential if we are to survive and evolve as a species. We need to restore the Earth's ecological system and recognize that humanity is but one among millions of species of plants and animals. Our future depends on the integrity of the overall ecological system, whose strength, in turn, depends on the presence of a broad diversity of plants and animals. To move from indifference and exploitation to reverential stewardship will require reconciliation with the larger community of life on the Earth.

- **Political reconciliation**—Assuming democracy is the natural political expression of a mature society of self-determining individuals, we must reconcile ourselves to working with diverse expressions of democracy and with the different views and values among the people of the world. With reconciliation we can sustain a vigorous conversation among the citizens of the Earth regarding our collective pathway into the future.

- **Spiritual reconciliation**—Religious intolerance has produced some of the bloodiest wars in human history. Vital to humanity's future is reconciliation among the world's spiritual traditions (for example, Catholics and Protestants in Northern Ireland, Arabs and Jews in the Middle East, Muslims and Hindus in India). We need to learn to appreciate the core insights of each tradition and to see each as a different facet in the common jewel of human spiritual wisdom.

- **Racial, ethnic, and gender reconciliation**—Racial, ethnic, and sexual discrimination profoundly divide humanity against itself. To work together for our common future, we must build a global culture of mutual respect that enables us to work together as equals. This does not mean that we will ignore sexual, racial, and ethnic differences; rather they will no longer generate the social gridlock that prevents us from building a sustainable and satisfying future.

- **Generational reconciliation**—Sustainable development has been described as that which meets the needs of the present without compromising the ability of future generations to meet their needs.[1] Because many industrial nations are consuming non-renewable resources, such as oil and natural gas, in a way that will diminish the ability of subsequent generations to meet their needs, we must begin to reconcile ourselves consciously with generations yet unborn. A wise example of reconciliation across generations is provided by the Iroquois Indians, who made major decisions based upon their expected impact seven generations into the future.

Although we can already see the broad outlines of what is required to build a sustainable future, the human family is a long way from being ready to work together to create such a future. We need an unprecedented level of communication, understanding, and reconciliation before we can work together cooperatively. Yet it is often very difficult for a person, community, or nation to accept responsibility for their past excesses and to seek new and healthy relationships. The world is filled with instances of genocide, religious intolerance, racial and gender discrimination, oppression of ethnic minorities, abuses of political and economic power, environmental destruction, and the extinction of other species. Some of these tragedies have festered for many generations and this makes the bridging of differences very difficult. Nonetheless without deep and authentic communication across these barriers of suffering, humanity will remain divided and mistrustful—and our collective future will be gravely imperiled.[2]

Each dimensional epoch challenges us to realize a new level of human maturity. There is no doubt that great personal and social maturity will be required in order for people to give up their claims of resentment for past abuses and to make a good-faith effort to resolve injustices and injuries so that the human family can work together for its common good. Bringing legitimate grievances into public awareness, mourning the mistakes of the past, taking responsibility for participation in them, and then seeking just and realistic remedies—these difficult actions are at the heart of the era of reconciliation. We need unprecedented communication to discover our common humanity from a place of uncommon humility. With reconciliation, social energy that was immobilized in resentment will be freed up and become available for productive working relationships.

THE FIFTH DIMENSION: REFLECTIVE CONSCIOUSNESS

It is important to differentiate the reflective consciousness of awakening hunter-gatherers from that of modern humans entering the fifth stage. The reflective consciousness of the hunter-gatherer was extremely limited and was focused primarily on the bare fact of physical existence in the here and now. Consciousness (or the knowing faculty) was not sufficiently developed to be able to deliberately reflect on much more than the simple reality of bodily existence and sensations. Thousands of years of development were then required before most humans were able to reflect knowingly upon an emotional life (so fundamental to the agrarian era), and additional thousands of years were required before humans were able to reflect upon a mental or intellectual life (so basic to the scientific-industrial era). With the fifth stage or communications era, the capacity for self-reflective functioning takes another quantum leap forward as humanity consciously recognizes the existence of consciousness. Evolution and learning begin to embrace realms beyond those of the physical senses as consciousness is seen as a unique aspect of the universe whose transmaterial potentials involve far more than brain chemistry and biology. As the distinctive nature and evolutionary importance of consciousness (or the witnessing capacity) become firmly established, the validity and reality of the polarity of observer and observed (or knower and known) will become anchored in mass social consciousness. In turn it is the detachment and perspective provided by this polarity that will support the process of communication and reconciliation that is unique to the evolutionary unfoldment of the fifth stage.

Where the four-dimensional, scientific view of reality bleached the life from nature and left a machinelike cosmos filled mostly with dead matter and empty space, the experience of the fifth dimension awakens the intuition that a living presence permeates the universe. In the spacious mirror of reflective consciousness we begin to catch glimpses of the unity of the interwoven fabric of the cosmos and our intimate participation within the living web of existence. No longer is reality broken into relativistic islands or pieces. If only for a brief moment at a time, existence is glimpsed and known as a seamless totality. To explore our gradual awakening to the aliveness and unity of the universe, it is important to introduce five basic concepts:

1. There is a deep **symmetry** in the geometry of the cosmos; consequently, the attributes of the next three stages of development mirror important aspects of the previous three stages.

2. A **trinity** of constituents comprise our reality: matter, consciousness, and the Meta-universe. **Matter** and **consciousness** are co-equal and mutually revealing of one another, whereas the **Meta-universe** is fundamental and is the Life-energy that infuses and sustains our cosmos.

3. The totality of the cosmos is being **continuously re-created** at each moment.

4. We are involved in a process of **coevolution**, or the synergistic unfolding of both the material and the consciousness aspects of existence.

5. A primary evolutionary goal is to fulfill our unique potential for **self-referencing consciousness** and thereby to experience our core nature.

By combining these five ingredients of symmetry, trinity, continuous creation, coevolution, and double-wisdom, we can describe the next three stages as we work to develop our full capacities as self-referencing beings and civilizations. Because these core aspects of dimensional cosmology are discussed at length in the second section of this book, I will give here only a brief overview of the first three of these assumptions (the latter two were discussed in the introduction).

Symmetry

The first three perceptual paradigms were straightforward: The second dimension revealed the **flat** fact of material existence; the third dimension revealed **depth** qualities of that existence; and the fourth dimension revealed the **dynamism** of material existence. Given the deep symmetry of the cosmos, I assume these three attributes are repeated again at a higher level to reveal the simple fact, depth, and dynamism of the consciousness aspects of existence (while continuing the coevolutionary unfolding with the material aspects of existence). This symmetry is essential if life-forms are to know themselves accurately and fully and thereby pull themselves together into self-referencing and self-directing organisms. Extrapolating from principles of symmetry, where the second dimension revealed the simple fact of form, I assume the fifth dimension reveals the simple fact of consciousness. In turn, where the third dimension revealed the depth of form, I assume the sixth dimension reveals the depth of consciousness. Finally, where the fourth dimension revealed the dynamism of form, I assume the seventh dimension reveals the dynamism of consciousness.

Trinity

In the first chapter matter and consciousness were described as co-equal aspects of reality that emerge and develop together. Matter and consciousness are mutually supportive and enabling of one another in the process of coevolution. They arise together from an infinitely deep, generative ground of pure awareness that I call the Meta-universe. Our evolutionary journey unfolds as we identify first with our material aspects (the second through fourth dimensions) and then with our consciousness aspects (the fifth through seventh dimensions). Finally we discover, in freedom, that our deepest nature is unbounded, pure awareness (the eighth dimension and beyond). To help clarify these important distinctions, the diagram in Figure 7 shows the synergistic relationship between matter and consciousness and the underlying generative ground or Meta-universe.

The entire universe (matter and consciousness as well as the fabric of space and time) is a single "standing wave" or resonance pattern

Figure 7: The Relationship Between Matter, Consciousness, and the Meta-universe (Whose Essence Is Pure Awareness)

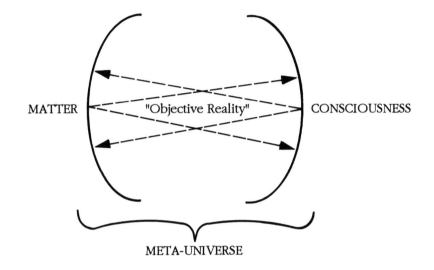

that is regenerated continuously by the Meta-universe. The continuing existence of the universe around us depends upon the unbroken generative power of the Meta-universe. Because all that exists continuously arises anew, each person, object, and place has a characteristic resonance that is produced in the process of continuous creation. Every person and place has a unique personality, or "song," that is intrinsic to its nature.

Neither the material nor the consciousness aspects of life are primary, as both continuously arise from the underlying Meta-universe. Basic to this view of reality is a subtle though crucially important distinction between "consciousness" and "awareness:"*

Consciousness—This is the "knowing faculty" and is *always* connected with an object of knowing. Elementary consciousness as well as rudimentary matter both emerged with the Big

---

*The distinction between consciousness and awareness is discussed further in Chapter 8, page 201, and in Appendix I, pages 325–326.

Bang. Matter and consciousness then coevolve to reveal their underlying source—the Meta-universe, whose nature is pure awareness.

Awareness—This is the ability to "know that we know." Because awareness does not depend upon reference to anything to be self-confirming, it is "pure" or "unconditioned." Awareness is an intrinsic property of the Meta-universe and is the clear Life-energy out of which both matter and consciousness arise.

Our thinking capacity is associated with the biological brain, the reflective capacity is associated with consciousness, and the ability to know that we know—the capacity for direct awareness—is associated with the generative ground or Meta-universe. The Meta-universe is the Life-force whose creative intelligence underlies, sustains, and transcends the self-bounding system that is our cosmos. Stephen Levine, a seasoned meditator and counselor to the dying, makes this clear distinction between awareness and consciousness:

Awareness is like a beam of light that shines endlessly into space. We only perceive that light when it is reflected off some object and consciousness is produced. . . . Awareness is the light by which we see the world. . . . We mistake the clear light of pure awareness for the shadows that it casts in consciousness. . . . We forget that we are the light itself and imagine that we are the densities that reflect the light back to us.[3]

Levine also explains that while consciousness depends on awareness for its existence, awareness depends on nothing, for it is the ground of existence.[4]

Although we are created from the transparent energy of the generative ground—pure awareness—we may not recognize that this is our true nature. We are like clouds that do not realize that we are made from the sky. It is the gift of this world to provide us with innumerable opportunities to encounter ourselves so that we can discover the remarkable nature of our being. *When our knowing so knows*

itself that it can recognize itself even without our physical body to pro-
vide an aligning structure for knowing, then we are identical with the
Meta-universe, whose nature is infinite and eternal.

Coevolution

Consciousness and matter are inseparable. Matter always arises with
the mirroring potential of consciousness, and consciousness always
arises with the expressive potential of matter. Matter and consciousness have an *instrumental nature;* that is, they mutually serve each
other in revealing the origins from which both arise. Awareness has an
intrinsic nature and is identical with the deep ground of Life-energy,
which is both infinite and eternal. The ultimate function of matter
and consciousness is to provide a learning context whereby we can
freely discover our infinite and eternal nature.

I assume that every material manifestation of whatever form and
scale—from an atom to a human being to a galaxy to the entire cosmos—has a reflective capacity appropriate to its nature.[5] This does
not mean that an atom reflects on existence in the same manner as a
human; rather it means that for an atom to hold itself together, it has
a reflective capacity consistent with its nature and structure. In the
words of physicist Freeman Dyson, "Matter in quantum mechanics is
not an inert substance but an active agent, constantly making choices
between alternative possibilities. . . . It appears that mind, as mani-
fested by the capacity to make choices, is to some extent inherent in
every electron."[6] While it is stunning to consider that every level of
the cosmos has some degree of consciousness, it is no more extraordinary than the hypothesis that our cosmos emerged as a pinpoint from
nothing some fifteen billion years ago. If anything, it seems less of a
miracle to propose the cosmos contains a pervasive self-referencing
capability than it does to propose (as does quantum physics) that the
cosmos was made from a "vacuum fluctuation"—where nothing
pushes on nothing to create everything.

Given its translocal potentials, consciousness is not confined
within the physical body or brain. As a property of the fifth dimension, reflective consciousness extends beyond the material world of
the first four dimensions. Because reflective consciousness transcends

(but interpenetrates) the material realm, it is able to stand back and mirror it. It is this enlarged capacity of consciousness that enables the observer to look at the world with a greater degree of detachment or objectivity. In the fifth dimension, then, the polarity of observer and observed (or knower and known) is established unmistakably. Because identity is no longer totally confined within a materialistic mind-set, the fifth dimension provides a perceptual paradigm within which we can work toward personal and planetary reconciliation.

Continuous Creation

Another core premise is that the entirety of our universe is a single living organism that is being regenerated in a flow of continuous creation. Metaphorically we inhabit a cosmos whose visible body is billions of light-years across, whose organs include billions of galaxies, whose cells include trillions of suns and planetary systems, and whose molecules include an unutterably vast number and diversity of unique life-forms. The entirety of this great body of being, including the fabric of space-time, is being continuously regenerated as a self-consistent whole at each instant. This is not a new insight. All of the world's spiritual traditions affirm in different ways that we exist within a continuing miracle of creation. The fact that anything exists at all is an ongoing miracle—moment by moment the entire cosmos is being sustained by the flow-through of a vast amount of energy. The Life-force that sustains this extraordinary process is the infinitely deep Meta-universe. If the Meta-universe were to halt the flow-through of Life-energy for even a moment, the entire physical universe born with the Big Bang would disappear.

Continuous-creation cosmology is not deterministic. At the quantum level, physicists describe our universe as a set of probabilities, not certainties. Quantum uncertainty reveals that a basic ingredient of our universe is freedom of choice. The Meta-universe will uphold a Hitler or a Mother Teresa equally, a society at peace or a society at war, a society living in excess or one in poverty. The Meta-universe is compassionately open-handed and immensely patient. We can choose how our lives will unfold without arbitrary interference or manipulation. We are born in a context of great freedom and can choose how we will respond to the evolutionary opportunities before us.

Given the core concepts of symmetry, trinity, coevolution, and continuous creation, we can now describe the perceptual paradigms of the fifth through seventh dimensions. Simply stated, in the fifth stage we discover that: (a) consciousness mirrors matter (symmetry); (b) aliveness and flow characterize all that exists (continuous creation); (c) behind the momentary flux of this world there is a deep and eternal reality (the Meta-universe); and (d) our challenge is to cooperate with the instrumental nature of matter and consciousness in order to realize, in freedom, our true nature as eternal beings (coevolution leading to double-wisdom or pure awareness).

As with movement into other dimensional stages, the experience of time in the fifth dimension is again transformed. The fragmented and relativistic time of the fourth dimension is now unified into snapshots of cosmic-scale manifestation. Although the many qualities of continuous creation are not fully evident until the seventh stage, in the fifth stage people can experience the subtle though simple fact of holistic regeneration of the cosmos. In knowing the universe is being regenerated as a self-consistent whole, the relativistic activity in four dimensions is bridged, at least momentarily, into an embracing unity in five dimensions.

REFLECTIVE IDENTITY

With the trustworthy mirror of reflective consciousness, we can see ourselves as if from a distance. From this perspective we see that while our **bodily experience** is one part of ourselves, we are more than our body and its sensations, desires, pleasures, and pains. We also recognize that while our **emotional experience** is one part of ourselves, we are more than our experience of anger, joy, happiness, and sorrow. Additionally we see that while our **mental experience** is one part of ourselves, we are more than our lightning-fast flow of thoughts, ideas, and images. By identifying with the conscious observer or witnessing self, we find a new degree of freedom, as we are no longer identified exclusively with bodily sensations, emotions, and the inner stream of mental dialogue.[7] We are able to disidentify from sensations, emotions, and thoughts sufficiently to recognize that our identity also includes a witnessing consciousness.

In a process of immense simplicity requiring the utmost self-acceptance, we discover that, to the extent that we can see our habitual patterns of sensation, emotion, and thought, we are less bound to repeat them. We must become intimate friends with ourselves and reconcile ourselves with who we really are—embracing even those aspects we may want to forget or deny (for example, lustful desires, angry feelings, and harsh mental judgments). We cannot move beyond the habitual pushes and pulls of these forces until we can consciously see them operating in our lives.

An analogy suggests how reflective consciousness can function in our lives. Imagine that you are driving your car on a very rainy day. While driving, a moment of conscious attention is akin to a single sweep of the wiper blades that clear the windshield and show the road ahead. The consciousness of the industrial era is akin to having the wipers turned off much of the time, allowing the rain to pour in sheets across the windshield, blurring our vision of the road. With reflective consciousness, or metaphorically when the windshield wipers are running, the features of the road become crisp and sharp. Nothing changes except the ability to see more clearly. With attention, then, the contents of our lives remain the same, but the capacity to see those contents is sharpened and expanded. Instead of a confined and blurred vision, an entire panorama is opened up. Our existence becomes more spacious, and we can respond more quickly and skillfully to all manner of changes along life's way. As this analogy suggests, living more consciously brings with it a range of enabling qualities. We become more:

- **Responsive**—If we are paying attention, then we don't have to be bludgeoned by a personal crisis before we recognize the need for adaptive change. In watching more carefully, we can respond more quickly to subtle feedback.

- **Creative**—If we are noticing our habitual patterns of response, then we are not so locked into them and we can respond with more creativity and freedom.

- **Self-determining**—In paying attention to our passage through life, we can rely increasingly on our own judgment and take responsibility for our decisions.

- **Accepting**—In seeing the cosmos as a learning system intending our evolution in freedom, we can embrace our mistakes along the way as valuable feedback. Instead of insisting on always being right, we can acknowledge our errors and learn to move through life with increasing skill.

- **Balanced**—In being able to stand back from an obsessive attachment to ideas, people, and actions, we are able to respond with greater equanimity and not be pulled off center or off balance.

- **Connected**—In identifying with consciousness, we begin to see ourselves as an integral part of the universe, and we experience greater caring for the life of which we know we are an inseparable part.

Humanity must be as awake, responsive, error-embracing, reflective, balanced, creative, forgiving, and engaged as possible if we are to move through the time of perilous transition represented by the fifth stage of development. These enabling factors illustrate how the awakening of double-wisdom is not a mystical capacity divorced from the hard realities of life. To the contrary, it is an immensely practical faculty whose development is central to achieving planetary reconciliation around a sustainable future.

A practical example of the impact of living more consciously is how it changes our relationship with the material side of life. By identifying with the observer part of ourselves, we have more perceptual distance and can choose more consciously where we want to invest our precious life energy. In seeing more clearly which activities truly bring deep satisfaction—conversing with a friend, playing with children, making music, cooking and sharing food, walking in nature— many aspects of the high-consumption lifestyle of the industrial era begin to lose their appeal and glamour. With reflective consciousness we can build a foundation in experiential riches that frees us from the single-minded obsession with material riches.

REFLECTIVE CONSCIOUSNESS AND
A COOPERATING SOCIETY

In its barest terms the social challenge of the fifth dimension is to achieve sufficient long-term cooperation among the human family to ensure the survival and basic health of the species and planet. The question of questions is whether humanity will actually reconcile itself to working together to build a sustainable future. In a testament to the exquisite design of the learning stages embodied in the sacred geometry of the cosmos, the reflective consciousness of the fifth dimension contains the very qualities that are most needed to overcome the shortcomings of the fourth dimension. Reflective consciousness provides the transpersonal glue that can bond the human family into a mutually appreciative whole while simultaneously honoring our differences. All beings share a common ground that transcends differences of gender, race, wealth, religion, and political orientation. Reflective consciousness supports a powerful process for rebuilding human relationships, for reconnecting with nature, and for knowing our communion with life.

The detached nature of reflective consciousness will bring a new tenor and feel into cultures. Instead of an aggressive, materialistic, and self-promoting orientation, there will be a more receptive, trans-material, and relationship-building orientation—a shift from masculine to feminine qualities. Embracing the feminine archetype (which tends to be more open, allowing, forgiving, bodily sacrificing, and integrating) will enable humanity to move beyond the aggressive, competitive mind-set of the industrial era and to promote the caring and cooperation that are the vital foundation for a sustainable future.

The emergence of a strong feminine archetype does not mean that women will come to gender dominance over men; instead a healthier balance of archetypes will develop. The masculine role model can evolve beyond the competitiveness and status seeking of the industrial era and can provide leadership for the coevolution of culture and consciousness. The masculine archetype can expand to include a "husbanding" intention. To be a "husband" means more than simply being a married man; it also means to be a frugal manager and steward.[8] Husbandry refers to the judicious use of resources—the ability consciously to conserve, economize, and safeguard the land and other resources. It is a way of describing a responsible relationship with nature that will enable us to build a sustainable future. Overall, in the fifth stage a strengthened feminine archetype could join with a revitalized masculine archetype to create a new ecological mind-set.

An important aspect of the strong feminine archetype is symbolized in the willingness of a woman to make bodily sacrifices for the sake of another. Just as a pregnant woman makes bodily sacrifices for the child that grows within her, so, too, is humanity called upon in this stage of evolution to sacrifice our bodily comforts and conveniences to develop a sustainable global civilization. We are asked to accept the physical discomfort, insecurity, stress, and trouble of giving birth to a planetary civilization and to work toward a new level of cooperation, caring, and creativity. To give of ourselves in this way requires a nurturing and compassionate approach that is nearly unthinkable in the competitive, achievement-oriented mind-set of the industrial era. It is the feminine archetype—with its emphasis on relationships, reflective listening, and nurturing—that supports the trust and understanding that are the true foundation for an enduring global civilization.

To be responsive to the radically changing conditions on the planet, the feminine archetype will need to evolve beyond the ancient Earth Goddess to a more expansive expression of the feminine. The universe could perhaps be symbolized as a "Cosmic Goddess" that provides a nurturing home for trillions of planetary systems. By expanding the feminine archetype to a cosmic scale, the universe is seen as a single, living organism. Instead of an impersonal machine that is devoid of consciousness and purpose, the cosmos is seen as a living entity infused with, and animated by, a subtle Life-energy. Within this respiritualized framework it is natural to view the Earth as a sacred, self-regulating organism.

Turning from archetypal to worldly concerns, an era of global reconciliation is also an era of global communication. Electronic technologies will play a pivotal role in achieving the breadth and depth of human communication necessary for discovering a shared vision of a sustainable future. With instantaneous computer translation of languages coupled with inexpensive and easy communications, a vast array of connections will be established with persons and institutions around the planet—in business, scholarship, play, political action, spiritual community, cultural progress, and friendship. These multimedia communication networks will constitute a vital ingredient in the social glue essential for a strong global culture. An electronic intimacy will infuse the planet as people increasingly work, play, and govern themselves as citizens of a global society. These diverse, overlapping, and intertwined communication networks will enable a level of global social cohesion and sense of community to emerge that has never before existed.

In the fifth stage the Earth-centered view of the universe will be further loosened by satellites positioned in deep space that send back live pictures of the Earth and give humanity a new perspective on our place in the universe. With wall-sized TV screens showing with stunning clarity live pictures of a slowly turning Earth suspended in the immensity of space, the human family will see that we really do inhabit a tightly interconnected biosphere—that we are all part of a single, living organism. The transformative impact of being able to view the Earth from afar was described by astronaut Rusty Schweickart as he was returning from the moon:

> [The Earth] is so small and so fragile and such a precious little spot in that universe that you can block it out with your thumb, and you realize on that small spot, that little blue and white thing, is everything that means anything to you—all of history and music and poetry and art and death and birth and love, tears, joy, games, all of it on that little spot out there that you can cover with your thumb. And you realize from that perspective that you've changed, that there's something new there, that the relationship is no longer what it was.[9]

With a continuous view of Earth from deep space, humanity will see that we must choose between mutually supportive development and destructive competition. A view of Earth from deep space will help us reveal to ourselves the preciousness of our planet and will motivate people to find solutions that respect the fact that we are united in a single biosphere.

CONSCIOUS DEMOCRACY

A conscious democracy pays attention. Recognizing that "the price of freedom is eternal vigilance," a conscious democracy is vigilant, watchful, and wide awake. A semiconscious democracy was characteristic of the fourth dimension and industrial era: Leaders and citizens wandered through the social landscape half asleep, inattentive to critical trends and events, and only momentarily awakened by the shock of some catastrophe. A great tragedy, triumph, or scandal was required to break through the complacency and distractedness of the masses. Once the public was aroused into momentary wakefulness, it was not long before a new issue, emergency, or scandal would dominate social consciousness, pushing aside or obscuring previous concerns. Because the body politic was not in charge of its own consciousness, industrial-era civilizations often stumbled into the future—forgetful of the past, fearful of and reacting to enemies often more imagined than real, and aggressively pursuing short-run interests even when they conflicted with long-run well-being. A semiconscious democracy is no match for the new global challenges. We must cultivate the double-wisdom at the heart of our species-potential if we are to take charge of our evolution and negotiate the narrow passageway of the near future.

Just as the evolution of consciousness is highly adaptive for an individual, so, too, is an evolving consciousness highly enabling for entire civilizations. The following are some of the important enabling qualities of a reflective society and conscious democracy:

- **Self-determining**—One of the most basic expressions of a maturing consciousness is an enhanced capacity for self-determination—the social expression of which is democracy. A conscious society is able to stand back and look at its choices as well as observe itself in the choosing process. A reflective democracy is able to observe itself "from the outside," much as one nation can stand back and view another from a distance. A conscious society knows its own mind and does not blindly trust in a particular ideology, leader, or political party; instead it regularly reorients itself by looking beyond superficial slogans and vague goals to choose anew its preferred pathway into the future.

- **Informed**—A conscious society is well informed. Instead of moving through life half-asleep and ignorant of the challenges it faces, a conscious citizenry is disciplined in learning about important trends and issues.

- **Confident**—Because a conscious society knows its own mind, it can move ahead with greater confidence and assurance. Because social policies are developed with public input, a conscious bond is formed among citizens who support those policies, and this promotes the social strength necessary to implement them.

- **Error-embracing**—A conscious society recognizes that social learning inevitably involves making mistakes. Therefore errors are not automatically rejected or denied as being "bad"; rather they are accepted as useful feedback and recognized as grist for the mill in the process of social learning.[10]

- **Detached**—A conscious democracy is objective, impartial, and reacts calmly to the stressful pushes and pulls of trends and events. A society with a witnessing consciousness has an evenness, detachment, levelheadedness, and confidence that is not pulled off center by the passions of the moment.

- **Inclusive**—A conscious society continually searches for the synergy of the highest common denominator. Differing ethnic and racial groups, geographic regions, and ideological perspectives are actively invited into dialogue as vital ingredients for a society that seeks a vigorous common ground.

- **Anticipatory**—In viewing the world more objectively and from a larger perspective, alternative pathways into the future are considered consciously.

- **Creative**—Because a conscious democracy is able to stand back and look at its choices, it is not locked into habitual patterns of thinking and behaving. A conscious democracy does not respond with preprogrammed solutions, but explores options and priorities with a fresh and flexible frame of mind.

- **Responsive**—A conscious society does not wait passively until some crisis forces action; instead it is already energized and actively engaged. A self-reflective society does not have to be shocked into remedial action by some catastrophe; instead more subtle warning signals of danger (and opportunity) are sufficient to lead toward self-corrective action.

These straightforward attributes of a conscious democracy are of immense functional value, as they support an empowered, active, and capable process of self-governance. We need all our strength as a species if we are to build a future of mutually assured development. Most of all we need conscious democracies if we are to take charge of our evolution, negotiate our way through the crises of the future, and remain on a path of ever-surpassing development.

GLOBAL COMMUNICATIONS AND THE SOCIAL BRAIN

Humanity cannot make the sweeping changes that are required for a sustainable future (for example, in consumption patterns, energy and transportation policies, the redesign of communities, international relations, and much more) without a dramatic increase in the intensity and quality of human communications. Only after a cathartic process of communication will people be ready to act with the level of energy, creativity, and cooperation that our circumstances demand. Initially people will need to express their anger that the ecology of the planet has been so devastated, their resentments for broken dreams of material prosperity, and their unwillingness to make sacrifices unless there is greater fairness. However, once people have worked through their anger, sorrow, and fear and have developed a working consensus in support of a sustainable future, then both citizens and their representatives in government can act with authority. When citizens can tell their leaders, with confidence, where they want to go and how fast they want to get there, then leaders can do their job. The first requirement, however, is an unprecedented increase in human communication.

Fortunately a communications revolution is already sweeping the planet. The most prominent technology in this revolution is television (although it is rapidly evolving into a computer-integrated, interactive multimedia system). Because we are a visually oriented species ("seeing is believing," "one picture is worth a thousand words"), the visual power of television creates a common language that makes it humanity's primary source of shared information and understanding. As of 1990 roughly 60 percent of the world had access to television, and this percentage is growing rapidly. In the United States 98 percent of all homes have a TV set, the average person watches more than four hours per day, and a majority of people get a majority of their news about the world from this medium. Just as consciousness is not "just another human capacity," television is not "just another technology." Television is at the very heart of our capacity for self-reflective consciousness at a civilizational scale. Television is our social witness—our vehicle for "knowing that we know" as nations and as a human family. Television is more powerful than either the schools or the workplace in generating our collective view of reality and social identity. If issues or trends do not appear on television, then for all practical purposes they do not exist in mass social consciousness.

The closeness and intimacy of television's window onto the world can give people a feeling of connection with the fate of the Earth. With the speed of light, television can extend our experience of involvement to the entire planet. Through the eyes of television we can see the reality of a starving villager in Africa, the destruction of rain forests in Brazil, urban decay in New York City, the effects of acid rain in Germany, and fighting in the streets of Northern Ireland and Israel. Television makes every viewer an active witness—a knowing and feeling participant in what is being shown. *Television has become the "social brain" or "central nervous system" of the human family.* Given the power and pervasiveness of television, we already possess the tools of local-to-global communication that can transform our semiconscious drift toward catastrophe into conscious actions to build a sustainable future. A direct measure of our social intelligence as a species is the intelligence with which we use our social brain—the rapidly evolving telecommunications system.

All of the major challenges of the current era are, at their core, communications challenges. The human family will not respond to global warming, ozone depletion, toxic pollution, rain-forest destruction, and other environmental problems until we can visualize their impact through the mass media and thereby mobilize the will of the body politic to bring about changes. Humanity will not respond to homelessness, hunger, and poverty around the world unless we continue to see compelling and persistent images of suffering and need. The visual power of television can lull us into complacency or it can stir us to action.

Television (or the fast-emerging, interactive, multimedia telecomputer system) will play a pivotal role in creating a more conscious democracy. Three ingredients are critical to a conscious democracy: an informed citizenry, a dialoguing citizenry, and a citizenry that gives regular feedback to its leaders.

An Informed Citizenry

A first requirement for creating a more conscious democracy is a quantum leap in the quantity and diversity of televised communication concerning issues vital to our common future. Currently the vast majority of commercial television time is devoted to entertainment (typically 95 percent or more of prime time on network TV in the United States). *We are entertainment rich and knowledge poor. By programming television for commercial success, the television industry is programming our civilizational consciousness for ecological failure.* Our situation seems similar to that of a long-distance runner who prepares for a marathon by eating junk food. We are trying to run modern democracies almost exclusively on a diet of TV entertainment at the very time that we confront challenges of marathon proportions.

We desperately need a hearty and robust diet of socially relevant television programming that informs us about the critical trends and choices facing communities, nations, and the planetary society. We need far more documentaries and investigative reports that give citizens an in-depth understanding of the challenges we face. We need scenarios of the future that vividly portray what life will be like within a generation if nothing is done to alter current trends. We need positive visions of what life could be like if we begin designing ourselves into a sustainable future. We need to balance the onslaught of aggressively proconsumerist commercials with a regular diet of "Earth commercials" that awaken an ecological consciousness and encourage us to live more compassionately.

Commercial television makes money by delivering a mass audience to corporate advertisers. Understandably, then, this industry is reluctant to devote air time to programs or commercials that question the appropriateness of high-consumption lifestyles. Because an ethic of sustainability runs counter to the aggressively proconsumerist mentality of commercial television, a major increase in government funding for public television seems essential in order to generate the level and quality of communication needed to support a conscious democracy in its process of choosing a sustainable future.

A Dialoguing Citizenry

Beyond an adequate diet of information, a conscious democracy must also know its own mind. If democracy is the "art of the possible," then we don't know what's possible until we have an accurate sense of what the overall community of citizens thinks and feels about different issues and priorities. Without an accurate understanding of what other citizens think about key issues, we drift aimlessly in a sea of ambiguity and are powerless to mobilize ourselves into collective action.

Power in a democracy is the power to communicate and build a working consensus. Only when the public knows what it thinks as a whole can it confidently communicate a working consensus back to its elected representatives. An informed public can be trusted. After reviewing his half century of polling public opinion in the United States, George Gallup, Jr., found "the collective judgment of the people to be extraordinarily sound."[11] Often, he said, "people are actually ahead of their elected leaders in accepting innovations and radical changes."[12]

To know its own views and values, a citizenry must go beyond the information revolution (with its one-way flow that enables us "to know" as individuals), to the communications revolution (with a two-way flow that enables us to "know that we know" as entire communities). As computers, satellites, fiber optics, telephones, and high-definition television technology merge into globally interconnected multimedia systems, the potential for interactive citizen communication will grow exponentially. With weekly or monthly electronic town meetings held locally, nationally, and globally, an entirely new level of accountability can be established between the public and decision makers.

A Feedback Democracy

Once a citizenry knows its own mind and has confidence in its views and values, then it can use electronic forums to give feedback to elected leaders. Assuming citizen feedback is advisory or nonbinding, it respects the responsibility of representatives to make decisions and the responsibility of the citizen to make inputs to those that govern. In a conscious democracy a working consensus among citizens would presumably guide (but not compel) elected representatives. The practical role of electronic town meetings is not to provide a vehicle for citizens to micromanage government; rather it is to provide a forum for citizens to build a working consensus on the major issues of the day. For example: Do citizens want an alternative energy future (relying primarily on solar power, wind generation, and increased efficiency as well as conservation) or do they want an energy future that relies heavily on nuclear power? Do citizens want to commit themselves to a dramatic reduction in greenhouse gases? Do citizens want to make major cutbacks in military expenditures in favor of social and infrastructure expenditures, or do they want to maintain a strong military? As citizens refine their views on these kinds of issues through regular, electronic dialogues, elected representatives can then move decisively to do their part in building a sustainable future.

A conscious democracy requires the active consent of the governed, not simply their passive acquiescence. Involving citizens does not guarantee that the "right" choices will always be made; however, it does assure that citizens will feel involved and invested in those choices. Rather than feeling cynical or powerless, citizens will feel engaged and responsible for society and its future. A conscious democracy that is empowered by the creative use of its tools of mass communication can respond wholeheartedly to the momentous challenges facing our planet. Perhaps the biggest challenge facing humanity in the communications era is to evolve the art and practice of conscious democracy.

EQUITY AND ECONOMICS

At the close of the twentieth century—a time when industrial-era views and values are still paramount within economically developed nations—it is nearly impossible to imagine a shift toward equity and justice in the use of the world's resources. People in economically developed nations are now so focused on safeguarding their gains that achieving a new global ethic of economic justice and sharing will first require a transforming experience of global proportions. Given the unyielding trends whose iron grip now tightens around the planet, there is little doubt that we will soon get the wrenching experience required to awaken us to the need for new approaches to global economic development. The alternative is bleak: If wealthy nations seek their well-being at the expense of those who are poorer, it will produce chronic wars over resources, massive migrations of people in search of food and work, and devastating ecological damage.

With the window of global television opening ever more widely, differences in wealth and well-being around the world will soon become glaringly and persistently evident to all. We are entering a superheated and supercharged world where issues of economic justice will be paramount. Global reconciliation requires that the basic material needs of the entire human family be met, and achieving this goal will require a profound shift in the levels and patterns of consumption in developed nations. Minor adjustments will not suffice.

With equity, simplicity, and efficiency, the world has adequate resources to sustain humanity into the foreseeable future.[13] In the words of Gandhi, "We have enough for everyone's need, but not for everyone's greed." We cannot achieve our maturity if humanity remains divided into a minority with great wealth and a majority consigned to the prison of absolute poverty. Each individual has a basic right to a reasonable share of the world's resources. Achieving this revolution in fairness will require an unprecedented increase in human communication and reconciliation. We need to work for a future of "mutually assured development" or economic progress that leaves no one behind but instead strengthens the entire human family and the ecosystem on which our common future depends. If all people and nations work to promote the development of everyone else, the world will move beyond passive coexistence to active mutual assistance.

Adopting a "golden rule of consumption"—consume as you would want others to consume if you were in their situation—will take on increasing importance as global communications reveal vast inequities in material well-being. Economic justice does not imply replicating the industrial-era manner of living around the world; instead it means that every person has a right to a fair share of the world's wealth adequate to ensure him or her a "decent" standard of living—enough food, shelter, education, and health care to be considered sufficient by a reasonable standard of human decency.[14] Given intelligent designs for living lightly and simply, a decent standard and manner of living could vary significantly depending on local customs, ecology, resources, and climate.

In the fifth stage of evolution we will invent new patterns of living that transform every facet of life—the work we do, the communities and homes in which we live, the food we eat, the transportation we use, the clothes we wear, the symbols of status that shape our consumption patterns, and so on. We could call this new way of living "voluntary simplicity" or "creative simplicity" or "ecological living."[15] However defined, we need more than a change in our style of life. A change in *style* implies a superficial or exterior change—a new fad, craze, or fashion. We require a far deeper change in our *way* of life. We could call this an ecological way of living that recognizes the Earth is our home and must be maintained for the long-range future. Ecological living begins with the understanding that we all live in mutual contingency and that we create the safety, comfort, and compassion in our lives together.

An aesthetic simplicity of living is a direct expression of civilizational growth as well as a requirement for a sustainable, planetary civilization. After a lifetime of studying the growth and decline of the world's civilizations, historian Arnold Toynbee concluded that the conquest of land and/or people was not the true measure of civilizational growth; instead he said the essence of civilizational growth could be summarized in what he called the Law of Progressive Simplification.[16] True growth occurs as civilizations transfer an increasing proportion of energy and attention from the material side of life to the nonmaterial side and thereby develop their culture, capacity for compassion, sense of community, and strength of democracy. Toynbee said that authentic growth consists in a "progressive and cumulative increase both in outward mastery of the environment and in inward self-determination or self-articulation on the part of the individual or society. . . . In other words the criterion of growth is a progress towards self-determination; and progress towards self-determination is a prosaic formula for describing the miracle by which life enters its Kingdom."[17]

A more conscious economy will shift its emphasis from sheer physical expansion to more qualitative growth. Products will be designed with increasing efficiency (doing ever more with ever less) while simultaneously increasing their beauty, strength, and ecological integrity. Economic justice need not imply a life of poverty, deficiency, and deprivation when living can be transformed through intelligent design into an elegant simplicity.[18] The level of satisfaction and beauty in living can be increased while lowering the quantity of resources consumed and the amount of pollution produced.

By learning to maintain ourselves ever more efficiently and aesthetically, greater increments of energy and attention will be available to develop along the psychological, cultural, and spiritual dimensions of life. In turn, by creating living and working environments that are sustainable, aesthetic, and nurturing, we can live more consciously. In living more consciously, we will feel less attached to material possessions and more able to live lightly and simply. In living more simply, there are fewer distractions, and we are more able to bring our undivided attention into the process of living. Each aspect builds upon the other. A self-reinforcing spiral is set into motion that promotes the coevolution of both the material and the consciousness aspects of life. As theologian Matthew Fox writes, "Luxury living is not what living is about. *Living* is what living is about! But living takes discipline and letting go and doing with less in a culture that is overdeveloped. It takes a commitment to challenge and adventure, to sacrifice and passion."[19]

REFLECTIVE SPIRITUALITY AND RECONCILIATION

Thus far the foundation for spirituality has evolved from the *Earth Goddess* orientation of the second dimension to the *Sky God* orientation of the third, the *Scientific Humanism* of the fourth, and now the *Reflective Knowing* of the fifth dimension. A reflective spirituality, with its capacity for detachment and objective witnessing, seems uniquely suited to meeting the primary challenge of this epoch of evolution—the global reconciliation of the human family.

Whatever one's spiritual path, in the fifth stage there will be a broad recognition that the experience of insight cannot be given by another person or institution but ultimately must be acquired through one's own efforts. We are each responsible for developing our potential for "knowing that we know." While spiritual traditions and teachers are valuable, the final responsibility for insight rests with the individual and his or her relationship with the Meta-universe, or "God," or whatever name we give to this ultimately unnameable presence. In the fifth stage the individual recognizes that there is no substitute for one's own process of self-discovery. The great value of spiritual teachers and traditions is to provide insights about coming into rapport with the living universe and to bolster our confidence in the most challenging search life has to offer.

Given the vital role of reflective spirituality, a science of consciousness will blossom in the fifth stage that will include: exploring the mind-body connection with sophisticated biofeedback; improving peak performance in sports, business, and other aspects of life; learning how to restore health using ancient healing traditions; studying the nature of mystical or peak experiences; exploring ways to enhance creativity and intuitive insights; collecting cross-cultural insights into the nature of near-death experiences; studying parapsychology or the mind-cosmos connection; and exploring interspecies communication. As scientific research progresses, a new view of consciousness will emerge.

Instead of viewing consciousness as a by-product of biochemical processes in the brain, consciousness will be seen by most as a natural force that infuses the cosmos and transcends, but interpenetrates, the material and biological realms. Many will accept that, via our knowing faculty, everyone connects with the larger universe. With the development of this subtle science, consciousness will no longer be relegated to a secondary position but will be seen as a coequal partner in evolution, and we will integrate that understanding into our visions and plans for our future as a species.

Seasons of Growth

The fifth stage of human evolution (and beyond) has yet to be realized at the scale of entire civilizations. We can therefore only speculate about the future. What follows is *not* a prediction, but only one plausible scenario. As I will discuss in Chapter 9, there are many pitfalls on the path to species-maturity, and the people of the Earth could choose any number of civilizational detours that would take us far from the pathway outlined here. With that caveat, here are the seasons of growth that I anticipate for the fifth stage.

Spring

As we approach the turn of the century, we are already experiencing the labor pains that mark the birth of a more conscious species-civilization. We are enclosed within an ailing and traumatized ecosystem. There is no escape from critical problems such as growing population, spreading pollution, dwindling resources, changing climate, massive famines, civil unrest, ozone depletion, soil erosion, rain-forest destruction, drug addiction, urban crime, and wars over access to resources. Caught in the grip of these forces, the springtime of growth will bring a protracted conflict between: rich and poor, Northern and Southern hemispheres, environmentalists and industrialists, fundamentalists and liberation theologists, advocates of military solutions and those favoring nonviolence, advocates of strong government and those seeking decentralization and greater citizen participation, and many more.

The tensions between the Northern and Southern hemispheres seems particularly problematic. The North wants the South to halt the destruction of rain forests, to preserve biodiversity, and to reduce population growth, and conversely the South wants the North to reduce the pollution that is producing climate change and to moderate high-consumption lifestyles that are wasting precious resources. Because each hemisphere must make major changes to create a planet habitable for all, it may be very difficult in the short run to achieve reconciliation around a common agenda for action. The springtime of the fifth dimension will be a hard time for the human family, filled with conflict, confusion, and despair. While the ideal of a new covenant and commitment among the human family will remain alive, the reality will likely be the continued disintegration of the global economy, society, and ecology.

A destabilized global climate may undermine the ability of the Earth to feed humanity. In turn, with world population approaching ten billion, the possibility of overshoot and collapse with a great die-off in human numbers could become a shocking and terrible reality. However, before such an awful Malthusian conclusion is reached, hundreds of millions of desperate persons will seek to migrate into resource-favored areas such as Europe and North America. Leaders in these regions will be so busy trying to maintain faltering cities and nations that they will have little time to look ahead and think creatively about the future. The world will seem to be going insane. Alienation and cynicism will escalate as a growing number of people feel utterly helpless and that our situation is hopeless.

Particularly in industrial nations, a deep psychological crisis will develop as people feel enormous guilt and shame for the devastation of the planet and the diminished opportunities for future generations. Many will be in mourning for the Earth and feel that humanity has failed in its grand experiment in evolution. After tens of thousands of years of slow development, many will feel that within the span of a single generation we have ruined our chance at evolutionary success. While many are grieving this lost opportunity, some will refuse to accept personal responsibility for this crisis and instead look for others to blame. Only gradually will deep soul-searching begin among the larger human family. Only gradually will people recognize that this is evolution in the raw—that we all face a future of unending bleakness and despair unless we collectively rise to this time of challenge.

The suffering, distress, and anguish of these times will become a purifying fire that burns through ancient prejudices and hostilities to cleanse the soul of our species. I expect no single, golden moment of reconciliation to suddenly descend upon the planet; instead waves of ecological calamity will reinforce periods of economic crisis, and both will be amplified by massive waves of civil unrest. Instead of a single crescendo of crisis and conflict, there will likely be momentary reconciliation followed by disintegration and then new reconciliation. In giving birth to a sustainable species-civilization, humanity will probably move back and forth through cycles of contraction and relaxation until we utterly exhaust ourselves and burn through the barriers that separate us from our wholeness as a human family. Eventually we will see that we have an unyielding choice between a badly injured (or even stillborn) species-civilization and the birth of a bruised, but relatively healthy, human family and biosphere. In seeing and accepting responsibility for this inescapable choice, we will enter the summertime of the fifth dimension.

Summer

In the summertime of growth humanity will discover a new sense of reality, identity, and social purpose held in common. Finding this new common sense while we are in the midst of major crises will be a messy, demanding, and drawn-out process. The summertime of growth will be an immensely trying season in which we will learn and relearn lessons, again and again, until they are anchored in the soul of our species. In life-and-death dramas played out around the planet, the human family will begin to build mutual understanding, begin to communicate its genuine desire for reconciliation, and begin to coalesce a simple though compelling vision for a sustainable world future. Only after we have exhausted all hope of partial solutions will we be willing to move forward with an open mind and open heart toward a future of mutually supportive development.

It was communication that enabled humans to evolve from early hunter-gatherers to the verge of planetary civilization, and it will be communication that enables us to become a bonded human family that is committed to the well-being of all. Because virtually all of the world's problems are human-caused, they are—at their core—communication problems. At the very time that we need an unprecedented capacity for local-to-global communication, we find that we have the necessary tools in abundance. Electronic town meetings will blossom from the local to national to global scale and make the sentiments of the body politic highly visible to itself. Less and less will citizens feel they are helpless victims of policies developed by remote bureaucracies.

The telecommunications revolution will become a powerful force for promoting reconciliation. Martin Luther King, Jr., said that to realize justice in human affairs, "injustice must be exposed, with all of the tension its exposure creates, to the light of human conscience and the air of national opinion before it can be cured."[20] Injustice and inequities flourish in the darkness of inattention and ignorance, but when the healing light of public awareness is focused on them, it creates a new consciousness among all involved. When everyone knows that the "whole world is watching"—when economic, ethnic, ideological, and religious violence is brought before the court of world public opinion through the mass media—then it will bring a powerful corrective influence into human relations. The global media will soon have the ability to provide the world with access to news and information about virtually any place, person, issue, or event on the planet within a matter of seconds. In a communications-rich world, old forms of political repression, human rights violations, and warfare will be extremely difficult to perpetrate without having a massive avalanche of world public opinion descend upon the oppressors.[21] As people and nations see their actions scrutinized and judged by the rest of the world community, they will become more inclined to search for more ethical and nonviolent approaches for both domestic affairs and international relations.

With intense global communication, economic restructuring, and conscious redesign of our living and working environments, small successes will grow into larger victories, and we will see the real potential for achieving a future where the engines of the world's economy work in harmony with the ecosystem of the planet. People will be designing themselves back into nature by creating sustainable ways of living that are adapted to the unique ecology, resources, and cultures of each bioregion. Prototype microcommunities will flourish that place a premium on living in ways that are ecologically conscious and nurturing of the human family, community, psyche, and spirit.

Autumn/Winter

Numerous times we may go to the very edge of ruin as a species, hopefully to pull back in time with new levels of maturity and insight. Eventually we will realize there is no final truce and lasting harmony and that, instead, goodwill and cooperation must be won freshly each day—forever. When we realize there is no final rest and that we have the skills and stamina for an ongoing journey, we will then rise to a new level of responsibility. Because people must work through the adversities of this stage together, it will foster feelings of global community and a shared commitment to a sustainable future.

If humanity is successful in realizing the evolutionary potentials of this era of communication and reconciliation, we will have achieved a foothold in building a planetary civilization. Our long-term future will be far from secure. We will have established little more than the collective intention to create a sustainable future and the capacity for mass communication necessary to realize that intention. It will be the task of the next major stage of human development—the sixth dimension—to make this hard-won possibility a reality. With reconciliation comes not the guarantee of success but the realistic opportunity to try to succeed. However, if "a problem recognized is a problem half-solved," then in recognizing the sweeping changes required to build a sustainable future, we will have come a long way toward realizing such a future.

After the intense feelings of guilt and self-doubt experienced during the springtime of this epoch, we will feel a new self-esteem as a species. We will feel as though we have "paid our dues"—the price of admission into the next stage of global maturity—through our immense suffering. Great anxiety as to whether our species would survive will be replaced by intense feelings of global community, solidarity, and kinship. "We made it through together," we will say. "Our species moved through the time of greatest danger that we could imagine, and we survived. We have truly begun to know ourselves as a human family, with all of our faults and idiosyncrasies. We have begun to realize our potential for double-wisdom—to know our own mind as a global family. We know there will be no rest—that forever we must work to reconcile ourselves with ourselves—but we also know that we are equal to the challenge."

Summary

It is the power of a witnessing or reflective consciousness that provides the practical basis for building a sustainable future. Reflective consciousness will enable humanity to stand back from counterproductive behavior and to choose more ecological ways of living. With reflective consciousness we can objectively witness environmental pollution, religious intolerance, poverty, overconsumption, racial injustice, sexual discrimination, and other conditions that have divided us in the past. With a more detached perspective combined with the skills of conflict resolution and the tools of mass communication, we can achieve a new level of human understanding. With understanding we can discover an authentic vision of a sustainable future that serves the well-being of all.

OCEANIC CONSCIOUSNESS AND THE BONDING AND BUILDING ERA

The **sixth dimension** will be a stage where consciousness seeks to know its own origins and discovers its connection with the deep ecology of the universe. In experiencing an intimate connection with the underlying universe, our sense of identity will move beyond the polarity of observer and observed to the experience of unbounded Beingness. An *oceanic consciousness* fosters feelings of love for all life, and this will promote bonding among the human family. Social compassion will become a practical basis for organizing and building a sustainable future. With a deep sense of bonding and community, humanity will work to build a sustainable future premised on mutually supportive development. This will be an era of intense cross-cultural learning, global celebration, and species-bonding.

CHAPTER 6

OCEANIC CONSCIOUSNESS AND THE BONDING AND BUILDING ERA

In our current era of scientific skepticism and social cynicism, it strains credibility to describe a future time when we might achieve a "golden age" of compassionate understanding and deep bonding among the human family. Legitimate skepticism is tempered with the recognition that immense suffering will be required to burn through age-old hostilities and achieve an authentic feeling of community among the human species. Evolution toward our initial maturity as a planetary civilization is not an abstract philosophical concept—it is a reality of the flesh that, at each stage, must be paid for in the blood and lives of countless individuals. There are no free gifts in evolution. We must genuinely earn access to each new stage of development.

Where the fifth stage will surely represent one of the most difficult and painful stages of human development, the blossoming of the sixth stage will, I believe, represent one of the most joyful and satisfying. Assuming we have not damaged irreparably the ecological foundations of life, in the sixth stage we will work in earnest to build a sustainable future. While reconciliation must still be renewed continuously, the sixth stage begins with great confidence in knowing we made it through a perilous transition and now share a common vision of a workable future. The world will blossom with a new enthusiasm for life and learning. We will take pride in building human-scale, sustainable communities that are nested within larger urban areas. Innumerable projects will get under way to restore the ecosystems of the Earth. A compassionate consciousness will infuse the world, bringing a new sense of caring and hope.

The same love that binds together an ordinary family is the unifying force that makes global reconciliation and commitment possible. It is this love that transcends the contentious and quarrelsome behavior of humanity and that can bind us into an authentic world community. It is love that enables us to join together consciously in a purposeful marriage of global scope in order to ensure a sustainable home for all life. Teilhard de Chardin described the essential role of love in building a mature species-civilization in his prophetic book *The Future of Man*. He said that love is "the fundamental impulse of Life . . . the one natural medium in which the rising course of evolution can proceed. With love omitted there is truly nothing ahead of us except the forbidding prospect of standardization and enslavement— the doom of ants and termites. It is through love and within love that we must look for the deepening of our deepest self, in the life-giving coming together of humankind."[1]

In the sixth stage of evolution humanity will recognize that a broad spectrum of choice exists for how we will live together: At one extreme we can become a dysfunctional and abusive global family that fails to support its members in rising to their individual and collective potentials. At the other extreme we can become a highly functional, nurturing, and loving family. Like a family, the amount of love we bring to the process will have a direct bearing on the outcome— we can either grow together through compassion or descend into conflict together through greed and fear.

The intense crises of the fifth stage will be necessary to awaken the power of love as a binding force for planetary civilization. These crises will push people to realize that technical solutions are inadequate to remedy our situation and that fundamentally we face a crisis of compassion. Only by building upon our shared spiritual experience as a species—the enduring wisdom found across cultures and through history—can we hope to make a successful turn toward a sustainable and meaningful future. It will be the task of the fifth dimension to confront this crisis of spirit squarely, and it will be the task of the sixth dimension to then rebuild human civilization from a soulful foundation. Compassion will no longer be seen as a spiritual luxury for a contemplative few; rather it will be viewed as a social necessity for the entire human family. The perceptual geometry of the sixth dimension is basic to this transformation of consciousness and culture.

THE SIXTH DIMENSION: OCEANIC CONSCIOUSNESS

Where the fifth dimension draws out the potential for reflective consciousness, the sixth dimension draws out the potential for a compassionate or oceanic consciousness. We do not enter the sixth stage with our capacity for compassion fully developed; instead it will be through our day-to-day work together as a human family that we evolve our capacity for loving engagement with the world. Over generations we will build a caring and nurturing planetary community. In turn it will be the strength of this union that will enable us to withstand the enormous stresses that will be unleashed by the creativity of the seventh dimension—our last stage of growth before we achieve our initial maturity as a species-civilization. Where the dispassionate consciousness of the fifth stage was sufficient to enable us to achieve embryonic reconciliation, it is the compassionate consciousness of the sixth stage that enables us to move ahead to actually build a global civilization.

To describe the foundations of compassionate consciousness, we need to recall a basic premise of this cosmology; namely, that our cosmos is a living organism that is being regenerated in its entirety in a continuous flow of creation (a theme discussed at length in Chapter 11). Oceanic knowing emerges naturally when we penetrate beneath the surface of life and experience the underlying ecology of Life-energy out of which all is continuously arising. This expansion in knowing occurs when the object of consciousness is consciousness itself—when knowingness seeks to know its own origins. With knowing centered upon knowing, we begin to penetrate into the realm of pure awareness, whose intrinsic nature is love—an experience always available to us at the center of our moment-to-moment existence.

When, through disciplined effort, we learn the skills of quieting our mind and turning the knowing faculty squarely back upon itself, a profound transformation in consciousness occurs—the distance between observer and observed is gradually reduced to nothing. Knowingness ultimately becomes identical with and transparent to the deep generative ground that continuously gives rise to all that exists. To describe this crucial though subtle process in visual terms, recall Figure 7 from the previous chapter, which portrayed the trinity of matter, consciousness, and the underlying Life-force of the Meta-universe. Figure 8 suggests how the experience of "self" moves from the back-and-forth dynamic of the observer and observed (or bodily existence and reflective consciousness) to become identical with the underlying Meta-universe, whose nature is compassionate awareness.

With highly focused attention to our moment-by-moment experience, the distance between the observer and the observed gradually diminishes until they become a single flow of experience that continuously arises anew. As the knower and that which is known become one in experience, we become identical to the infinite Life-energy from which all continuously emerges. When we are fully present in the precise center of our moment-to-moment experience, we automatically come into a living relationship with the unbounded Life-force—an experience that is intrinsically pleasurable and satisfying. At the center we find the simple joy and contentment of being alive. Our intimate connection with all of creation naturally awakens feelings of wholeness, aliveness, and compassion.

Our experience of time is again transformed with entry into the spaciousness of the sixth dimension. Time moves beyond the momentary snapshots of holistic manifestation in the fifth dimension to the abiding fullness of creation in the sixth dimension. Instead of skipping along the surface, we move into the oceanic depths of con-

**Figure 8: The Evolution of Identity from the Polarity of
Observer/Observed to Oceanic Awareness**

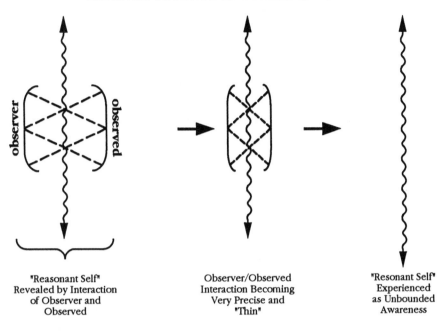

| "Reasonant Self"
Revealed by Interaction
of Observer and
Observed | Observer/Observed
Interaction Becoming
Very Precise and
"Thin" | "Resonant Self"
Experienced
as Unbounded
Awareness |

sciousness, experiencing the ebbs and flows of a larger life and tasting the experience of great Being. Yet the boundless experience of Being in the sixth stage does not complete the evolution of our self-referencing capacity—we still have to close the loop and bring the boundless ocean of compassionate knowing back into the everyday, material world of the here and now. The oceanic experience of Being in the sixth stage has yet to become fully transformed into the flow consciousness of "Being-Becoming-Being" characteristic of the seventh stage.

OCEANIC IDENTITY

Many paths can lead to the discovery of the oceanic scope of our being—for example, meditation, prayer, and service in the world. A common challenge in all paths is to develop the skills of coming to our centered sense of self. As we become practiced in opening to this center, our sense of self expands commensurately. We no longer see ourselves as contained entirely within a physical body. We recognize that the true scope of our being extends into the deep ecology of the underlying Meta-universe and that we have an identity of vast magnitude. We know from direct experience that we are inseparable from the unbounded Meta-universe and that we are infused by a silent hurricane of Life-energy that moves through and sustains all things. With penetrating attention we recognize that a subtle fact of cosmic proportions has been ever-present in our experience but largely overlooked. In our previous state of mental distraction—thinking about the past and worrying about the future—we did not appreciate the importance of the subtle self-experience that was always available to us. In the sixth stage, however, a knowingness that was initially almost imperceptible grows in strength and clarity. Just as a nearly universal, written literacy would have seemed almost impossible during the agrarian era but the norm in the industrial era, so, too, can a "literacy of consciousness" seem almost unimaginable today but become widely accessible only a few generations into the future.

Although awakening to an expanded sense of self can be marked by profound mystical experiences, this does not mean people in the sixth stage move through life "blissed out" or in a state of rapture that is disconnected from bodily and worldly existence. To the contrary, by being fully present within our bodily experience, we settle into the miracle of existence and discover the subtle aliveness, delight, and joy of sheer being. While powerful and transformative experiences may mark our passage into an oceanic self-sense, the everyday experience and expression of this compassionate mode of being tends to be down-to-Earth and practical.

An important aspect of the conscious learning of the sixth dimension comes as people stray from their centered experience and seemingly "lose" themselves, only to rediscover themselves again and again until they have unshakable confidence in their capacity for "knowing that they know." Many times a day we will forget the fact of our oceanic Being but with a few moments of focus, intention, and grace we can take a breath, notice the smile and love that arises spontaneously in our hearts, and reaffirm our capacity for approaching the world with loving kindness. Through diligent practice we learn that once we discover the oceanic dimension, we are not cut off from this experience of reality. Even though we may move up and down the spectrum of dimensional stages many times during the course of a day, we can be confident that we know where to look within our felt experience to discover freshly the oceanic nature of our Being. In a self-reinforcing spiral of development we become increasingly secure in knowing this ordinary miracle, and we recognize that we are beings of cosmic dimension, connection, and purpose.

A WORLD OF FRIENDS

With a compassionate consciousness as a widely shared foundation for human relations, a feeling of community will naturally expand to a global scale. Most people will feel they are among friends, no matter where they are in the world. A common bond will exist beneath the outward differences of culture, race, gender, age, and occupation. Everywhere people will be working to craft their individualized art of living more consciously. In a grocery store, walking along a street, working in an office, driving along the road—wherever—a majority of people will be found going about their lives more consciously and intentionally. A world culture that values the potential for double-wisdom will be everywhere evident.

Entirely new levels of community will be generated by the electronic networks with their complex array of overlapping associations and connections among people. Communication networks will be so inexpensive to use that it will be nearly as easy to connect with someone on the other side of the planet as with someone down the street. Electronic communities and cultures will flourish, transforming research, friendship, arts, education, business, play, and governance. Electronic networks will leap over traditional organizational and social boundaries to move knowledge through the global society like water passing through a sponge. A strong feeling of global family will emerge from the collective influence of these diverse electronic communities. With communication networks enveloping the world, humanity will have the "global brain" it needs to build a future of mutually supportive development.

With the rise of a compassionate consciousness, humanity will be so busy creating sustainable communities and restoring the ecosystems of the Earth that physical warfare will lose much of its potency and purpose. All war will be seen as civil war. With a commitment to nonviolent means of resolving conflicts, the world will shift its resources away from military arsenals and will focus on critical needs for world health, environmental restoration, rebuilding cities, global literacy, lifelong education, and expanding the communications infrastructure.

In the sixth stage the differences that previously divided humanity—in religion, politics, ethnicity, race, and gender—will now be what bring us together. This will be an era for celebrating diversity within a context of overarching unity. In the sixth stage a rich and diverse global culture will emerge as music, theater, literature, dance, and other arts proliferate. With a flood of exchange among the cultures of the planet, there will be a worldwide interest in understanding and preserving the deep historical roots of every culture to ensure that we do not forget the unique origins and contributions made by various peoples throughout history. There will be widespread interest in archaeology and paleoanthropology as humanity makes a systematic effort to discover its roots and to protect knowledge of the unique genealogy and history of all the world's cultures.

In the sixth stage a fermenting global culture will emerge that is pulsing with life and activity. The richness of the global culture will compensate for severe material limitations. Regular rites and rituals will celebrate the recurring cycles of the planet. "Earth Days" will acknowledge our bonding as a human family and our connection to the living planet, "Gaia." In global concerts and gatherings people will celebrate their reverence for life and affirm their solidarity with the planet. Regions and nations will take turns hosting gatherings that celebrate our covenant with the Earth and our commitment to one another.

World games will become increasingly popular as spirited competition replaces armed conflict as an important way of working through tensions and aggressions. New games will be invented with challenges and refinements that push contestants toward ever higher levels of excellence—from the cerebral (for example, highly sophisticated electronic-simulation games where, in virtual reality, players undertake challenges more dangerous and difficult than they could in real life) to the more physical (perhaps racing advanced forms of solar, wind, and human-powered airplanes).

The culture of the sixth stage will embody a balance between masculine and feminine archetypes. The feminine archetype will be expressed in the priority given to building nurturing relationships among the members of the human family and in restoring the global ecology. The masculine archetype will be expressed in the priority given to practical projects required to build the new planetary infrastructure. Overall, there will be a life-serving intention as most persons seek to serve the well-being of the living planet. A culture of kindness will become the social norm as more and more people become "guerrillas of goodness" and spontaneously express their caring for one another and for the Earth in countless small actions.

A compassionate or life-serving intention will have practical impacts on how social relationships are structured and managed. During the industrial era, people were expected to behave in a self-serving manner, and external forms of regulation (intrusive bureaucracies, laws, and monitoring systems) were needed to moderate the negative impacts of actions taken without regard to their impact on the world. However, in this era of compassionate consciousness many people will bring a life-serving intention to the affairs of everyday life, and consequently the need for intrusive bureaucracies will be diminished and human freedom will be enhanced.

One practical expression of designing ourselves into a sustainable future will be the rebuilding of massive cities with neighborhoods in the form of intentional microcommunities. By creating economically and socially integrated microcommunities at roughly the scale of a city or suburban block, new forms of living and working environments will emerge that utilize local space far more intensively and creatively. A suburban block may, for example, be transformed into an aesthetic and organic clustering of buildings, gardens, and areas for living and working. Because the population of many of these "ecovillages" would roughly approximate the tribal scale of living (with several dozen to a hundred or so persons), this design and scale of living will, for many, feel very comfortable and "fitting." With an architecture sensitive to the psychology of modern "tribes," a new sense of community will begin to replace the alienation of massive urban regions. Microcommunities will also be designed with gardens, trees, and courtyards that invite nature back into the living environment.

Each microcommunity might specialize in a particular area of interest to provide fulfilling work for many persons (for example, crafts, health care, child care, gardening, education, publishing, and so on). Common to all ecovillages could be a community garden for local food production, solar collectors or some other source of energy production, an efficient system of recycling and waste disposal, and a telecommuting center. Instead of isolating people in single-family dwellings or apartments, people could find a satisfying sense of place within an immense variety of different ecovillages designed to reflect the values and interests of various communities of people. Sustainability would be achieved through different designs that are uniquely adapted to the culture, economy, interests, and environment of each neighborhood and region. These microcommunities will have the feeling and cohesiveness of a small town and the sophistication of a big city as they are nested within a communications-rich setting. One vision of a sustainable community is shown in Figure 9 on the following page.

Revitalization at the microscale would be accompanied by the growth of other institutions that expand the sense of belonging and meaningful association: voluntary groups, churches, clubs, and other organizations will flourish and give people a strong sense of connection and community. In a spirit of local self-help, grass-roots organi-

Figure 9: Envisioning a Sustainable Community

zations will take charge of many activities formerly preempted by centralized bureaucracies: education, health care, child care, crime prevention, job training, and much more. With a strong sense of community at the scale of the neighborhood and local bioregion, there will exist a resilient and sturdy foundation upon which to build a planetary-scale civilization. A compassionate society that is organized and largely governed at the local scale has another high social payoff: It will enable people to maintain their freedoms and avoid impersonal control by remote bureaucracies—the "the doom of ants and termites."[3]

An Ocean of Voices

Democracy will be highly participatory in this communications-rich society. The alienation and cynicism of the past will be transformed as people are offered innumerable ways to participate in dialogue and decisions at every level—local, regional, national, and global. Where the fourth stage (or industrial era) was characterized by massive citizen withdrawal from civic duties, and where the fifth stage (or communication and reconciliation era) will be characterized by bursts of intense public dialogue and consensus building followed by periods of relative quiet and distraction, the sixth stage will be characterized by an ocean of voices that, with ebbs and flows, gives ongoing feedback vital to building a sustainable future. As the global village comes of age, the conversation of democracy will broaden and deepen through the powerful electronic networks that surround the planet.

Because competition between nation-states that is unrestrained by any effective form of overarching governing process will produce conflict, a more democratically organized world-governing body will emerge in the sixth stage. A natural progression in the scale of government seems to accompany each stage of dimensional evolution:

- **Second Stage**—In the era of the awakening hunter-gatherer humanity moved from tribes to the small-village scale of activity.
- **Third Stage**—In the agrarian era we moved from the scale of city-states to loosely connected empires.
- **Fourth Stage**—In the industrial era we moved from strong nation-states and confederations of nations into a weak form of international governance.
- **Fifth Stage**—In the communications era we are seeing the emergence of strong economic alliances among groups of nations, creating important transnational entities as well as a strengthened United Nations.

As the scale of social organization enlarges, issues of domination and sovereignty must be overcome at each stage of evolution. A strong system of global governance is unlikely to be accepted easily or quickly. The historical progression from villages to city-states to nation-states to regional alliances and beyond has been accompanied by terrible wars and human suffering. It took the horror of World War I to generate support for the ineffective League of Nations. It took the millions of lives lost during World War II to generate support for the largely symbolic and relatively weak United Nations. If history is our guide, it may require another great tragedy before a global consensus emerges that supports a system of effective global governance.

A system of global governance could be developed with appropriate checks and balances so that it has adequate power to enforce laws but not enough to become a global dictatorship. It could be modeled, for example, after the design of the United States government, where a democratically elected legislature develops laws, an appointed court interprets those laws, and an elected executive agency enforces those laws. With a democratically constituted vehicle of global governance, the world could move from peace achieved through threat (mutually assured destruction) to peace achieved through promise (mutually assured development). Despite a compassionate orientation, it seems unlikely that conflict will be eliminated entirely; instead, other forms of violence will persist (for example, information wars, eco-terrorism, economic injustice, and racial discrimination) that will create the need for ongoing conflict resolution.

Nonviolent action will become increasingly important as a way to awaken the conscience of a community, corporation, or nation. For example, a majority of persons in an entire city, region, or nation might engage in a hunger strike to awaken other people of the Earth to a particular human need or injustice. Previously unthinkable levels of compassionate mass action and national self-sacrifice might blossom in efforts to raise the world's consciousness and achieve life-enhancing ends. As people make successful use of the principles of nonviolence, it will further soften the heart of humankind and wean us away from violence.

The actions of governments around the globe will be scrutinized by people around the planet. The constant flow of information and dialogue will create a palpable global consensus. The body politic will increasingly know its own mind and grow ever more sophisticated in its collective thought processes. Regions, nations, and transnational alliances will work to forge understandings that can be injected into the global decision-making process. Given the overlapping nature of communication networks and the strength of a highly decentralized global economy, it is unlikely that any single group or nation will be able to dominate. In this new world everyone will be in charge—and no one will be in charge. We will have a mature, self-organizing system where no one nation, group, or leader dominates and yet everyone participates.

COMING HOME TO THE EARTH

The root meaning of the word *economy* is "home management," and it is in the sixth stage that we will learn to manage our affairs as a species in a way that truly makes the Earth our home. To prevent the Earth from going into catastrophic decline and failure, we will recognize that we must maintain the Earth's capacity for self-repair. We will understand that if we don't safeguard the natural healing ability of the planet, the long-term costs will far outweigh short-term advantages. After the trauma of the last epoch people will understand that there are no quick fixes and that restoration of the ecosystem will require the patient effort of billions of individuals over many generations. A primary goal will be to develop ways of life that ensure that the planetary biosphere can support the weight and pressure of humanity's civilizing activity.

In the sixth stage humanity will continuously adjust its overall levels and patterns of consumption to keep within the carrying capacity of the Earth. Voluntarily paring back on consumption will not be done in a spirit of sacrifice, as people will recognize that we are here for reasons far beyond consuming and being entertained. In the oceanic era there will be widespread understanding that we are here to experience life fully, to engage the world purposefully, and to contribute to life wholeheartedly. There will be broad recognition that an unquenchable spark of life burns within each of us and that we cannot satisfy the drive of our inner Life-force for soulful engagement with the world by simply consuming more stuff. People will understand that the feeling of wholeness comes from authentic union with the world—when our inner aliveness comes into conscious and fulfilling connection with the miracle of everyday existence.

A SPIRITUALITY NAMED COMPASSION

The spirituality of the sixth stage is grounded in the transpersonal experience that emerges when consciousness is turned back upon itself. As consciousness seeks to know its own origins and nature, we penetrate into the realms underlying a living universe. Cosmic consciousness—or knowing our connection with the consciousness of the living cosmos—becomes a widely shared, experiential foundation for the global culture.

Oceanic knowing provides a new common sense for a more compassionate society. A core meaning of the word *passion* is "to suffer." Therefore the word *com-passion* literally means "to be with suffering." In the sixth dimension we will directly experience our connection with the suffering of the rest of life in its struggle for existence and liberating awareness. Where the fifth stage is marked by a dispassionate distance between the observer and that which is being observed, the sixth stage is marked by feelings of intimate connection between the self and the rest of reality. It is this experience of connection that enables us to respond naturally with a more open mind and heart to the suffering of the world.

The lives of Martin Luther King, Jr., and Mother Teresa provide two examples of the practical expression of a compassionate consciousness and suggest how it might transform life in the sixth stage. King would sometimes quote Gandhi, who said, "Rivers of blood may have to flow before we gain our freedom, but it must be our blood." King also said that the willingness to bear suffering transforms resister and oppressor alike and avoids the bitterness that comes from hate. "Along the way of life, someone must have sense enough and morality enough to cut off the chain of hate. This can only be done by projecting the ethic of love to the center of our lives."[4] Mother Teresa has devoted her life to working with the poorest of the poor around the world and is a powerful example of the practical expression of compassion. She says, "Love is a fruit in season at all times, and within reach of every hand. Anyone may gather it and no limit is set."[5]

The oceanic consciousness of the sixth stage will enable humanity to see beyond the differences in religious dogma that were so divisive in the past. Each spiritual tradition will be appreciated for how it invites people to experience a different facet of the divine Life-force: **Christianity** inviting us to bring love, forgiveness, and a concern for social justice into our community life; **Judaism** inviting us to appreciate the divine force that is not aloof from this world but lives in and through human history and society; **Islam** inviting us to recognize the great value of the awakened individual whose life is surrendered to God; **Buddhism** inviting us to discipline our thinking minds and to develop the capacity for penetrating insight that reveals the core nature of our Being as an unbroken flow of pure awareness; **Hinduism** inviting us to experience the absolute reality behind all appearances and the moment-to-moment dance of creation and destruction of the cosmos; **Taoism** inviting us to appreciate the subtle, unceasing flow of reality and the wisdom of yielding to that flow; American Indians and other **native peoples** throughout the world inviting us to experience the living presence infusing all of nature's expressions— plants, animals, Earth, wind, fire, and water. Each of the world's wisdom traditions reveals a different facet of humanity's experience of the divine Life-force.

An oceanic spirituality emerges when knowingness seeks to know its own source and we discover that our core nature is the unbounded Life-force or "God," the "Tao," "Brahman," and other names for this ultimately unnameable presence. Modern physics hints at this deeper nature and describes our seemingly solid bodies as whirlwinds of subtle energy that are orchestrated with exquisite harmony so as to dynamically sculpt a living presence. The creative power of this invisible Life-energy is unnoticed because of its transparent nature. We can easily overlook the fact that at the center of the flow of thoughts, feelings, and sensations there is a clear "knowing-resonance"—an artesian well of pure Life-energy that continuously pours into existence. Yet, just as when the clear light of the sun is passed through a prism and blossoms into a bright rainbow of colors, so, too, when the clear light of our centered existence shines through the prism of this material world and our unique personality, we each manifest a broad spectrum of textures and qualities of being. To experience ourselves as unique expressions of this infinite Life-energy, we must learn the skills of quieting our mentally constructed I-sense so that the spontaneously given I-sense may become evident in awareness.

The opportunity to develop our inborn capacity for double-wisdom is the most precious gift this world offers. In knowing that we know, we discover the gateway into the unbounded Meta-universe—into eternity. Because a supreme evolutionary imperative is to support life in its ascent toward self-referencing knowing, to die before coming to self-referencing consciousness represents a profound lost opportunity.

To discover the subtle Life-energy at the center of our being requires periods of undistracted attention and contemplation. Our world of busy schedules, distractions, noise, and conflicting purposes makes it very difficult to cultivate the refinement of attention needed to discover the presence of eternity. In the culture of oceanic consciousness people will consciously simplify their lives to create the time and space to contemplate and celebrate the subtle but unmistakable Life-force at the core of our being. Increasingly people will recognize that our greatest satisfaction comes from experiencing the aliveness at the center of our existence and in sharing that experience with others.

THE SEASONS OF THE SIXTH DIMENSION

As a compassionate consciousness infuses our worldly actions, restoration of the Earth becomes a project as compelling as was the domination of the Earth in the industrial era. Here are the seasons of growth involved in building a sustainable planetary culture and bonding ourselves into a global family.

Spring

In the springtime of the sixth stage we will be challenged to realize the visions of a sustainable future that were developed at the close of the fifth stage. Humanity will have one overriding world project in the opening of this new epoch: achieving basic minimums of well-being for all people with regard to food, shelter, health care, education, environmental quality, and access to communication systems. Although great disparities may persist for several generations, these could be tolerable if there is a clear plan and intention to achieve ethical minimums. In order for humanity to live within the ecological limits of the biosphere, enormous goodwill and self-discipline will be required to restrain the engines of economic growth in both developed and developing nations. Overall, the human family will need the powerful bonding force of love to hold itself together during these challenging times.

Summer

The summer of growth will be a season of intense activity and determined invention. After several generations of work on restoring the integrity of the Earth's ecosystem, a feeling of satisfaction and accomplishment will infuse the planet. The people of the Earth will know that they are capable of creating a civilization in harmony with the biosphere, one that can endure into the far future.

With the Earth recognized as a living organism, an ecological ethic will continue to develop that recognizes the rights of all life-forms. We will accept responsibility for the well-being of all creation—from the trees, dolphins, and whales to the microbes and plankton. Because the strength of an ecosystem depends upon a diverse biosphere with a broad spectrum of life-forms, many people will adopt, and seek to protect, a particular bioregion or particular species of plants or animals as part of their lifework.

The growing breadth and depth of world communications will continue to awaken a global consciousness. World festivals, fairs, Olympics, and observances will abound. Cycles of celebration will mark out the year and infuse the world with a perceptible consciousness. World meditations and mass rituals will deepen the sense of global cohesion and union. Local to global rites and rituals will flourish with innovative music, theater, and ceremony that celebrate the solidarity and bonding of the human family.

Autumn/Winter

As the golden summer and abundant autumn of this epoch move toward winter, there will be a growing recognition that the evolutionary journey is not yet complete. Although the dream of species-bonding and a sustainable future will have been realized, the global civilization that once looked so appealing will now show another face: Bonding turns to bondage. Union turns to uniformity. Cohesiveness turns to constraint. Increasingly people will feel suffocated and controlled—on a leash of love, bound by the golden chains of a compassionate society. Having learned to maintain ourselves, a billion or more creative individuals will now want to explore the possibilities for surpassing themselves.

Until we reach our initial maturity as a species-civilization in the eighth stage, we will find that after we harvest the potentials of each of the preceding stages of growth, there emerges a dark side that leads to a civilizational crisis, which in turn pushes us to a new stage of development:

- **Fourth Dimension**—We realized the potential for material development only to find that we were destroying the ecosystem on which our existence depends.

- **Fifth Dimension**—We may realize the potential for a lawful world order only to find our freedoms threatened by a global computer and communications network that tightly monitors and controls human affairs.
- **Sixth Dimension**—We may realize the potential for a compassionate and sustainable world only to sink into a stagnant society where living becomes "only not dying."

In communities around the planet empowered and capable persons will seek to move beyond maintaining themselves to surpassing themselves. Acting from love, they will push creativity to its limits with an unprecedented range of projects (for example: genetic engineering that creates hybrid forms of animals and plants; developing superintelligent computer systems that are set free to advance learning into uncharted areas; "uplifting" other species into new levels of consciousness and competence; and building communities of genetically augmented humans with vastly increased brain power and physical capacities).

At the close of this epoch a psychic entropy will begin to pervade the planet. World civilization will become a loving but lukewarm amalgam. Still, for a time, most will be content with a compassionate civilization and not want to jeopardize the welfare of the world for the sake of seemingly fringe experiments. Many people will recall that reconciliation around a sustainable future was achieved only after horrible suffering and will fear that a new era of "progress" will actually lead to chaos and regress. The world will be locked into the subtle shackles of mass consensus. As mass celebrations drown out the voices and visions of creative individuals and communities, a division in dimensional perspective will grow between a contented majority and creative minority. Ultimately even the golden chains of a compassionate civilization must be broken as people recognize that if we are unable to liberate the soulful creativity of individuals, then we will not discover the potentials of our species and we will be consigned to live out our future in fearful self-restraint.

SUMMARY

The perceptual paradigm of the sixth dimension provides a spacious context for people and civilizations to experience their oneness with the universe. In turn it will be the compassionate consciousness of this stage that will enable humanity to make the sweeping changes required to build a sustainable world civilization. Most people will find a sense of community and connection that more than compensates for material limitations. People will feel bonded with one another through their biological family and psychospiritual families; through their microcommunity or neighborhood ecovillage; through voluntary associations, churches, schools, and other local organizations; through the many communication networks to which they belong (learning, politics, play, research, and so on); and through their common task of building a workable future.

In the sixth stage we will look outward to understand the cosmos and inward to understand the depths of our own experience. We will look back to understand our ancestors and origins, and we will look around ourselves to appreciate the diversity of people and cultures. Above all, we will celebrate the fact that we are, at last, home.

FLOW CONSCIOUSNESS AND

THE SURPASSING ERA

The **seventh dimension** will be the stage where the diffuse, oceanic consciousness returns to its center and becomes *flow consciousness*—and a force for concentrated and creative expression in the world. The planetary civilization will move beyond a concern with maintaining itself to surpassing itself. The strength of human bonding and the sense of global community achieved in the sixth stage will be critical for enabling the world to liberate its creativity without tearing itself apart. The oceanic consciousness of the sixth dimension will be focused into practical action as people delight in the process of fully engaged participation in the world. World civilization will seek continuously to balance creative diversity with the need for a sustainable unity.

$\mathcal{F}$LOW CONSCIOUSNESS AND THE SURPASSING ERA

Despite the elevated experience of oceanic consciousness in the sixth dimension, this is not the end of our journey of personal and civilizational awakening. Our next challenge will be to bring the knowing of the sixth stage fully back into the world. Opening into the spaciousness of the sixth stage will still leave us with the task of "closing the loop"—of achieving full self-possession. Metaphorically, in the sixth stage the drop dissolves into the ocean, and in the seventh stage the ocean returns to the drop. In more practical terms, when global civilization moves into the seventh stage, we will be challenged to liberate the creativity of our species without destroying ourselves. A growing proportion of the world's people will be increasingly frustrated with the lukewarm civilization that emerges in the sixth stage and will be busy discovering ways to surpass themselves, both personally and cooperatively.

Examples of some of the creative ventures that might be unleashed in this epoch include: large-scale genetic engineering to create new types of superhumans or other dramatically altered life-forms; extensive use of self-replicating nanotechnologies (microscopic machines) that have the potential of growing like a virus and getting out of control; extreme forms of sexual behavior that become widespread and threaten social norms; so-called sporting events that appeal to the dark side of the human psyche and that go beyond testing ordinary human endurance and skill. To open this overflowing Pandora's Box of possibilities is to invite both destructive as well as creative potentials into the world with consequences that are nearly impossible to imagine.

In the seventh stage we will be challenged to achieve centered self-possession as a planetary civilization. In coming to the center of our experience as a species, we will inevitably encounter many disowned or shadow aspects of ourselves (the violent, bizarre, or extreme) that we may want to forget or to diminish. Humanity will take an important step toward the early adulthood of our species when we learn how to remain open to the creative ferment of flow consciousness without losing our balance and spinning out of control (for example into destructive warfare or species-neurosis).

Given a global marketplace and the ability to connect instantly through electronic networks with like-minded persons around the planet, innovations that would have taken decades to move from idea to implementation in the industrial era will now move through the world culture in years or even months. The speed of change will be so great that differences of culture, religion, aesthetics, politics, and so forth will need to be reconciled continuously to maintain the integrity of the Earth as a sustainable system. The Earth will seem impossibly small for containing the ever-mounting diversity. To align and harmonize the dynamism and creativity of this stage, humanity will have to move beyond compassionate consciousness to flow consciousness and learn the skills of moving through life with an integrated awareness that supports a new level of self and social mastery.

The difference between the compassionate consciousness of the sixth dimension and the flow consciousness of the seventh dimension is akin to the difference between the diffuse light that comes from a reading lamp and the focused light that comes from a laser. Just as laser light can be focused with enough intensity to even cut through steel, the compassionate consciousness of the sixth stage can be focused with enough intensity to even cut through the golden chains of a compassionate culture.

The power of the seventh stage will not be unleashed blindly on the world—it will be guided by whatever degrees of learning, love, and insight were developed in the preceding epochs. This wisdom will provide an important moderating influence for the creative energy liberated in the seventh stage. The Earth will have become so small, and the surpassing projects so many, that there will be a constant need to rediscover the balance between planetary unity and human diversity, between enterprising action and compassionate restraint.

Not everyone will be pushing the edges of their creative potentials—many will be content to be supportive sustainers who provide a nurturing context within which the creativity of others can prosper. Nonetheless, instead of a relatively few powerful innovators and entrepreneurs, this will be a world with billions of empowered and capable people—each extremely strong and inventive. In this epoch humanity will break free from the compassionate stability that characterized the sixth dimension and enter a final time of testing and learning before reaching the dynamic stability of a self-organizing, planetary civilization.

THE SEVENTH DIMENSION: FLOW CONSCIOUSNESS

A basic premise of this cosmology is that the geometry of the universe is neither indifferent nor arbitrary but represents an exquisitely designed structure and highly purposeful framework through which we progressively develop our capacity for double-wisdom. Just as it required three dimensions to develop the material aspects of life (the second, third, and fourth), it requires three additional dimensions to coevolve the consciousness aspects of life:

- **Fifth Dimension**—Reveals the simple fact of the profound interconnection of the universe, and this is experienced through **re-**

flective consciousness. The primary challenge of this epoch is to build a world consensus around, and commitment to, a shared vision of a sustainable future through mass communication and global reconciliation.

- **Sixth Dimension**—Reveals the infinitely deep Life-force that infuses the universe, and this is experienced through **oceanic consciousness**. The primary challenge is to build a sustainable world community and culture with a deep feeling of belongingness and bonding.

- **Seventh Dimension**—Reveals the dynamism of the universe in its process of continuously arising anew, and this is experienced through **flow consciousness**. The primary challenge is to liberate the creative potentials of the species without destroying the foundation of global unity and sustainability developed in the previous stages.

With the opening of the seventh dimension we will take the final step in the evolution of perceptual geometry by embracing the full dynamism of the cosmos. The last vestiges of the passive observer will be transformed into the fully engaged participator. There is no longer an observer that stands outside the rushing flow of creation. At the center is the experience of becoming where each moment is fresh and alive, forever arising anew. In the seventh stage, the loop of self-knowing fully closes upon itself and the capacity for dynamically "knowing that we know" will be realized. By coming to the center of oceanic consciousness (the "great Being" of the sixth stage), we discover the flow of the living cosmos in its process of "great Becoming" (the seventh stage). Being and Becoming are both true. To complete our learning, we must learn the skills of movement, of flow, of riding the wave of time's integrated flow, of "reality surfing," of Being Becoming Being—discovering the stillness within motion and the motion within stillness.[1] Enlightening experiences emerge naturally when attention rides the precise edge of the endless, cresting wave of continuous creation. (Continuous-creation cosmology is discussed at length in Chapter 11.)

What does flow consciousness feel like? Here's an analogy: Imagine you are riding a bike along a road with a twenty-mile-per-hour wind blowing directly at your back. When you are pedaling slower than twenty miles per hour, you feel the wind pushing you from behind. When you are pedaling faster than twenty miles per hour, you feel the wind pushing from the front. But at perfect speed—when the speed of your bike matches the speed of the wind—the world suddenly becomes very still, and your movement along the road becomes nearly effortless. In a similar way, when our flow of awareness comes into precise synchronization with the arising of the cosmos, then the world suddenly becomes very quiet and our passage through life becomes calm and easeful. When we are aware of the stillness within motion, we are in the center of the flow of continuous creation. In flow consciousness we experience a deep harmony as the personal and the universal move together in mutual synchrony.[2] Because any activity done with fullness of attention offers an opportunity to connect with the cosmic flow, this experience is always available to us.

Our bodily existence is alive with the motion of continuous creation. The trillions of atoms that comprise our body are each phantoms of energy that cohere into a single symphony of expression that is our unique material form. At each moment we are a unique manifestation of the music of creation. We have a paradoxical existence: We are **stable** entities (as macrolevel biological beings) as well as completely **dynamic** entities (as ungraspable whirlwinds of energy at the quantum level). In addition we are totally **unique** (everything that exists is a singular expression of a flowing Meta-universe) as well as totally **integrated** (we are interior to and inseparable from the dynamically arising universe and the sustaining Meta-universe).

The perception of time also evolves a step farther in the seventh dimension. The Buddhist sage Ananda K. Coomaraswamy described the flow of reality this way: "We are deceived if we allow ourselves to believe that there is ever a pause in the flow of becoming, a resting place where positive existence is attained for even the briefest duration of time."[3] Time moves from the "abiding Beingness" of the oceanic experience to the "Being-Becoming-Being" of the flow experience.[4] Here is how this culminating experience of time is described in the Buddhist tradition by Lama Govinda, an artist, philosopher, and meditator: "[In the precise present] the 'one-after-another' is transformed into 'the-one-within-the-other,' a relationship . . . in which all things reflect and penetrate each other as well as the experiencing subject, without losing their respective individuality. Thus the universe and the experiencer of the universe are mirrored in every phenomena."[5] This is not an insight exclusive to the East. The Greek philosopher Heraclitus made the same point when he said, "No one can step twice into the same stream, nor touch a living object twice in the same condition. In swift and repeated change, things disperse and gather again. . . . So it is that becoming never ends in being."[6]

With flow consciousness we engage the "natural time" of continuous creation. Natural time has its own pacing and can be experienced as moving either faster or slower than mechanical or clock time. For example, it is not unusual for top athletes to report that with intense concentration time slows down considerably. Former pro-football quarterback John Brodie described how in the most intense moments of a football game "time seems to slow way down, in an uncanny way, as if everyone were moving in slow motion. It seems as if I had all the time in the world to watch the receivers run their patterns."[7] Time can also seem to move along more quickly than clock time, particularly when an activity loses any sense of drudgery and becomes an engaging and satisfying experience. A chess master described his experience of play as almost dreamlike because "time passes a hundred times faster."[8] With flow consciousness the experience of time can also seem to stop. Practitioners of the Chinese art of T'ai Chi—a form of moving meditation—report there is a common experience "of seemingly falling through a hole in time. Awareness of the passage of time completely stops, and only when you catch yourself, after five or ten minutes, or five or ten seconds is there the realization that for that period of time the world stopped."[9] Immersion in the moment-to-moment flow opens a window onto new dimensions of time experience.

Overall, each dimension has revealed a different facet of time. With the culmination of the seventh dimension (or the beginning of the eighth) time achieves its fullness of expression. The word *timeless-ness* has often been used to describe the nature of time at the center of experience. However, *time-less-ness* implies that time is somehow "lessened" or even absent. A more accurate word is *time-full-ness*. At the center of the flow of creation all aspects of time are fully revealed—the simple present, natural cycles, relativistic dynamics, the pulses of cosmic-scale manifestation, the expansiveness of oceanic time, and the focused thread of creational time. All the time we could ever want and need is experienced as being fully present in the center of existence. No time is missing. All time is available. Therefore in "timefullness" we can relax fully into the NOW without any sense of temporal loss or omission. At the center, in timefullness, we experience wholeness. Time is not going beyond itself but is unfolding from within, forever new, like an artesian spring that bubbles up and over itself.

THE FLOW SELF: BALANCING UNITY AND CREATIVITY

The pace of change in the seventh stage will be breathtaking, as, regardless of whatever limits existed in the past, people will seek to reach "beyond the beyond the beyond." In athletics, the arts, ecology, biology, business, and more, people will continuously work to expand the envelope of accepted human potentials. This will be an epoch of continuous transformation as people and groups seek to discover the immense power at the center of consciously lived existence. The previous era of compassionate conformity will be surpassed as billions of individuals dare to be original—to be as fully themselves as they are capable—and to bring their unique life-expression into the world.

Flow identity can be experienced anywhere: while running, making a cup of tea, listening to music, dancing, driving a car, watching a sunset, washing dishes, walking, or relating to another person. No matter how subtle or slight, every activity presents an opportunity to combine our experience of being and the process of doing into a single flow. Because everything we do is involved in the flow of creation, with wholehearted involvement in any of life's activities, we can discover our flow identity as a unique hum of resonance—a singular symphony, characteristic to each being, that is forever new and alive.

Flow consciousness has long been recognized by athletes when they achieve a high level of concentration and synchronization. The long-distance runner Dr. George Sheehan states that after a half hour of running, "I see myself not as an individual but as part of the universe."[10] Flow consciousness is paradoxical in that it often requires great effort and concentration to achieve a result that is seemingly effortless and spontaneous. With effort we move beyond effort and find stillness. Here is how Steve McKinney described his experience of breaking the world downhill ski record: "I discovered the middle path of stillness within speed, calmness within fear, and I held it longer and quieter than ever before."[11]

Work also provides important opportunities for flow experiences. All kinds of manual labor—whether that of a farm hand or a surgeon—are an invitation to the flow. During difficult operations, surgeons sometimes have the experience that "the entire operating team is a single organism, moved by the same purpose; they describe it as a 'ballet' in which the individual is subordinated to the group performance, and all involved share in a feeling of harmony and power."[12]

A personal example illustrates how the flow experience can be encountered in even the most seemingly mundane circumstances. While growing up on a farm in Idaho, I spent many years working in the fields doing manual labor—weeding crops with a hoe, digging furrows, tending plants by hand, and so on. For a long while I found this work boring and painful drudgery. Only gradually did I learn important secrets about work (and life) from a few old-time farm hands (mostly women) who taught me how to find joy and satisfaction in any task.[13] Each day they demonstrated that every task, no matter how menial, offered an opportunity for experiencing the joy of working well, at perfect speed, with disciplined spontaneity. Minute by minute and hour by hour we would work through the sun and dust, pushing our capacities in an unspoken ballet of supreme effort—neither frantically fast nor ploddingly slow, but at a pace that could be sustained at the limits of one's ability. Casual comments and playful teasing disguised the great intensity that filled the rhythmic flow as we worked side by side through the fields. The unspoken purpose was to experience our maximum capacity to work with excellence. In pressing the limits of our ability, tasks were transformed into an intensely satisfying meditation. No one had to philosophize about this—it was a self-evident experience for all who came to the fields and approached work in this manner. Although for many farm work continued to be drudgery, I learned that even the most simple tasks can be deeply satisfying and can express the inherent dignity of flow consciousness.

These few examples illustrate a basic insight: *Everything* we do is an occasion for flow experience—working, walking, relating, driving, dancing, playing, contemplating. In the seventh stage, therefore, the dominant attitude will be that anything worth doing is worth doing well. Mastery of the art of daily living will be paramount. People will seek to experience and express their mastery of everyday life by investing each moment with attention and love. Even the most mundane task will be seen as an opportunity for self-mastery and fullness of living. In countless small ways the emotional climate and social character of the world will be transformed—in the smile and care of a grocery clerk, in the help and courtesy of a stranger, in the joyful movement of an athlete, in the compassionate choices of a businessman, or in the loving attention of a teacher. Quietly and unpretentiously people will be integrating flow consciousness into their everyday lives.

Flow experience will be viewed as its own reward, its own purpose. Although some people may continuously seek the "runner's high," most will be satisfied with small and subtle experiences of resonant presence as sufficient feedback from the cosmos that they are living with union and harmony. Finding fulfillment in life's simpler pleasures will provide an important counterforce to the excesses that will result from the liberation of the creative imagination of the seventh dimension.

Flow consciousness requires balancing concentration and mindfulness. Concentration is the ability to focus on the precise center of our unfolding experience. Mindfulness is the ability continuously to embrace the panoramic totality of life. The flow experience is somewhat analogous to riding a unicycle—we must concentrate on where the rubber hits the road and at the same time be mindful of the surrounding environment within which we are riding. We can maintain our equilibrium, poise, and stability by balancing the particular and the whole—by harmonizing concentration and mindfulness. Concentration without the balancing influence of mindfulness results in the mind sinking into an activity and getting lost in the details, losing perspective. Mindfulness without the balancing influence of concentration results in the mind becoming so diffuse and expansive that the person is "spaced out" and unable to be present within the precise center of the flow experience. With a dynamic balance—the part and the whole, the center and the context—both come into wholesome alignment, each acting as a corrective against the excesses of the other. Mindfulness awakens the experience of cosmic connection and thus compassion. Concentration grounds the spaciousness of mindfulness with a center of focus and intention, and thus creative expression. In concert they support a healthy flow of balanced participation in the world.

FLOW SOCIETY: TAMING EXPLOSIVE CREATIVITY

With continuous global communication, the human family can evolve with unprecedented openness, energy, and dynamism. However, if sheer vibrancy is not to degenerate into violence, then the planetary culture will have to reconcile itself with the full range of humanity's potentials, both creative and destructive. Only by acknowledging both the light and the dark side of our species character will we be able to achieve ongoing reconciliation. A new level of social maturity and mastery will be required to prevent society from tearing itself apart. By integrating and harmonizing the growing social diversity into an overarching unity, purposeful and spirited evolution will infuse every area of life.

There will be a double-edged nature to life in the seventh stage. On the one hand, flow consciousness will enable people to find satisfaction in even the smallest details of life. On the other hand, flow consciousness will also enable people to bring their highest level of intentionality into their creative expressions. While many will seek to achieve mastery through unpretentious work in the world (feeling the experience of the moment to be its own reward), many others may seek the fullest expression of their creative potentials. The compassionate consciousness nurtured in the sixth stage will be crucial for maintaining a healthy society in the seventh stage. Most people will recognize that in serving life we serve ourselves and so will attempt to express their creativity in ways that contribute to the well-being of the world.

Although the cultivation of flow consciousness does not guarantee that actions will be ethical, it will *incline* persons (and societies) in an ethical direction consistent with the admonition Do unto others as you would have them do unto you. Because the flow experience emerges from our transpersonal connection with the cosmos in its process of regeneration, it naturally fosters a sense of felt union with all that exists. In knowing that we are inseparable from the universe, we know that whatever we do to the world we do to ourselves. In feeling the Earth is a part of our extended body, we will tend to act in ways that express our care for its well-being. Flow consciousness tends to be naturally harmonizing and ethical, for people understand intuitively that their actions are constantly being written into the deep structure of the Meta-universe. The subtle hum of knowing-resonance that is our core identity and character (our so-called con-science) indicates, moment by moment, whether we are living in ways that are serving the well-being of the universe.

Flow consciousness is a proevolutionary force, as it promotes honesty. When our greatest satisfaction and happiness is found in the direct experience of the process of living, then to be dishonest is to be out of alignment with, or out of accurate relationship with, the stream of life. Dishonesty is felt as dis-comfort and dis-ease. The more we appreciate the comfort and ease of aligned living, the more we will seek to bring honesty and integrity into our passage through life.

Although the flow experience emerges from authentic connection with the living cosmos, this does not guarantee "positive" results, even at this stage of development. The seventh dimension will not bring a magical transformation of human nature that eliminates misperception, error, and misapplication. We are here to learn a series of lessons, and the seventh dimension will have its share. The heightened creativity of this stage, coupled with our unavoidable humanity, will make this an epoch always on the verge of going out of control. Individual self-purpose will constantly need to be brought into compassionate alignment with unfolding social purpose. Because the vast majority of people in the seventh stage will value synergy and creative harmony, physical warfare will be viewed as profoundly destructive to flow civilization. Conflicts will still exist, but people will feel an evolutionary responsibility to resolve them in ways that preserve the continuity and synergy of life on the planet.

An avalanche of creative expression will need to be harmonized continuously with the requirements for sustainability. A complex process of local-to-global communication and communion will be required to hold together the fabric of a maturing world civilization:

- Electronic town meetings on critical social issues
- World Olympic games and other athletic contests
- Worldwide musical events and dramatic productions
- Historical remembrances of people and civilizations to bond with the past
- Shared visualizations of the planetary future through drama and ritual
- Planetary rituals that celebrate the ineffable and mysterious nature of life
- Communal efforts in support of major world projects (for example, unique "world cities" or the regeneration of the biosphere of Mars)

With nearly continuous opportunities for cultivating and celebrating the flow consciousness of the planet, the world will develop innumerable overlapping networks of association and connection. These diverse networks (cultural, political, spiritual, ecological, and economic) will be a vital ingredient in the social glue that binds the human ecosystem into a coherent and dynamically stable community that lives in harmony with the larger ecosystem of the Earth.

THE THINKING EARTH

The world of the seventh stage will be so volatile and changing so rapidly that it will be imperative for the body politic continuously to pay attention to where it is going. To cope with the ferment of creativity, there must be a level of social attention that is equal to the complexity and enormity of the challenges generated by that creativity. The alternative to conscious self-regulation by the global citizenry will be control by a computerized global bureaucracy that suffocates creativity and drains the vitality from world civilization.

A flow democracy will require ongoing local-to-global electronic gatherings that support a vigorous expression of the views and values of the body politic and maintain a unified thread of social awareness and intention. Flow democracy will also require continual envisioning of the long-range future. Because actions in this era (such as extreme genetic engineering) can have such far-reaching consequences, it will be essential that the world make an unrelenting effort to explore their future implications. This will be a futures-responsive world civilization that places a premium on making visions of the future explicit, anticipating their impacts, and choosing preferred pathways ahead consciously.

By the seventh stage a palpable feeling of conscious self-possession will infuse the planet, and the Earth will effectively become a thinking entity. From the vantage point of the industrial era (where there exists only a glimmer of a planetary consciousness and decision-making capacity), it is very difficult to imagine the breadth and depth of the global mind that will emerge to consider the ongoing interests of the Earth. Centuries after the communications revolution began, the Earth will have become an integrated, reflective organism with thought processes that have a life of their own and that transcend any individual or nation.[14] Massive flows of information and communication will envelope the Earth and will include every imaginable human concern. Quite literally a new order and kind of life-form will emerge—the Earth will have become a planetary-scale, self-reflective organism.

THE ECONOMICS OF FULFILLMENT

In the sixth stage the human family will develop the skills and tools needed to maintain ourselves into the deep future. By the seventh stage those who live frugally will be confident that their material needs will be met and that they can live within a nurturing community with many opportunities to contribute to the well-being of the world. For most people work will be balanced between serving the local microcommunity (through gardening, child care, teaching, maintenance, and so on) and serving the larger world (through cultural, political, scientific, and other activities). Highly decentralized microcommunities or ecovillages (of several dozen to several hundred persons) will be nested within larger urban settings and offer a diversity of living and working environments sufficient to suit nearly every interest and personality. Intentional communities will provide, along with the family, the basic building blocks of global society.

In the seventh stage, process will be seen as its own reward. The experience of life in the moment will be its own satisfaction. By living more simply, people will be able to engage life more directly and fully. In experiencing life more fully, people will have less desire for nonessential possessions. Flow is fulfillment. The tenor of economic life will be transformed as people increasingly look for fulfillment in flow experiences rather than through the consumption of things. Other sources of satisfaction—food, sex, entertainment, and so on—will be recognized as secondary to "flow" as the primary source of satisfaction. We know that until we learn the skills of directly encountering the Life-force at the core of our being, we will feel empty and hollow.

The economy of the seventh stage will be distinguished not only by what it does but by what it does not do. Unlike the manipulative advertising and marketing of the industrial era, this economy will not seek to amplify and exploit human insecurities by aggressively working to divide people from themselves. Instead of working to split us apart from ourselves with substitute longings that are not relevant to our core journey in life, an economy will emerge that intends our wholeness as persons and civilizations. Instead of a high-tech world filled with endless inventions and labor-saving gadgets, this will be a world of aesthetic simplicity with highly sophisticated designs that are sustainable for the long haul. Although the material circumstances of everyday life will be unassuming—even modest—this disciplined way of living will enable humanity to mobilize an enormous amount of social and creative energy for an unprecedented range of global projects.

One long-envisioned world project that seems likely to develop in this epoch is the terraforming of Mars. To awaken Mars from its prison as an icy, lifeless planet and transform it into a flourishing biosphere will require a concerted effort over centuries. Terraforming Mars presents the people of Earth with the kind of creative challenge that will be the hallmark of the seventh stage. Theoretically, by introducing greenhouse gases to produce an atmosphere, the planet can be warmed gradually, melting trapped ice that will produce rivers and lakes and allow hardy plants to be introduced. They in turn will further accelerate warming and the production of oxygen. After several centuries the biosphere will presumably develop to where it could support a population of several hundred thousand persons.

With the terraforming of Mars, our solar system could acquire a new society with its own views, values, culture, and history. For example, Mars may need plants and animals that are genetically adapted to living conditions with significantly less gravity and oxygen. If plants and animals were genetically engineered to prosper in this unique environment, an evolutionary trajectory could be set in motion that may increasingly diverge from that on Earth. Our solar system will then have a second planetary civilization that could interact with and influence the development of life on Earth in ways we cannot now imagine.

FLOW SPIRITUALITY: RIDING THE WAVE OF CONTINUOUS CREATION

In the seventh dimension, spirituality will be everywhere. Every act of living will be seen as "spiritual" as it connects with the universe in its flow of continuous creation. Spirituality will become a matter of fact and a practical aspect of life. People will not be self-absorbed in mystical consciousness; rather they will recognize that every situation presents an opportunity for directly experiencing the living universe of which they are an inseparable part—cooking, eating, walking, taking a shower, talking, driving, and so on.

People will understand that although they may lose the thread of knowing many times each day and may move up and down the spectrum of dimensional experience, they know where to return. There is never an end, but there is always a middle. And the middle will be known so intimately that it will never be forgotten completely. People will be confident that they can always look within the center of their moment-to-moment experience and re-member, or become whole with the flow of creation. There will be no need for existential anxiety when the Life-force is known directly as an artesian spring that continuously bubbles up, bringing the entire cosmos into existence.

A simple but demanding practice is found at the heart of the awakening of double-wisdom. Whatever our path may be—meditation, prayer, devotion, service, and so on—there is one essential requirement: cultivating a continuous flow of attention. If we are to live in the flow of continuous creation, then we must be awake to the living present—and the present is extremely precise, as "sharp and thin as a razor's edge."[15] In being precisely present, the distance between the observer and the observed is progressively lessened until both merge into a single flow and disclose the underlying Life-force as direct awareness. Enlightenment will no longer be seen as a different *state* of consciousness (happening inside our brain); it will be seen as a whole-being *flow experience* that naturally emerges when we come into dynamic alignment with the universe in its process of continuous creation. There will be contentment in riding the wave of creation with an open heart whose warmth expands in proportion to the continuity of consciousness.*

At the center of creation's flow, individuality and wholeness are not competing but are complementary aspects of the universe. With the culmination of the seventh dimension individuals will not dissolve into a formless ALL; instead we will achieve a stage of healthy self-possession and self-connection with the Meta-universe—ready to begin an entirely new cycle of discovery and learning.

When we are in dynamic and conscious accord with the always-emerging cosmos, then there is an opening, and our beingness becomes the "lens" through which reality is appreciated and celebrated. Philosopher Ken Wilber said, "A person is an opening or clearing through which the Absolute can manifest."[17] No other individual being in all the corners of creation has the same view or perspective through which the clear light of existence pours continuously. Just as there is no limit to the wholeness of reality, so, too, is there no limit to the uniqueness of each being. We are each creative musicians, artists cultivating an eternally living body of harmonious resonance, infusing it with a singular texture, presence, and vitality.

In the seventh dimension we will know that we are learning to live in eternity. By consciously coming to our center and realizing our inborn potentials as *Homo sapiens sapiens* for "knowing that we

---

*This experience has been beautifully described by, for example, the monk Theophan the Recluse (1815–1894): "For so long as the mind remains in the head, where thoughts jostle one another, it has no time to concentrate on one thing. But when attention descends into the heart, it attracts all the powers of the soul and body into one point there. This concentration of all human life in one place is immediately reflected in the heart by a special sensation that is the beginning of future warmth. This sensation, faint at the beginning, becomes gradually stronger, firmer, deeper. At first only tepid, it grows into warm feeling and concentrates the attention upon itself. And so it comes about that, whereas in the initial stages the attention is kept in the heart by an effort of will, in due course this attention, by its own vigor, gives birth to warmth in the heart. This warmth then holds the attention without special effort. From this, the two go on supporting one another, and must remain inseparable: because dispersion of attention cools the warmth, and diminishing warmth weakens attention."[16]

know," we will recognize that we no longer require the aligning structure of a physical body to realize our capacity for double-wisdom. When our knowingness so knows itself that it knows itself without reference to the material body, then we discover that we are identical with the Meta-universe and realize that our true nature is eternal, unbounded, and infinite.

SUMMARY

The seventh stage is so far into the future that I hesitate to speculate on its seasons of growth. Nonetheless it seems likely that only after much trial and error will humanity learn the skills of both maintaining and surpassing itself in a balanced flow of evolution. The launching of a planetary-scale, high-synergy flow civilization will be a challenging undertaking. Like a person learning to ride a bicycle, we will need to move beyond the mechanics of global functioning and experience the poetry of the global flows as our guide to appropriate action. Only after humanity acquires a capacity for unflappable self-possession will the world body politic learn neither to rush ahead of itself nor to lag behind but to engage in a conscious dance of unfolding that can be sustained for the long haul.

An explosion of innovation will occur in the seventh stage. This will be a dangerous and vulnerable time, as humanity's collective consensus could dissipate quickly and bring social chaos. Yet, having established a compassionate consciousness as the social norm in the sixth stage, humanity will be ready for a new degree of freedom and experimentation in the seventh stage. The challenge will be to liberate this creativity while simultaneously maintaining planetary unity—no small task given the many pitfalls that lie ahead on our evolutionary journey.[18]

In the culmination of the seventh dimension, consciousness emerges fully from the oceanic depths to a dynamic center and achieves focused expression in the world. The observer no longer stands apart from any aspect of reality but instead is the fully involved participator. Meaning is found in the process of creative and conscious living. The more diffuse, life-sensing and life-serving orientation of the sixth dimension will coalesce into creative and conscious expression in the seventh dimension.

With the culmination of the seventh stage all aspects of double-wisdom will be developed and internalized:

- The **bodily**, or sensory, experiences of the second dimension
- The **emotional**, or feeling, qualities of the third dimension
- The **mental**, or intellectual, capacities of the fourth dimension
- The **reflective**, or dispassionate, knowing characteristic of the fifth dimension
- The **oceanic**, or compassionate, knowing of the sixth dimension
- The **flow** consciousness and liberated creativity of the seventh dimension

When the potentials of all stages have been sufficiently fulfilled, humanity will have the scope of learning and experience needed to make wise choices for the long-term future. We can then begin our next cycle of discovery as a newly mature, planetary civilization.

INTEGRAL AWARENESS AND THE INITIAL MATURITY OF PLANETARY CIVILIZATION

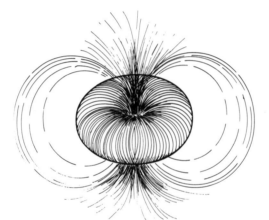

The **eighth dimension** will be the stage where humans acquire the perspective, wisdom, and compassion to sustain themselves into the deep future. A dynamically stable, self-referencing and self-organizing species-civilization will emerge that has the maturity to become a participant in the larger arena of galactic-scale evolution. This stage represents both the completion of a long process of development (from prereflective to postreflective consciousness or *integral awareness*) and the foundation for a new beginning. A wisdom-culture will emerge with sufficient maturity to be able to endure into the distant future by balancing across polarities of being and becoming, unity and diversity, the eternal and the momentary.

CHAPTER 8

INTEGRAL AWARENESS AND THE INITIAL MATURITY OF PLANETARY CIVILIZATION

The eighth stage represents the completion of a long process of learning—and a new beginning. By integrating the full range of potentials made possible by reflective consciousness into the heart and soul of human civilization, we will establish the foundation for an entirely new phase in the human adventure. Just as reaching adulthood marks the beginning of creative work in the world for individuals, so, too, will attaining our early adulthood as a planetary civilization mark the beginning of a new phase in humanity's exploration and learning.

For an aligning majority of the Earth to arrive at the eighth stage will require humanity to travel an enormous evolutionary distance. Nonetheless the essence of this stage is already familiar to many. The words of the Buddha after his enlightenment suggest what we might find in a future era of "social enlightenment." When other monks saw his newly discovered radiance and knowing, they asked him, "Are you a God?" He replied, "No." They then asked if he was an angel. Again he answered, "No." "Then what are you?" they asked. The Buddha replied simply, "I am awake."[1] In a similar way, when we establish ourselves as a sustainable and creative planetary civilization, we will not have become gods or angels or saints; we will simply be awake to the fullness of who and what we already are. Even the most awakened master of integral awareness will still experience the full range of emotions: sorrow and joy, hope and fear.[2] However, these emotions will arise within the spacious awareness of the Meta-universe —a context whose vastness welcomes the full experience of feelings without generating undue reactivity, whether grasping or aversion.

To appreciate the eighth stage, we need to demystify the mystical and see life in its unpretentious wakefulness. The unassuming character of everyday life in the eighth stage is illustrated by the culminating image in a series of Zen paintings that describe the stages of enlightenment.[3] In these paintings the spiritual aspirant is depicted as moving through ten stages, each of increasing refinement and depth of insight. In the final stage of enlightenment he is not shown as lost in meditation but instead as a potbellied and happy man who returns to the marketplace and, without ceremony or pretense, lends a helping hand wherever he can. With little concern that his clothes are ragged and dusty, he carries a broad smile for all that he meets. His primary intention is to bring the joy and great treasure of awakening to others. In a similar way, once we know the creative aliveness and wonder of the universe, great satisfaction can be found in the ordinary activities of daily life. An awakened person or species-civilization is happy to live unpretentiously and return to the everyday world to assist others.

The wisdom culture of the eighth stage is more "ordinary" and accessible to us than we may think. Analogously, during the stage of the awakening hunter-gatherers, our ancestors would have been incredulous if someone suggested that millions of persons could learn to live and work in the manner now considered ordinary in advanced industrial nations: living in massive cities, driving cars on freeways, operating computers, watching television, and working in organizations with tens of thousands of persons. We now take our urban-industrial way of perceiving, living, and working for granted. But to the ancient hunter-gatherer, who had yet to establish a settled village way of life with a productive agriculture, the thought of people being able to function in a manner common to the industrial era would have seemed utterly impossible. In a similar way, attaining our initial maturity as a species may appear equally unachievable; however, we seem to be designed with the potential for successful evolution.

Our innate evolutionary potentials are apparent when we consider persons who have been born into Stone Age cultures (for example, as hunter-gatherers in New Guinea) and see how quickly they have been able to adapt to the perceptual, emotional, and intellectual demands of living in a modern urban-industrial society. Within a single generation many have made the transition from a Stone Age culture and now drive cars, operate computers, and help govern a large society. Their example suggests that humanity is already biologically endowed with all the perceptual capacities necessary to rise to the highest levels of maturity described by the theory of dimensional evolution. Individuals in today's world can acquire learning within a few years that previously had taken civilizations tens of thousands of years to accumulate. The point is that we should not place our initial maturity as a planetary civilization any further beyond our current reach than we should place the urban-industrial experience beyond the reach of contemporary Stone Age peoples.

While it could take many centuries to reach our initial maturity, it seems plausible that a majority of persons could move rapidly to this stage if there already existed an advanced civilization that could instruct us on our next steps. However, because we are our own teachers—pulling ourselves up by our own bootstraps—learning will necessarily be slow and haphazard. But, like a highway built over many years through dangerous and difficult terrain, as our learning is realized, there will be a pathway for succeeding generations to follow that can convey them swiftly to this further destination.

In completing the seventh stage we will come into self-referencing alignment with the cosmos. As our descendants emerge into the eighth stage, the people of the Earth will know that, through our own efforts, humanity has established a wisdom-culture with the potential of enduring and learning into the distant future. The gift of life is freely given, but our ability to develop into the deep future as a species must be earned. We will have attained our initial maturity through an immensity of struggle and suffering. Humanity will have a feeling of self-assurance and planetary self-esteem that could not have developed except through the merit of honest labor across many generations. After epochs of great self-doubt, we will have gained a steadfast belief in ourselves as a species. We will recognize our place within the web of life. An immensity of time will stretch out before us, welcoming our creativity with opportunities of galactic proportions.

In the eighth dimension the polarities of life will be integrated continuously into a higher synthesis: Being and becoming, unity and diversity, the eternal and the momentary, transcendence and immanence—the ongoing integration of these polarities will produce a strong and dynamically stable world civilization. Life in the eighth dimension will be comparable to a controlled chain reaction in a nuclear reactor. Always on the verge of going critical and exploding destructively, global civilization will be forever pulsing with creative life energy. In this culminating stage, humanity will have developed the wisdom, acquired from hard-earned experience, to act in ways that maintain an ever-evolving planetary equilibrium.

THE EIGHTH DIMENSION: INTEGRAL AWARENESS

In the eighth stage the cosmos will be viewed as a single living organism that is being regenerated by the constant flow-through of an infinitely deep and unfathomably intelligent Life-force (which I have called the generative ground, or the Meta-universe).* Once we see the entire universe as continuously woven together as a single, flowing creation, space will no longer be viewed as the simple absence of form but as an intensely active process that continuously opens to make room for matter to present itself. Consciousness will be viewed as a natural property of the cosmos that, to varying degrees, is present everywhere. Whether it is an atom, microbe, animal, galaxy, or the entire cosmos, every aspect of the universe will be recognized as having a knowing capacity that is consistent with its nature.

---

*See pages 296–298 for an expanded description of the "Meta-universe."

Although the universe is a completely flowing system, it is able to manifest itself as stable forms at every scale. There is one particularly useful way of visualizing a flowing process that is able to manifest itself as a dynamically stable form: *The "torus," or doughnutlike shape, is the simplest geometric form of a completely flowing, self-referencing system.*[4]

Figure 10: The Torus as the Simplest Geometry of a Self-Referencing System

The characteristic toroidal shape of self-referencing systems is perhaps the most common structure found throughout nature and can be seen everywhere—from the structure of atoms, tornadoes, whirlpools, and planetary magnetic fields to the shape of galaxies and quasars.[5] Figure 11 illustrates how this characteristic shape is found throughout nature.

As a simple geometric form, the torus can help us visualize and gain insight into the nature of self-referencing and self-organizing systems. Like a tornado—where two air flows mutually contain and focus each other—the torus seems to symbolize the ability of matter and consciousness to work together to create a dynamic structure with a reflective capacity and great power to persist despite its completely flowing nature. To create a dynamic torus, two flows that would

Figure 11: The Torus as the Most Common Shape Found Throughout Nature

Earth's magnetic field

Air currents in a tornado

The magnetic field around a person

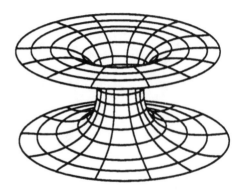

The curvature of space around a black hole

Cross-section of an orange

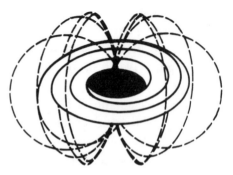

The magnetic field around a spiral galaxy

**Figure 12: Cross-section of a Torus Illustrating
Its Self-Holding and Self-Referencing Nature**

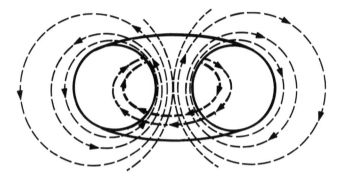

otherwise rapidly dissipate become self-containing of one another.

Each flow brings focus and coherence to the other, and together they create a self-perpetuating, flow-through process that has the ability to endure as a stable system. In a similar way the material and consciousness aspects of life are mutually focusing and reinforcing of one another in a dynamic process. Human beings are flowing systems designed to achieve full "self-possession," or the double-wisdom of "knowing that we know," by becoming dynamically centered in the Life-force from which we continuously arise. Our challenge is to "get ahold of ourselves" by integrating the material and consciousness aspects of life into a self-bounding process that is dynamically drawn from, and exists within, the Meta-universe. The cosmos and Meta-universe mutually serve each other. The cosmos is made from and sustained by the Life-energy that is the Meta-universe, and this Life-energy achieves creative, self-referencing expression through the living systems continuously growing within the self-bounding cosmos.

Despite the seeming simplicity of its structure, the torus embodies two paradoxical attributes consistent with our complex, flow-through nature: We are both *dynamically closed* (as self-organizing and self-bounding systems) and *dynamically open* (directly connecting with the Meta-universe). The torus symbolizes this self-referencing closure while simultaneously remaining open to the flow-through of infinite Life-energy.

The universe appears to be a flowing system composed of dynamically stable and interconnected toroidal structures. At its center each toroidal form draws energy from the underlying Life-force, so each is a system existing within and connected to the grand system of the Meta-universe. Because each toroidal system is open at its center to the Meta-universe despite separation in space and time, at their center all toroidal structures are open to and connected with all others (see Figure 13).

Figure 13: Toroidal Structures as the Building Blocks of the Universe Connected with One Another, Center-to-Center

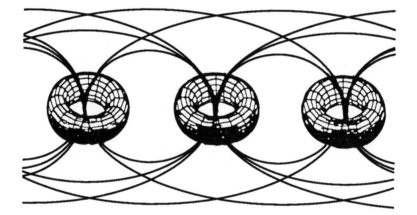

At the center we are each completely open, and in this openness we connect with the Meta-universe. When we meet another person center-to-center, we call the experience love. In his book *The Future of Man* Teilhard de Chardin writes that an integration of the human spirit can only be achieved through the meeting, center-to-center, of all human beings. He says that the only way for billions of diverse individuals to love one another is "by knowing themselves all to be centered upon a single 'super-center' common to all."[6] Teilhard asks what is the highest work of humanity "if not to establish, in and by each one of us, an absolutely original center in which the universe reflects itself in a unique and inimitable way?'" An elegant and evocative rendering of a toroidal view of reality is portrayed in Figure 14 by the artist Alex Grey, in his painting entitled the *Universal Mind Lattice.*

The flowing construction of the torus enables us to explore the crucial distinction between "consciousness" and "awareness." When the self-referencing process is fully centered upon itself, the experience at the center is one of pure awareness or "knowing that we know," or "consciousness-without-an-object." Therefore the term **awareness** is used here to describe *direct knowing,* while the term **consciousness** is used to refer to a *reflective process that stands apart from, and has some object of, knowing.* Awareness is unconditional and self-validating while consciousness always arises with an object of reference. Awareness exists at the center of the torus and does not require self-confirming feedback from an external source.

A toroidal geometry also provides a way to visualize the convergence of Eastern and Western views of reality. On the one hand, because the individual is seen as a dynamic being that is fully open at the center, the symbol of the torus supports the Eastern view, which holds there is no fixed or concrete identity. On the other hand, because each individual is seen as a unique, self-referencing system, the toroidal metaphor also supports the Western view, which sees each being as distinct and real.

In the past eight chapters we have traveled from a condition of prereflective knowing through seven stages of filling out the capacity for reflective consciousness and finally to full self-referencing knowing, or integral awareness. Prior to the eighth stage humanity's future was in grave doubt. In "knowing that we know" as an entire Earth community, we will have the double-wisdom essential for taking charge of our evolution and enduring into the distant future. We will understand our great power as a species and we will also understand the power of restraint. Knowing the difference, we will have confidence in our ability to participate in a journey that extends outward to a galactic scale.

Figure 14 : *Universal Mind Lattice,* from the *Sacred Mirror* series by Alex Grey, 1981, acrylic on canvas, 84 x 46 in.

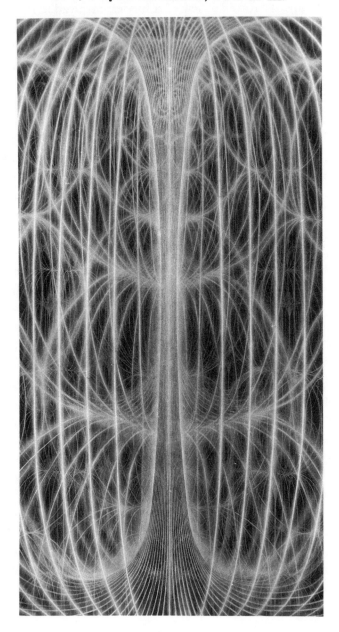

INTEGRAL SOCIETY AND AESTHETIC SIMPLICITY

Although the eighth stage will surely be distinguished by an elevated consciousness and great technological advances, it will not be unimaginably remote from contemporary experience. As a Zen saying states, "After awakening, we sweep the floor." After awakening in the eighth dimension we will recognize the extraordinary nature of the reality that surrounds us. In appreciating the ordinary miracles of everyday life, "sweeping the floor" will be sufficient. We will be far more content with life as it is and not seek manufactured miracles to entertain us.

Simplicity reveals the master, says an old adage. When we become masters in the art of living on Earth, our mastery will be evident in the simplicity of our way of living. If we could look ahead in time and see life in the eighth stage, its simplicity might deceive us into thinking that relatively little change had occurred. Given outward appearances, life may seem so unassuming that we could overlook the conscious sophistication of design required to create a mode of living that is sustainable into the distant future.

Recall from Chapter 5 that historian Arnold Toynbee said the most fundamental expression of civilization growth was neither the conquest of land nor people but rather the process of "progressive simplification." Toynbee described this as a process whereby the material side of life is progressively simplified so that increasing amounts of energy and attention are freed up to develop the cultural and spiritual aspects of life. The aesthetic refinement of the material side of life (learning to do ever more with ever less) develops in concert with the refinement of the consciousness side of life (learning to touch every aspect of life ever more lightly and gently). Through this coevolutionary process we will be able to create a true wisdom-culture that is rich in beauty, nurturing relationships, caring communities, and other arts of elevated living.

Despite all the wonders and breakthroughs of intervening stages of growth, I do not expect us to become superhumans, vastly different from who we are today. Granted, we will surely have extraordinary capacities for global communication (and community). We will also have vastly expanded our knowledge about the Earth and the universe and we will have a much clearer understanding of the evolutionary journey in which we are involved. Nonetheless I think we would be surprised by the outwardly unassuming nature of life as this new phase of evolution begins. Life in the eighth dimension will exhibit an unpretentiousness that expresses a deep wisdom, and disciplined enthusiasm, for life.

To see the eighth stage as characterized by a progressive simplicity of living does not mean there will be little technological advance. To the contrary, the universe is filled with emergent potentials that are not apparent until a perceptual stage is achieved that can recognize and develop those potentials. For example, until recently few would have guessed that silicon could be transformed into tiny computer chips that could contain an entire library, or that we could send moving pictures through the air via television, or that we could jam together fifteen pounds of a metal called plutonium and release the explosive force of the atomic bomb. These extraordinary possibilities have always been embedded within the structure of reality, waiting for us to discover them. In a similar way there are surely countless additional surprises now hidden within the universe, waiting to be found. The cosmos embodies an extraordinarily high level of design and subtlety, so it seems likely that we will continue to discover extraordinary new potentials. We may, for example, find unexpected ways to traverse the fabric of space-time and connect with other civilizations beyond those of Earth.

COSMIC COMMUNITY

We can put the human journey in perspective by considering the possibility of life evolving elsewhere throughout the cosmos. Given the remarkable level of creative intelligence expressed in the design of our cosmos, there seems to be a high probability that life-forms—including mature civilizations of planetary scale—are flourishing throughout the universe. Astronomers estimate there are hundreds of billions of galaxies, and each galaxy is estimated to contain a hundred billion or more star systems like our sun. One galaxy was recently found that contains an estimated 100 trillion stars! Our cosmos could therefore easily contain thousands of *trillions* of planetary systems upon which life could potentially evolve. With such an overflowing abundance of planetary systems, the universe appears designed to seed innumerable life experiments. It seems likely that sprinkled throughout our cosmos there are countless other civilizations that are struggling to secure a sustainable and surpassing future for themselves.

I do not think humans are special creatures; rather we are probably run-of-the-mill miracles—relatively commonplace beings. In our vast cosmos, with its trillions of planetary systems, the planet Earth is probably only one among innumerable places where the capacity for reflective knowing is now evolving. Encountering other beings and civilizations, sharing our stories about the journey of awakening, and cooperating in creating a community of galactic scale seems likely to be part of our evolutionary journey. Each world civilization will surely take pride in adding its unique story to the larger cosmic drama that describes the emergence and unfolding of life in the universe.

Because an encounter with a much older and more advanced civilization could distort humanity's trajectory of development and undermine our self-concept as a species, it seems unlikely that a wiser civilization would make overt contact with Earth until we have achieved our initial maturity—the eighth stage. We will need this level of social integration and ego strength as a species-civilization to be able to withstand the shock of encounter with advanced civilizations beyond Earth. The human family could doubt its capacity ever to achieve, in its own right, the level of reflective consciousness and self-organization achieved by civilizations beyond Earth. Therefore it seems improbable that we will have substantial contact with extraterrestrial civilizations until we have developed a self-organizing planetary culture that is able to tolerate and assimilate the learning of other civilizations without devastating the fabric of Earthly civilization.

Importantly, the theory of dimensional evolution gives hope that we may be able to relate to civilizations beyond Earth. Because dimensionality is a fundamental characteristic of all existence, dimensional evolution has universal relevance. Despite wide differences in chemistry, biology, and culture, all life in the universe shares in the same geometric framework as it works to become self-aware and self-determining. The fabric of reality is a rich and purposeful pattern that provides an evolutionary framework for life-forms to achieve self-referencing knowing. If, throughout the universe, beings and civilizations are moving through a common structure that produces a similar pattern of learning, then countless variations on a general evolutionary theme will be repeated again and again as life-forms work through a shared dimensional context that supports the coevolution of culture and consciousness. Totally alien psychologies may not exist if all life moves through the same learning pattern to achieve its maturity as self-organizing and self-referencing organisms.*

Would we trust extraterrestrial civilizations if, in their evolutionary history, they had not moved through the same kinds of trials and tests that humanity has experienced? Probably not. However, if we all have had a similar pattern of experience and learning produced by the same dimensional environment, then we could relate to one another and develop feelings of trust and kinship. Dimensional evolution may describe a common pathway for all expressions of life. If so, no matter what forms of life we meet in future journeys throughout the cosmos, we could each reminisce about our ancestors' struggles to work

---

*Some think contact with civilizations beyond Earth is unlikely. They argue there are great odds against finding another mature civilization in the vicinity of Earth within the same time frame in which we achieve our maturity (and before we go into decline and eventual extinction). Given our historical record of devastating warfare, this seems a reasonable conjecture. For example, Teilhard de Chardin has stated, "Unless, *as seems infinitely improbable,* we are destined by contact with other thinking planets, across the abysses of space and time, some day to become integrated within an organised complex composed of a number of Noospheres, humanity, having reached maturity, will remain alone, face to face with itself" [emphasis added].[9] Nonetheless I am optimistic that if we achieve our species-maturity, we can have a very long life as a planetary civilization. I suspect as well that the emergence of civilized life-forms is not a random process but a purposeful part of the elegant design of the cosmos.[10] If so, the development of a galactic-scale community could be as natural as the development of reflective life on Earth.

through these stages of growth. A sacred geometry may provide a universal framework and language for the evolution of life throughout the cosmos, and therefore a common basis for understanding.

If every life-form throughout the cosmos must move through seven dimensional stages to achieve its maturity as a planetary-scale organism—including the sixth dimension and the development of a compassionate consciousness—then all are obliged to achieve a basic level of ethical conduct. The dimensional structure of the cosmos seems to create a learning process with a fail-safe mechanism to weed out civilizations that are unsustainable and unethical. If we humans devastate ourselves with nuclear war, or pollute ourselves into near extinction, or stagnate in an authoritarian bureaucracy, or genetically cripple ourselves through inappropriate self-mutation, then it is unlikely that we will have the strength, endurance, and creativity to reach very far beyond the Earth. The cosmos seems to have been designed to provide the greatest degree of freedom while limiting the degree of damage that any one planetary civilization can do at the galactic or cosmic scale.

It is instructive to consider that the potential for developing nuclear weapons is inherent within the atomic structure of reality and is pervasive throughout the cosmos. Any species that reaches a rudimentary level of scientific and technological development will discover the nuclear potential and the ability to destroy civilization at a planetary scale. Was this potential deliberately designed into the cosmos, both as a way of weeding out unethical civilizations and as a catalyst to stimulate rapid evolution? The cosmos appears to be a self-regulating system with built-in safeguards to prevent civilizations from extending their technical reach too far beyond the scope of their ethics.

What might lie beyond initial contact with other planetary civilizations? Perhaps a new kind of conscious community can emerge in the distant future—a galactic-scale mind consisting of all the individuals and planetary civilizations who, in telepathic sympathy, bond together in knowing fellowship. Beyond a galactic-scale mind, we may ultimately join in a cosmic-scale community consisting of all the reflective minds in the billions of galaxies. A single field of cosmic knowing may then be woven together in telepathic communion.[11]

And then? Would an awakened cosmos exhaust the potentials of the underlying Meta-universe? I think not. Assuming we live in a Meta-universe of infinite dimensionality, our immense cosmos may be no more than one small island of self-organizing activity that is dynamically suspended within a boundless ocean of Life-energy containing innumerable cosmic systems.

Humanity is immersed within a flowing Life-force whose depth, subtlety, creative intelligence, and power utterly dwarf our imagination. This we can celebrate. We can accept where we are—confident in the design-intelligence of the Life-force that sustains us, no longer thinking we inhabit an indifferent and random universe but recognizing we live in a cosmos of immense sophistication, subtlety, and support for our evolution. We can return home and "sweep the floor"—satisfied to move ahead, one step at a time.

INTEGRAL SPIRITUALITY

In the eighth stage the cosmos will be known as a unified, living organism. The universe will be seen as a holographic entity, where all is contained within all—at each instant the totality is fully present within and expressed through each part, and each part is fully connected with the whole. People will be inclined to live ethically because they understand that everything we do is, moment by moment, woven into the infinite depths of the Meta-universe. Mikhail Nimay describes this insight beautifully in his *Book of Mirdad:*

> So think as if your every thought were to be etched in fire upon the sky for all and everything to see. For so, in truth, it is.
> So speak as if the world entire were but a single ear intent on hearing what you say. And so, in truth, it is.
> So do as if your every deed were to recoil upon your head. And so, in truth, it is.
> So wish as if you were the wish. And so, in truth, you are.[12]

Our spiritual perfection is in our wholeness. Our self-completion without any omissions—embracing both the light and the dark aspects of our being—is what gives the unique energy, character, and texture to our lives. The *Corpus Hermeticum,* dating back at least two thousand years, gives a stunning description of the scope of the spiritual challenge awaiting us in these further stages of dimensional unfolding:

> Unless you make yourself equal to God, you cannot understand God: for the like is not intelligible save to the like. Make yourself grow to a greatness beyond measure, by a bound free yourself from the body; raise yourself above all time, become Eternity; then you will understand God. Believe that nothing is impossible for you, think yourself immortal and capable of understanding all; all arts, all sciences, the nature of every living being. Mount higher than the highest height; descend lower than the lowest depth. Draw into yourself all sensations of everything created, fire and water, dry and moist, imagining that you are everywhere, on Earth, in the sea, in the sky, that you are not yet born, in the maternal womb, adolescent, old, dead, beyond dead. If you embrace in your thought all things at once, times, places, substances, qualities, quantities, you may understand God.[13]

Material reality provides a launching pad for eternity. Because we must live with ourselves forever, our self-awareness is of inestimable value—it is priceless. *Nothing is of greater value than to develop the capacity for double-wisdom that enables us to live consciously in the Meta-universe, which is our home in eternity.* That is the challenge—and the promise—of the eighth dimension. Once we discover, in freedom, our true nature, we can then journey forever through perpetually unfolding dimensions without losing ourselves.

SUMMARY

The seven major stages of growth can be summarized in a single graphic so that the overall pattern of the theory of dimensional co-evolution can be seen more clearly. Although the matrix shown in Figure 15 is largely self-explanatory, the reader may want to explore the four chapters in Part II on "Dimensional Cosmology." Three other comments about this matrix are important.

- This geometry may seem too simple to describe a process as rich and miraculous as human evolution. Yet this sacred geometry is akin to the disciplined simplicity of a musical scale, which allows new levels and varieties of music to emerge progressively as the skill, understanding, and creativity of the musician develop.

- As symbolized by the torus, dimensional coevolution does not progress in a linear fashion; instead development proceeds as an arc that turns back upon itself. In the initial stages, humanity's evolutionary challenge is to separate from nature and discover our capacities as a relatively autonomous species. In the later stages, our challenge is to reintegrate ourselves with nature and to learn to act in conscious harmony with the cosmos. Evolution moves through a nested series of perceptual environments, each with new challenges and potentials, that gradually turn back upon themselves to create self-referencing beings and civilizations that are intimately connected with the deep ecology of the universe.

- This is not a deterministic view of evolution. Although humanity is obliged to evolve through a preexisting pattern of perceptual paradigms, we are free to respond to this series of dimensional environments as we choose. This pattern of dimensional contexts provides an optimal sequence of perceptual environments for enabling us to evolve into self-referencing and self-organizing individuals and civilizations. However, given human freedom and frailty, I do not expect evolution to conform to the neat boxes and boundaries that are described in this matrix. The path we actually take through these various stages will surely be filled with many surprises, accidents, and twists of fortune that will make it uniquely human and characteristically unpredictable.

DIMENSION	IDENTITY
8 + D Meta-universe	**Integral Awareness [8th D]**—A dynamically integrated identity emerges that is both unique and whole. Knowingness so knows itself that there is no need for a material reality to push against to remind the self of one's unique resonance, nature, and identity. A self-referencing, self-organizing, and self-remembering identity. Meaning is found through participation in cosmic-scale evolution.
7th D ⎫ **6th D** ⎬ Consciousness Dimensions **5th D** ⎭	**Flow Consciousness [7th D]**—The observing process no longer stands apart from any aspect of that which is observed—the observer becomes the fully involved participator. Conscious "reality surfing." An unbroken thread of awareness runs through all existence. Meaning is found in creative and conscious expression in the world.
	Oceanic Consciousness [6th D]—Consciousness seeks to know its origins. The observer explores the source of self-referencing knowing and experiences immersion in the deep ecology of the universe. Feelings of compassion emerge with the recognition of unbounded connection with the rest of the universe. Meaning is found in directly experiencing the qualities of unbounded Being.
	Reflective Consciousness [5th D]—Conscious of consciousness. The sense of identity expands to embrace the polarity of observer and observed or knower and known. In being able to stand back and observe the ego self, this dimension fosters a sense of detachment and makes it possible to achieve authentic reconciliation. Meaning is found in the process of seeing.
4th D ⎫ **3rd D** ⎬ Material Dimensions **2nd D** ⎭	**Dynamic Consciousness [4th D]**—Conscious of thinking. An existential sense of self emerges through identification with the intellect. The individual feels unique and alone. The "wheel of time" becomes an open spiral of progression, and "progress" is widely recognized. Meaning is expressed through creative thought and material development.
	Depth Consciousness [3rd D]—Conscious of feelings. A social ego emerges with depth and texture. Individuals acquire their identity from affiliation with an extended social group. The wheel of time (seasons, cycles) is recognized and celebrated through rituals. Meaning is found through shared feelings and a sense of belonging to an extended group.
	Surface Consciousness [2nd D]—Conscious of bodily sensations and bodily existence. A tribal ego emerges with very limited concerns and attachments. The sense of self is flat and momentary. The world is experienced as a magical place. Meaning is found in the direct sensing of and engagement with life.
1st D Foundation Dimension	**Contracted Consciousness [1st D]**—People "run on automatic" and rely upon instinct. Not decisively conscious of a "self" that is separate from the rest of nature. No distinctly conscious observer. "Meaning" is not a meaningful concept.

Patterns of Symmetry

Figure 15 : The Pattern of Dimensional Evolution

SOCIETY

Establishment of Planetary-Scale Wisdom Civilization [8th D]—Humans acquire the perspective, compassion, and creativity to sustain themselves into the long-term future. A dynamically stable, self-referencing, and self-organizing species-civilization emerges that continually balances between planetary unity and individual, creative diversity.

Era of Balancing Species-Creativity and Unity [7th D]—Planetary civilization moves beyond a concern for maintaining itself to a concern for surpassing itself. The critical challenge is to maintain global unity while coping with the enormous stresses generated by liberating human creativity and diversity. Creative ventures might include the terraforming of Mars and genetic engineering that creates entirely new forms of life.

Era of Global Bonding & Celebration [6th D]—Social compassion becomes the practical basis for organizing a planetary-scale civilization. With a deep sense of bonding and commitment, humanity works to build a sustainable future premised on mutually supportive development. An era of intense cross-cultural learning and global celebration. Much effort is placed on restoring the global environment.

Era of Mass Communication & Global Reconciliation [5th D]—With reflective consciousness realized at a civilizational scale through the creative use of the communications media, humans are able to stand back and cope with the severe ecological stresses generated by the industrial era. With intense local-to-global communication comes reconciliation around a vision for a sustainable future for the earth. The potential for a planetary-scale civilization gains a foothold in human consciousness.

Industrial Era [4th D]—Society is dominated by a materialistic and intellectual worldview. As people perceive the potential for material progress, the mystery of nature gives way to science and the analyzing intellect. Economies of scale in production and an ideological basis for social affiliation combine to foster a nation-state scale of development. Material development becomes the primary measure of social "success" and meaning.

Agricultural Era [3rd D]—A surplus of food makes possible a growing population and the division of labor. The scale of social organization expands from the farming village to the city-state. With a time-sense that recognizes nature's cycles, a settled agrarian existence develops along with supportive forms of civic organization.

Awakening Hunter-Gatherer Era [2nd D]—Social organization is of limited scale and is influenced by the demands for a mobile existence. With very few possessions there is little basis for material differentiation or conflict. Social affiliation is based upon the tribal group involved in gathering and hunting. Nature is seen as filled with mysterious forces. Magical rituals are developed to harness nature's power.

Archaic Humans [1st D]—With consciousness collapsed into a one-dimensional point, there is no ability to stand back and reflect on self and nature; instead beings are fully embedded within nature and operate largely on automatic. Social organization is extremely limited and extends little beyond the biological family.

$\mathcal{T}$HE CHANGING DYNAMICS OF HUMAN EVOLUTION

To arrive at the eighth stage, we must travel an enormous evolutionary distance—going from our initial awakening as hunter-gatherers to our initial maturity as a planetary-scale civilization. Several questions naturally emerge about this journey: How long will it take us to move through the next three stages of reconciliation, bonding, and creativity so as to achieve our initial maturity? Is this a journey that is so long that it is nearly meaningless to speculate on the pace of evolution? Or is a planetary-scale, wisdom-civilization much closer than we may think? Are there major pitfalls along the way that could divert us from achieving our dynamic balance and stability as a global civilization? What can we do in the near term—within this generation—to assist in our own evolution? These are some of the questions considered in this chapter, and the answers may be both surprising and sobering.

THE ACCELERATING PACE OF EVOLUTION

How long will it take the human family to reach its maturity in the eighth stage? To explore this core issue, Figure 16 summarizes the dynamics of growth from our awakening as hunter-gatherers through the agrarian and industrial eras and then into the early stages of the communications era. Although simplistic, this chart reveals the extraordinary acceleration that has occurred in the pace of human evolution. With each successive dimensional epoch there has been a dramatic collapse in the span of time required to move through a given stage. Where roughly thirty thousand years were required to move through the epoch of awakening hunter-gatherers, roughly five thousand years were needed to move through the era of agrarian-based civilizations. With the scientific-industrial era now giving way to the communications era, it is possible to estimate that the time span required for civilizations to move through an industrial stage of development is no more than three hundred years. Evolution is quickening at a truly remarkable pace.

The extraordinary compression in the amount of time needed to move through successive stages of dimensional development indicates that *humanity has reached a critical mass in perceptual evolution and could move very rapidly through the stages of growth essential for realizing our initial maturity as a planetary civilization.* Because the pace of change is accelerating enormously, we should not assume that thousands or even millions of years will be required for us to achieve our initial maturity as a species. We have entered a time of explosive development, and historical experience does not provide an accurate guide for the span of time required to move through the dimensional transformations that lie just ahead. *In my judgment humanity has the potential to reach its initial maturity—the eighth stage—within another dozen generations or roughly five hundred years.* This appraisal of the pace of the coevolution seems to be a middle-of-the-road estimate—it is a far longer period than is expected by some and far shorter than is expected by others.

Figure 16: Dynamics of Dimensional Evolution

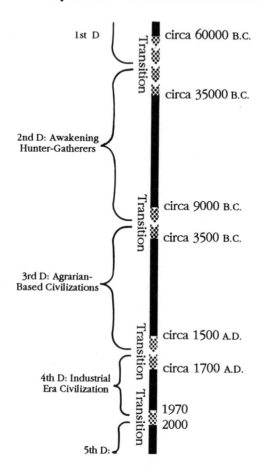

Illustrative of the view that humanity has the potential for awakening very rapidly are the estimates of Peter Russell. In his book exploring the future of human evolution *The White Hole in Time,* he states that "if we do survive our present challenges, and if our evolution does continue to accelerate, we could see the whole of our future evolution . . . compressed into a century or so."[1] Russell concludes that "we are in the last moments of our 50,000-year dash from emerging consciousness to full enlightenment."[2]

In striking contrast are the views of other keen observers of human evolution, who think that the evolution of culture and consciousness is a very slow process and that it will require thousands, and perhaps millions, of years for humanity to achieve our initial maturity:

- Teilhard de Chardin states in his book *The Future of Man* that "humanity will have completed itself and fully achieved its internal equilibrium only when it is psychically centered upon itself (which may yet take several million years)."[3]

- Ken Wilber states in his book on the evolution of transpersonal awareness *Up from Eden* that "it will probably be thousands, maybe millions, of years before mankind as a whole evolves into superconsciousness."[4] Wilber also states that "the next stage of growth is the beginning of the trans-personal. . . . I don't see this happening on a large scale for at least another century, if then."[5]

- Alan Watts explains in his book *The Spirit of Zen* that "in the East the effectiveness of a religion is judged by its success in producing a comparatively small number of thoroughly enlightened men, for it is not believed possible fundamentally to alter the lives of vast numbers of people within the span of a thousand years or so. Great social changes are not expected; the religions of the East are more concerned with the enlightenment of some few individuals than of society as a whole."[6]

- In his book *Civilization on Trial* Arnold Toynbee considers the future of humanity in thousand-year increments, and it is not until roughly three thousand years hence that, he suggests, humanity will find a new, common life springing out of the wreckage of the old civilizations.[7]

While these estimates of slow evolution may be convincing when considered from the perspective of the past, they overlook at least two critical facts about the future: First, exponential growth in electronic communications is providing humanity with the tools to support a witnessing or reflective consciousness at a planetary scale. Second, global crises are pushing the human family to evolve far more rapidly than we would have ever expected from looking back at historical dynamics. If we had neither the enabling pull of communications technologies nor the empowering push of necessity, it would be realistic to assume that the further stages in the coevolution of conscious-ness and culture would take many thousands of years.

An example illustrates how our species-evolution is moving ahead far more rapidly than is assumed by the conventional spiri-tual wisdom. Instead of requiring a century or more before a sub-stantial fraction of humanity moves into the realm of transpersonal consciousness, in my estimation a majority of humanity is *already* beginning to move into a transpersonal domain where people are cognizant of a witnessing or reflective capacity. Specifically, with the explosive growth of telecommunications technologies, we are developing a new capacity for a witnessing or observing conscious-ness as a species. Telecommunication technologies are transform-ing our perceptions of ourselves and the world with breathtaking speed. Rather than requiring a century or longer, a majority of hu-manity is already immersed in a rudimentary, transpersonal reality via the witnessing capacity of television. A seemingly profane me-dium is unavoidably transmitting the sacred message of reflective consciousness! As the saying goes, "It's a rare fish who knows he swims in water." The world is already swimming in the reflective consciousness generated by global television. By osmosis we are ac-quiring a new way of looking at the world. When communication systems reach a critical mass of development (through the integra-tion of computers, fiber optics, video, satellites, libraries, and elec-tronically supported democracies), they will provide humanity with an unstoppable voice and unshakable conscience that is concerned with building a sustainable future.

Television has already become an unprecedented force for pro-moting transformative shifts in social consciousness and institutions. Around the planet the unblinking eye of television is generating mo-mentous change by creating a shared perceptual framework that tran-scends national boundaries and ideologies. Television does more than report on events; it produces change by transforming social con-sciousness, and this in turn is propelling social revolutions forward at a breathtaking pace. For example, when asked what had caused the stunning collapse of communism in Eastern Europe, Polish leader Lech Walesa pointed to a nearby TV set and said, "It all came from there."[8] In the words of journalist David Remnick, "Information and images are the ultimate weapon now."[9]

The push of necessity is combining with the pull of opportunity to propel humanity forward to a new level of consciousness and communication. If we use the experience of the past as our guide for estimating the pace of change for moving into a transforming future, our reaction time will be so slow that we will seriously misjudge our situation and may suffer calamitous consequences.

While I believe the ascent to double-wisdom is reaching a critical mass and beginning a rapid takeoff, I do not believe that we will inevitably or automatically reach our early adulthood as a species. Evolution must now become conscious of itself, and we must deliberately choose our pathway into the future. There are many pitfalls on the path to maturity that can sidetrack us. It is conceivable that various evolutionary detours could absorb our attention for thousands of years and take us far from a healthy pathway. There is no cosmic requirement that we stay on an optimal track of development; instead we may squander precious years in empty pursuits that produce needless suffering.

How long might it take for humanity to traverse the next three dimensional epochs? Assuming that at least four generations will be required to move through each of the three fully remaining dimensional epochs (the fifth, sixth, and seventh stages), then this translates into roughly five hundred years as the minimum time for achieving our initial species-maturity. This is *not a prediction*, but an order-of-magnitude estimate of the opportunity before us.* The important point is that, compared with other estimates of thousands and millions of years, a half a millennium is an extraordinarily brief period of time. Although realizing our initial maturity could easily take far longer than five hundred years, we are nonetheless moving into a time of unprecedented compression and accelerated learning. We should not underestimate the potential for rapid evolution leading to our embryonic maturity as a planetary civilization.

---

*To obtain this rough order-of-magnitude estimate, I assumed that at least one generation would be required to work through the unique demands of each season of growth. Assuming three dimensional epochs, or twelve "seasons," plus a gradually lengthening life span (with an average generational span of forty years), then the minimum length of time required to move through these epochs to initial species-maturity would be roughly five hundred years. Again, this is *not* a prediction but an order-of-magnitude estimate.

Even if it takes several thousand years to reach the integrated functioning of the eighth stage with its dynamic stability, the entire span of time required for humans to evolve from a prereflective species to a postreflective or integrated species-civilization will have been roughly in the range of forty thousand years. Although this may seem like an enormous length of time, from a cosmic-scale perspective we are making a momentous transition in an extraordinarily brief period—the blink of an eye relative to our potential life span as a species.

If we do achieve our initial maturity as a species, how long might we then survive? We don't have other planetary-scale civilizations with which to compare ourselves, but we can get some perspective by looking at the longevity of early humans and other animal species. For example, our early human ancestor *Homo erectus* survived more than a million years before becoming extinct. The typical life span of a species has been estimated to be between 1 and 10 million years.[10] Some species live far longer. For example, dinosaurs survived roughly 140 million years before a natural catastrophe wiped them out. If humanity is as capable of survival as the dinosaurs, then we should be able to endure for a period equal to more than 25,000 times the span of recorded human history! Given these illustrations of longevity, there is no reason why *Homo sapiens sapiens* cannot endure for a million years or more. Millions of years of evolution preceded the emergence of beings with reflective consciousness, and it is conceivable that millions of years of development—perhaps even billions!—could unfold afterward. (Recall the three macrophases of evolution portrayed in Figure 1 in the Introduction.)

Although there is an immensity of time behind us and an equal immensity of evolutionary potential before us, it is important to recognize the pivotal period in which we now live. Humanity is making an evolutionary inflection toward planetary integration and sustainability. Our choices during these transitional times will profoundly influence human destiny into the distant future.

CONTEMPORARY REALITY— A SPECTRUM OF DIMENSIONAL PERSPECTIVES

Although the pace of evolution is accelerating, humanity is now spread out across a wide range of perceptual paradigms. We have an immense amount of work to do if we are to coalesce this diversity around a shared evolutionary agenda. Figure 17 shows the changing percentage of the world population that is estimated to live within the context of different dimensional paradigms. These are rough estimates, but they do give a feel for the dynamics of our evolution toward our species-maturity.[11]

Figure 17: Percent of World Population by Perceptual Stage

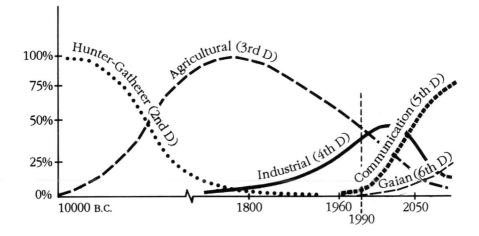

Two points stand out when we consider a contemporary cross-section of this chart. First, although the center of social gravity for humanity is now oriented around the perceptual paradigm of the industrial era or fourth dimension, we are moving rapidly into the fifth dimension—the era of a witnessing consciousness, with mass communication, and global reconciliation. Second, at least five different perceptual paradigms or "dimensional cultures" coexist on the planet as we approach the twenty-first century:

- **2nd Dimension: "Hunter-gatherer"**—Hunter-gatherers now account for less than a fraction of one percent of all people on the Earth. Until recently this way of life was found in areas as diverse as Southeast Asia, the Arctic, and Scandinavia.

- **3rd Dimension: "Agricultural"**—Roughly half of the world's population live in agrarian civilizations, but this fraction is declining rapidly with the spread of industrialization and urbanization.

- **4th Dimension: "Industrial"**—Urban-industrial cultures are developing swiftly around the planet, and by the year 2000 an absolute majority of the world's population will live in urban settings. Although many will live in urban slums, they will nonetheless be separated from an agrarian setting and challenged to survive in the urban-industrial world.

- **5th Dimension: "Communication"**—A new global consciousness and culture is emerging with the explosive growth of mass communications. By the turn of the century a majority of the world's population will be influenced by the mind-set of the communications era. Even those who are agrarians or industrialists in their daily work will nonetheless orient themselves increasingly within the perceptual framework created by the communications revolution.

- **6th Dimension: "Gaian"**—Although they constitute a very small fraction of humanity, there is a distinct culture growing around the world consisting of people who have a strong sense of global family and global bonding. These are planetary citizens that are dedicated to human service and celebrating our common humanity. Examples of Gaians with a compassionate, planetary view include many who worked for "Live Aid" for Africa (1985), many "Earth Day" groups (1990), and many of the "Earth Summit" participants in Brazil (1992).

As of the 1990s the people of the Earth are spread across five different perceptual paradigms. Yet by midway through the twenty-first century a majority of humanity could *begin* to coalesce within the fifth-dimensional perceptual context as a common organizing paradigm. For the half century or so in between, there lies a time of unprecedented transitioning among multiple perceptual frameworks. This will be a complex process, as, for example, developing societies may seek to avoid the pitfalls of the past, leap over the economic infrastructure of a traditional industrial society, and instead build the infrastructure for a sophisticated amalgam of agriculture, selective industrialization, and advanced communications. With complex patterns of change occurring simultaneously and with no overarching perceptual paradigm previously established to orient human activities, the early decades of the twenty-first century seem likely to be a time of intense conflict over which paradigm holds the greatest promise as an aligning vision for a sustainable future.

TECHNOLOGICAL ADVANCE AND EVOLUTIONARY ADVANCE

In Western societies there is a tendency to equate technological advance with civilizational development. However, for a number of reasons it is misleading to apply this limited criterion to the complex process of the coevolution of culture and consciousness. First, I do not automatically equate the use of advanced technology with an advanced civilization. Civilizations can be overdeveloped on the technological side and underdeveloped on the psychological, social, and spiritual side of life. Less technically advanced cultures may, for example, have an extremely sophisticated understanding and appreciation of nature and the cosmos. Native American Indians have an intimate and subtle sense of nature that seems far more advanced and wise than the commercialized and materialistic American culture that is rapidly destroying its ecological heritage. Second, scientific evidence suggests that people around the world are born with the same levels of cognitive ability and capacities for achieving self-referencing consciousness. Third, this is not a linear view of development—dimensional evolution proceeds in an ever-bending arc that turns back on itself so as to produce self-referencing beings and civilizations. In the poetry of T. S. Eliot:

> And the end of all our exploring
> Will be to arrive where we started
> And know the place for the first time.[12]

Any judgment of "lower" or "higher" is much less meaningful in this self-referencing evolutionary dynamic. Fourth, the "law of the retarded lead" suggests that societies that prosper in one evolutionary epoch often find themselves unable to adapt flexibly to the potentials of subsequent epochs, and civilizing leadership may then pass to others. Given that we are only roughly halfway through the stages of growth that lead to our initial maturity, it is far too soon to make value judgments regarding the relative contribution and status of any civilization.

While the innate abilities of people around the world are the same, and the wisdom-culture we seek will draw upon the insights of all cultures, there do seem to be significant differences in the character and structure of the perceptual environments generated by different stages of civilization growth.[13] For example, I do not think the perceptual framework of agrarian-based civilizations would be able to coalesce and sustain a democratically constituted, compassionate, technically advanced global-scale civilization. The point is not to devalue the wisdom of earlier civilizations; rather, it is to acknowledge the nature of the perceptual paradigm that is needed to support a planetary-scale civilization. For humanity to build a technically advanced, democratically constituted, sustainable, compassionate, and creative civilization *at a global scale,* I believe we will need the perceptual capacities of the seventh stage of dimensional evolution.

Although the world needs a shared perceptual framework from which to build a sustainable world economy and civilization, this does not mean we should seek homogeneity and uniformity. After surveying the growth and decline of the world's civilizations, Arnold Toynbee found a master process at work in the disintegration of societies, which he called a "tendency towards standardization and uniformity: a tendency which is the . . . opposite of the tendency towards differentiation and diversity which we have found to be the mark of the growth stage of civilizations."[14] As we seek global reconciliation around a sustainable future, we need simultaneously to support a broad range of cultural diversity. Each country needs to be free to develop in ways that are uniquely suited to its culture, ecology, climate, and so on.

While valuing diversity, it is important to anchor world civilization in the highest dimensional perspective possible, as this will provide the most inclusive, tolerant, and productive framework for peaceful reconciliation. The fifth stage and communications era—with its natural emphasis on social witnessing and reconciliation—provides a mediating and moderating influence to what otherwise could become intense, survival-oriented competition among egoistic nation-states seeking to preserve their power and status relative to the rest of the world.

EVOLUTION ELSEWHERE: A TOUR OF THE COSMOS

Given our great freedom, the future is genuinely uncertain. There is no guarantee that humanity will choose to climb the steep ascent to our initial maturity.[15] Viewed as a whole system, our cosmos may produce an overabundance of life-forms, understanding that many will not reach their full blossoming. A similar evolutionary strategy seems to operate for plants that produce hundreds of seeds, perhaps implicitly recognizing that only a very few will take root in nurturing soil and develop fully. Astronomers estimate there are more stars in the visible universe (and thus potential planetary systems to support life) than there are grains of sand on all of the Earth's beaches! Although there seems to be a wealth of opportunity for life to develop, many planetary-scale civilizations may not succeed in moving beyond a rudimentary stage. Instead they may stagnate psychologically, devastate their ecosystem, and physically collapse, or be wiped out by natural disasters (as were the dinosaurs). There are many twists and turns on the path to our species-maturity, and we cannot take our future for granted.

If we had a spacecraft that could take us through the cosmos at great speed, here's what I think we would see: On most planets the experiment in life would have never gotten under way or else failed early on. Like our neighbor Mars, these planets would be barren and incapable of supporting the complex ecosystem needed for life-forms to grow. As we continued our journey through the cosmos, on a small percentage of planets we would find habitable ecosystems and see a variety of life-forms struggling to reach an elementary stage of reflective consciousness. Finally, on a very small percentage of planets we would find civilizations of global scale that have acquired the wisdom, stability, and compassion needed to sustain themselves into the distant future.

Although the probability of life arising on other planets is intensely debated, it is useful to make this assumption in order to bring greater perspective to our current challenges. We live within a relatively young star system. Because there are many stars much older than our sun, it is reasonable to speculate that there may be many planets with civilizations far older than our own. Astronomer Carl Sagan and Russian scientist I. S. Shklovskii estimate that *there are between fifty thousand and one million civilizations in our galaxy that are in advance of our own!*[16] If there are mature species-civilizations scattered throughout the billions of galaxies of our cosmos, then the daunting challenge of achieving a sustainable planetary future must have been met successfully innumerable times before by other civilizations.

Still, each world civilization is unique. For better or for worse—on a small planet circling a relatively young, moderate-sized star located at the outer edge of a swirling cloud of a billion stars that comprises an average-sized galaxy—we are involved in the birth of a unique global civilization. Will we become one of the planets where life struggles forward only to fall back before achieving its full measure of development, our environment crippled by pollution, our abundant resources squandered, and humanity torn apart by chronic conflict? Or will we become one of the gems of the Milky Way galaxy, the Earth a place of great beauty and humanity choosing a path of mutually assured development? If we do not muster the social will and creativity to choose our pathway into the future consciously, we may well become one of the unfortunate cosmic seeds that has taken root but is so crippled by unconscious, self-destructive actions that it never flowers into the fullness of its potential. These are pivotal times for our species.

Dangers Ahead: Pitfalls on the Path to Maturity

Although humanity is on a path of exponential development that could lead rapidly to our initial maturity, there are a number of pitfalls on the way that could deflect our development onto an evolutionary detour, or even into a dead end. Opportunity is not destiny. There are no guarantees of success. We have entered a time of great testing of our evolutionary intelligence. It remains an open question whether we will develop the cosmic wisdom needed to survive. In addition to the widely recognized threats of nuclear war, overpopulation, and pollution, there are many other ways in which we can sabotage our own evolution. An illustrative sampling of the pitfalls on the evolutionary path reveals how precarious and uncertain is our pathway into the future.

Inflexibility and Delay

Arnold Toynbee concluded that civilizations are particularly vulnerable to disintegration after they have achieved a time of great success.[17] He said it is difficult for a successful civilization to let go of approaches that have worked well in the past; instead there is a tendency to deny the need for fundamental change and to redouble efforts along old lines that previously had been highly successful. Therefore one major pitfall is the inflexibility and delay produced by seeking to perpetuate the status quo. In Toynbee's words, civilizational growth requires "perpetual flexibility and spontaneity."[18] By waiting too long to adapt, humanity may lose a precious window of opportunity and find that the chance for creative change has been lost. For example, by delaying the inevitable need to respond to the combined impact of the depletion of world oil reserves, climate change, and world population growth, we will find our options increasingly limited and the challenge of adaptation increasingly difficult. The opportunity for creative evolution could turn into a scramble for survival.

Lack of Vision

We cannot consciously create a future that we have not imagined. When our collective visualization is weak and fragmented, then our ability to build a workable and meaningful future is commensurately diminished. To consciously evolve, we require a clear vision of a compassionate future that draws out our enthusiastic participation in life. The richness and reach of our social vision is a direct measure of our civilizational maturity. To evolve consciously as a global civilization, it is imperative that we extend our social imagination into the deep future and anticipate our development as a species. Looking only a few years into the future at a time when our decisions have long-run consequences is like trying to drive a car on a winding road at high speed while looking only a few feet ahead. To keep our bearings in a changing world where the pace of evolution is accelerating, we must consciously look multiple generations into the future.

Humans can bear many hardships when they are seen as purposeful. Futility and despair will grow, however, when people encounter a period of great material hardship and psychological stress that has no end in sight and that serves no meaningful purpose. Civilizations can disintegrate when forced to respond to overwhelming stress without a guiding vision for the future. Without a broad public consensus around a compelling vision of the future, cynicism can overwhelm trust and we can lose confidence in ourselves, our leaders, and our institutions. A disheartened and disoriented world civilization is a recipe for social unrest, religious fanaticism, and authoritarian domination.

Ecosystem Disruption

A combination of ecological trends may undermine or even collapse the biosphere on which life depends, pushing the world into chaos; for example:

- Rapid ozone depletion may cause critical damage to the entire food chain, both in the oceans (from the plankton upward to the fish that feed on the plankton) and on land (from plants, to the bees that pollinate plants, and upward to the higher animals that depend on the integrity of the overall ecosystem).

- Increasing quantities of greenhouse gases will likely produce major shifts in the climate and result in marked changes in rainfall patterns and growing seasons that in turn could produce drought and famine throughout the world.

- Loss of genetic diversity in agriculture through reliance on a few strains of rice, corn, and grain could make the world's food supply highly vulnerable to disease and result in crop failures of catastrophic proportions.

Disruptions to the ecosystem are exacerbated when people must struggle each day just to survive. For example, the growing population in many Southern Hemisphere countries desperately needs land to grow food—so people are cutting down the rain forests for farm land, even when most know this will produce an even greater calamity in the long run. Given survival pressures, it is conceivable that the global ecosystem could become so devastated that it could sustain only a fraction of the world's population, and this in turn could lead to massive famines and severe civil unrest and push the world toward an authoritarian form of civilization.

Resource Wars

Within a generation we will deplete a significant amount of critically important, natural resources; for example: (a) easily accessible and thus inexpensive supplies of oil are expected to be nearly exhausted within thirty years; (b) major ground-water aquifers are being pumped dry to support a high-intensity agriculture; and (c) widespread soil erosion is depleting precious topsoil. As our situation grows ever more critical, those areas that have essential resources (such as oil, water, and arable land) will become the focus of protracted conflict. The world could then disintegrate into warfare rather than coalesce into a process of mutually sustainable development. Easter Island provides a powerful warning about the impact of resource wars.[19] When the island was first populated in the twelfth century, it was covered with trees. These were eventually all cut down, which allowed the soil to erode, which in turn greatly diminished crop yields. Ultimately the food supply became so limited that warfare and cannibalism became widespread and the island's estimated population of eight thousand was reduced to a few hundred. There is the frightening possibility that, with resource depletion, some variation of this scenario could be repeated at a global scale.

Unsustainable Gap Between Rich and Poor Nations

In the media-rich world of the future, glaring differences between rich and poor nations will be painfully and persistently evident. People in the poorest regions will want a decent standard of living and may not tolerate chronic extremes of material inequity that result in conspicuous consumption for a relative few and starvation and misery for a billion or more others. The prosperity of wealthy nations is vulnerable to disruption by people of the impoverished nations, who have nothing to lose by expressing their discontent.

Thomas Aquinas taught that when people have more than they require for meeting the necessities of life, they have an obligation to give away the rest to the poor. Whatever people have in superabundance, he said, is owed, as a natural right, to the poor for their survival. "The bread which you withhold belongs to the hungry, the clothing you shut away, to the naked; and the money you bury in the Earth is the redemption and freedom of the penniless."[20] If a fairness ethic grows among poorer nations while wealthy nations attempt to maintain their privileged status and isolate themselves from the needs of desperate billions, it could produce a world that is so ethically and morally divided that it cannot achieve reconciliation around a common future.

Authoritarianism

Ecosystem breakdown and resource wars could deplete the trust essential for democratic governance among nations and push the world into such chaos that, to restore order, authoritarian forms of government could emerge at a national or even global scale. People may so mistrust others and so disbelieve in the potential for a compassionate future that instead of working for humanity's collective well-being, they may take a survivalist approach and work only for their own interests, thereby making authoritarian forms of government more necessary. Four ingredients seem to be likely elements in a new era of authoritarianism: a strong military or police force to secure borders and maintain law and order; a strong religious foundation to bring moral legitimacy to nondemocratic government; extensive use of computer networks to monitor and control people; and a land- and resource-based orientation as each community, region, or nation seeks to maintain its particular material advantage.

Information Wars

Humanity may forgo physical violence only to embrace other forms of violence that, in the communications era, could be extremely destructive. Warfare may shift to an electronic battleground where conflicts range from terrorist skirmishes to all-out assaults on the electronic integrity of the information systems of a corporation, nation, or the entire planet. Terrorists may resort to communication wars (propaganda and disinformation) or information wars (scrambling or damaging data critical to vital computer systems in government and business). To counter this threat, an electronically supported authoritarian government could emerge that uses superintelligent computers to scan global communications continuously, looking for abnormal flows or "communications storms" that indicate a threat against those in power. Chronic information wars could develop between authoritarian leaders and dedicated hackers seeking to restore democracy.

Genetic Challenges and Catastrophes

Unlocking insights into the genetic structure of both plants and animals will have profound consequences. Whether by accident or by intention, our interventions will have reverberations of immense proportions. Three major possibilities suggest the range of impacts:

- **Extreme Genetic Augmentation**—We may soon find that we can enhance people's physical strength, resistance to disease, longevity, and intellectual capacity. Genetic intervention and augmentation will then raise immensely difficult questions: Are genetically enhanced individuals still "humans"? Should individuals be required to disclose their family's history of augmentation so that there are no undue advantages in sports, work, education, and relationships? Should a caste system be established to differentiate between those who are highly augmented and the "normals"? Should those who are significantly at risk in their genetic factors be identified as a "biological underclass" or even as "untouchables"? As these questions suggest, once our genetic foundation is made explicit and accessible to conscious manipulation, it may lead us in entirely unforeseen directions.

- **Hybrid Species**—We may learn to create hybrid species of animals with an enhanced intelligence and consciousness. For example, by genetically modifying already advanced species—such as dolphins and chimpanzees—we may be able to engineer life-forms that have an increased capacity for self-reflective consciousness. In addition we may be able to create a new type of being that has just enough intelligence and consciousness to be able dutifully to perform menial and/or dangerous tasks, such as working with hazardous pollutants and nuclear wastes. In being able to "uplift" other species to a new level of intelligence and consciousness, humanity will be forced to learn a new measure of ethicality for inhabiting the planet alongside with relatively conscious life-forms whose evolutionary direction may diverge from that of humans.[21] Once set into motion, the development of hybrid species may have consequences that are impossible to foresee or to reverse.

- **Genetic Warfare**—A nightmarish possibility is that biological warfare will become the poor terrorist's nuclear weapon. Biotechnologies may allow scientists to create, for example, a "black-plague flu" that could devastate the world's population. An outbreak of an unknown virus with deadly potentials could bring the world to a halt, creating a quarantine condition where all physical movement and contact among people virtually stops. Groups could also hold the biosphere hostage by threatening to release genetically engineered and biologically damaging plants and animals into the ecosystem. Terrorists from desperately impoverished nations could demand that unless their citizens were able to share equitably in the economic well-being of the larger world, they would act to prevent the rest of humanity from enjoying those benefits.

As these extreme examples suggest, immense repercussions could flow from genetic interventions and could divert the people of the Earth onto a long and convoluted evolutionary journey.

Misuse of Advanced Behavior-Control Devices

By combining advanced computer technology with nanotechnology, or microscopic-scale machines, it is conceivable that "criminals" could be implanted with sophisticated biocomputer systems to control the limits of their behavior. A biocomputer could monitor a person's brain-wave and hormonal activity and, if it detected "antisocial" patterns and levels, it could automatically inject a tranquilizing chemical or electrical stimulus. In the context of an authoritarian society, the definition of a "criminal" could include social dissidents who challenge the legitimacy of those in power. Even the threat of using these biotechnologies could greatly inhibit social criticism and creativity.

Religious Fanaticism

Because so many of humankind's wars have been fought between people with differing religious views and because the world is entering a time of growing compression and proximity among people, religious differences will present enormous challenges for humanity. Under conditions of great planetary stress, different historical religions could coalesce around charismatic spiritual leaders and come into conflict. The planet could then descend into religious wars, perhaps with a new era of crusades intended to liberate the world from unbelieving infidels. Religious fanaticism could lead to spiritual tyranny and undermine trust in a compassionate and broadly shared spiritual ethic that can bind humanity into a single family.

Another possibility is that a significant fraction of the world may view extreme planetary distress as a sure indication of a coming apocalypse and feel relatively little concern for starvation, pollution, and resource depletion. If these are seen as the last days before a miraculous spiritual transformation, then people may assume that "God" will intervene and clean up the mess. Instead of mounting a vigorous and creative response to the challenge of sustainability, people may simply wait for the apocalyptic end, or abrupt transformation, of the world.

Planetary Psychosis

Another pitfall is that the world could "go crazy," experiencing such divergent views, voices, and paradigms of perception that it is unable to come together in meaningful dialogue and agree on the nature of a sustainable future. Instead of converging around a common agenda, the world could drift into ever more confusing and chaotic rhetoric and conflicting ideology. Unable to discover a shared consensus beneath the discord and pandemonium, the conversation of the planet could collapse to the lowest common denominator consistent with security and survival. With no transcendent and trusted source of perspective, the collective psyche of the human family could disintegrate, and the people of the Earth could descend into chronic conflict for the indefinite future, never achieving the species-understanding and consensus necessary to build a sustainable and surpassing civilization.

In the face of monumental stress—cultural, political, economic, ecological, and spiritual—the collective human psyche may disintegrate and split into multiple and conflicting subpersonalities. Some people may move into denial, refusing to acknowledge the tenuousness of our situation and fantasizing that somehow things will return to "normal." Others may feel such a profound sense of helplessness that they slip into fatalistic resignation. Others may look for ways to escape or to insulate themselves and their family from the deteriorating situation (for example, wealthy families may create walled-in enclaves in order to try to ride out the storm, while some poorer families may choose to develop survivalist skills and seek out less populated areas in an effort to get by on their own). Others may assume that some powerful group must be deliberately causing things to go awry; feeling angry and resentful, they may look for people to blame.

If these kinds of responses predominate and a majority is unable to cope constructively with a deteriorating world over generations, the conviction could grow that humanity is an ill-fated and luckless species that never had a chance to succeed. Each new generation could reconfirm the suspicion that we live in a hostile universe, that we do not share a coherent view of reality, and that humanity cannot work together. The human race could become so preoccupied and depressed with its guilt for the devastation of the planet that we could take self-fulfilling actions to confirm that we are a doomed species.

The difficulty of achieving a stable and integrated sense of collective identity for humanity could further be compounded by: (a) a significant subculture of genetically augmented beings who feel alienated from the dominant culture; (b) a significant subculture of virtual-reality fanatics who live in artificial, electronic worlds that diverge radically from consensual reality (and perhaps come into conflict with it); and (c) a significant subculture of religious fanatics who believe theirs is the only "true way" to insight or salvation. Multiple subcultures such as these could amplify the splits in our planetary personality and make our integration into a coherent species-culture extremely difficult.

Progress/Regress Confusion

Another pitfall is that movement to a higher stage of dimensional functioning may be misperceived as evolutionary regress instead of progress. For example, a shift from passionate engagement with the world in the fourth stage to the more detached perspective of the observer in the fifth stage may be viewed as a loss of passion and a turning away from material development. Instead of seeing the ob-

sessive material attachments of the fourth stage as ultimately dysfunctional and needing to be transformed through a witnessing consciousness, the detachment of the fifth stage could be interpreted as
indifference and disengagement. Instead of seeing the biological,
brain-encapsulated view of consciousness characteristic of the fourth
stage as excessively limiting, the translocal view of consciousness
(which accepts the potential for psychic functioning) may be misin-
terpreted as a return to the superstitions of an earlier, prescientific
age. A similar process of misperceiving the nature of evolutionary
advance can operate at the transition between each stage.[22] People
may frustrate or divert the evolutionary process by misinterpreting
evolutionary progress as a step backward to a previous level of functioning. Progress/regress confusion could produce enormous barriers to evolutionary advance.

This brief review illustrates the dangers and pitfalls that lie ahead.
Humanity can get sidetracked in many different ways on the path to
species-maturity. These detours are not mutually exclusive; for example, ecosystem breakdown could generate resource wars that lead to
global anarchy and promote the rise of religious and political fanaticism, which in turn could lead to the emergence of a new feudalism
that produces a long dark age for the Earth. These diverse and intertwined pitfalls illustrate how truly uncertain—and precarious—is our
evolutionary journey.

While it is conceivable that we could achieve our early adulthood
as a species-civilization within half a millennium, this does not seem
easily attainable. It is very plausible that our maturation could take
vastly longer. Given our great freedom to choose different pathways
into the future, we could move swiftly toward our species-maturity or
we could spend thousands of years wandering off on long detours. If
we are to keep from getting sidetracked, we will have to keep our wits
about us and act with intelligence, compassion, and creativity.

Although there are many pitfalls on our path to maturity, we
should not despair. It is true that, looking back through history, we
can see that our development from wandering tribes of food gatherers to a species with global impact has been filled with mistakes and
crises. Just as every growing child makes many missteps along the

path to adulthood, so, too, has humanity made many painful mistakes along its way to its early adulthood as a planetary society. Entire civilizations have collapsed, or have wandered off into a stagnant dead end, or have made horrendous use of newfound powers. Still, we humans have learned through our mistakes, and step by step we have moved ahead—ever more experienced, ever more seasoned, and ever more mature. Although our future is deeply uncertain and at risk, we should not be paralyzed with despair, as we have all the resources and capacities we need for our journey. I agree with the biologist Lewis Thomas that our species has great promise:

> We may all be going through a kind of childhood in the evolution of our kind of animal. Having just arrived, down from the trees and admiring our thumbs, having only begun to master the one gift that distinguishes us from all other creatures, it should perhaps not be surprising that we fumble so much. We have not yet begun to grow up. What we call contemporary culture may turn out, years hence, to have been a very early stage of primitive thought on the way to human maturity. What seems to us to be the accident-proneness of statecraft, the lethal folly of nation-states, and the dismaying emptiness of the time ahead may be merely the equivalent of early juvenile delinquency. . . . If we can stay alive, my guess is that we will someday amaze ourselves by what we can become as a species. Looked at as larvae, even as juveniles, for all our folly, we are a splendid, promising form of life and I am on our side.[23]

ALTERNATIVE FUTURES FOR HUMANITY

Pulling back from the deep future to the nearer term, there already exists sufficient information about emerging trends to get a useful sense of what lies ahead. Briefly, by 2025 two powerful sets of trends will converge: unprecedented material adversity will meet equally un-precedented communications opportunity. Because we evolve most rapidly when the push of necessity coincides with the pull of opportunity, this will likely be a time of dramatic change for the human family. To explore this further, consider these two sets of trends:

- **Material Adversity**—Current levels and patterns of growth in developed nations are not sustainable. Three driving trends illustrate our predicament: Within a generation (by roughly 2025), world reserves of easily accessible oil are expected to be depleted, we will add another three billion persons to the planet, and the climate is expected to become more variable due to global warming.[24] Without inexpensive petroleum to provide the pesticides and fertilizers for a high-yield agriculture, and with the prospect of disruption of food production due to climate instability at the very time we have added another three billion persons to the planet, the likelihood of massive famines and global civil unrest looms large. When many other trends are factored into this equation (ozone depletion, rain-forest destruction, soil erosion, acid rain, and so on), it is no longer a probability but a certainty that we face an immensely difficult and challenging time in human affairs.

- **Communications Opportunity**—The world will make a quantum leap forward in its level of communication when, by roughly 2025, a whole series of potent technologies will be in place that together will produce an unprecedented capacity for local-to-global communication.[25] Nearly every home and business in developed countries will be wired with high-capacity fiber-optic systems that can transmit the equivalent of entire libraries of information within seconds. Fiber optics will also support highly sophisticated forms of interaction (not only banking, shopping, learning, and entertainment but also near-instantaneous citizen feedback to decision makers). Computer systems will continue to make quantum leaps forward in their "intelligence" (for example, they will have voice-recognition capabilities and universal translators that will make it possible to network easily and inexpensively with persons around the Earth). High-definition television systems with flat, wall-sized screens will be integrated with the fiber-optic and computer systems to provide vivid, interactive connections with the rest of the planet. Massive data-base systems will be translated into formats that are universally accessible, creating a further knowledge revolution. Powerful satellite systems will link rural areas and developing nations into the global communications network. As all these revolutionary technologies merge into a single system, they will produce a global telecommunications network of stunning depth, breadth, and sophistication. In short, our "global brain" will burst forth and "turn on" during the first two decades of the twenty-first century.

Although greatly simplified, Figures 18 and 19 portray the meeting of these trends of adversity and opportunity. (See page 250.) Even though these curves are more symbolic than literal, they do illustrate a very promising fact: The communications curve is growing at a rate that seems to match the growth in the adversity curve. While it is hopeful to see that humanity is acquiring, just in time, the communication tools necessary to respond to a global crisis, it is unclear whether we will make effective use of these tools.

By 2025 we will begin to encounter the full challenge and potential of the era of communication and reconciliation. We have no historical precedent for the intensity of experience that lies roughly a generation into the future. On the one hand, material trends will converge to create megacrises that will roll around the planet, producing chains of actions and counterreactions that will leave untold death, sorrow, misery, and civil unrest in their wake. On the other hand, the telecommunications revolution will provide the human family with an extraordinary capacity to communicate its way through these difficulties and into a sustainable future. For example, if food is needed in Africa, the entire world will be able to communicate and discover where surpluses exist that can be shared. If medicine is needed in Brazil, hospitals around the planet can be notified in a matter of minutes and the responses monitored day by day.[26] If torture and human rights abuses are occurring in Iraq, for example, within hours or days the people of the Earth can put its government on notice that the whole world is watching their behavior and will respond accordingly. In sum, a quantum increase in communication will make it possible to develop a cooperative, efficient, ecologically conscious, and democratically governed world civilization.

Figure 18: Material Trends

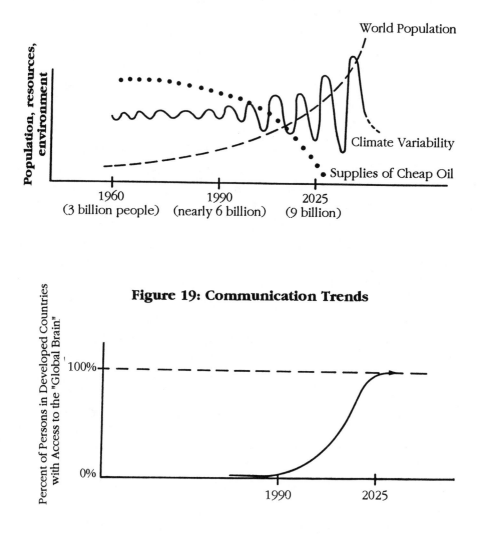

Figure 19: Communication Trends

Our collective future depends directly upon our level of communication and cooperation as a human family. *We face an invisible crisis of civilizational consciousness and communication that is as critical as any of the material challenges we confront.* If the world continues to drift along half awake and humanity fails to communicate about critical choices, we are effectively choosing a future of great calamity for ourselves and our children. If we awaken to our situation and diligently communicate our way through these dangerous times, there is a real opportunity to build an exciting and promising future of mutually supportive, global development.

Although I am hopeful about the long-range future, realism demands acknowledgment of the great uncertainty about the decades just ahead. Even with swift reconciliation among the human family, it seems likely that the world's ecosystems will soon be so damaged that it will require two or three generations for significant renewal and restoration. There will be no quick technological fixes that can solve our many, interconnected problems. Here are the three major scenarios that portray the most likely alternative-future possibilities for the coming decades:

1. **Collapse and Rebuild from a Devastated Base**—If humanity fails to respond to current challenges, the results could be catastrophic: ozone depletion might ravage the Earth's biosphere, runaway population growth might far outstrip the carrying capacity of the planet, climate change might devastate the Earth's agricultural base, and all of these forces might result in chronic and destructive wars over access to resources. There is no guarantee that humanity will achieve the level of cooperation required for long-term, sustainable development. We may first need to "hit bottom" and experience the reality of a devastated, mean-spirited, and dangerous world created through some combination of massive famines, civil unrest, and economic breakdown. Having tasted the bitter consequences of our short-sighted behavior, we may then be ready to work cooperatively for sustainable development. The danger is that we may so profoundly devastate the ecological base upon which world civilization depends that we will be unable to rise to our potentials.

2. **Dynamic Stagnation**—It is conceivable that humanity could muddle along with destructive trends balanced by constructive trends. We would then neither advance nor collapse but dynamically stagnate by making severe adaptations that enable us just to maintain the status quo.[27] All available social creativity and economic energy would be used up in the effort to prevent world

civilization from falling backward, resulting in arrested growth. Despite a dynamic balance, this would be a highly stressful future, as enormous efforts would be required to keep world civilization from collapsing. By making extreme adjustments, humanity might be able to maintain itself almost indefinitely, but would lack the energy and creativity to surpass itself.

3. **Mutually Assured Development**—Humanity could mobilize itself and communicate its way through to a future of sustainable development. Through intense communication the world economy could become much more cooperative and efficient. As standards of living are raised in poorer nations and the birthrate declines, survival-oriented pressures that cause environmental damage (such as slash-and-burn agriculture that destroys rain forests) would lessen. As the human family learns how to resolve conflicts through peaceful means, investments in weapons and armies could be reduced dramatically and investments in learning and development increased commensurately. Overall, a future of mutually assured development could emerge by restoring the integrity of the Earth's ecosystem, narrowing the gap between rich and poor nations, and respecting human diversity.

The human family faces at least these three starkly different pathways into the future—unyielding calamity (collapse scenario), unrelieved stress and boredom (stagnation scenario), or unprecedented development (communication-and-reconciliation scenario). These three pathways are illustrated simply in Figure 20 as outcomes from a traditional growth curve.

The choices made in the next few decades will profoundly shape the direction and character of human evolution. Just as the birth experience and first few years of life have a profound impact on the development of a child, so, too, will the manner in which our global civilization is born have a lasting imprint on the long-term evolution of the human family. Many centuries from now people will look back at these pivotal decades as the time when the people of the Earth made fateful choices that determined whether we were able to move swiftly and without needless detours toward a sustainable planetary civilization.

**Figure 20: Three Pathways into the Future
for the People of the Earth**

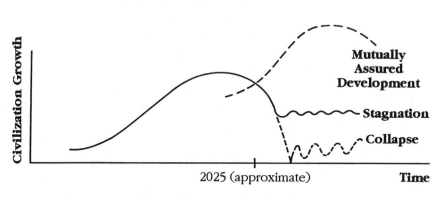

BUILDING A SUSTAINABLE FUTURE

The sustainability crisis is now viewed largely in terms of dwindling resources, mounting pollution, population growth, and other physical indicators that measure the Earth's ability to support the burden of humanity. Although these are of critical importance, they do not go to the heart of our situation. More basic is an invisible crisis in the consciousness and culture of humanity. Until we come to terms with the nonmaterial aspects of our crisis, we will not be able to make the many material changes required to build a sustainable future. Drawing on the insights of previous chapters, here are six priority needs for building a sustainable and satisfying future:

- **Breaking the Cultural Hypnosis of Consumerism**—The mass media are aggressively promoting a consumerist mentality in developed nations. In the United States the average person sees more than 35,000 commercials a year, most of which are ads for a high-consumption lifestyle as well as a pitch for a product. We need a new social ethic that holds the mass media accountable for its programming of our civilization's consciousness with antisustainability messages. We need to counter this cultural hypnosis with programming and advertising that foster a sustainability consciousness. From documentaries to dramas to "Earth commercials," we need to use the mass media to awaken and sustain a new understanding and caring for the planet and for the future.

- **Ecological Ways of Living**—We need actively to envision new ways of living that reflect our understanding that the Earth will be humanity's home for countless generations into the future. We need to invent new patterns of ecological living that moderate our impact on the Earth—from the design of our homes and neighborhoods to the food we eat, the clothes we wear, the transportation we use, the work we do, and much more. To design our way into the future consciously offers an inspiring challenge—an exciting experiment in intentional living that can bring forth our most creative potentials.

- **Compelling Visions of a Sustainable Future**—We cannot consciously build a future that we have not first imagined. Many people can visualize a future of worsening crisis—ecological destruction, famines, civil unrest, and material limitation—but few have a positive vision of the future. Without a hopeful future to work toward, people will tend to withdraw into a protected world for themselves and focus on the short run. We need to see that with new patterns of consumption, housing and community, work and livelihood, we can create a sustainable *and* a satisfying future. These visions of the future need to involve more than "only not dying"—we need to see how we can both maintain *and* surpass ourselves and thereby continue our evolution toward our initial maturity as a planetary civilization.

- **Conscious Democracy**—To choose a sustainable future, we need a revitalized democracy that engages citizens in a whole new level of dialogue and decision making through innovative use of our tools of mass communication. We need to energize the conversation of democracy by developing regular electronic town meetings with effective forms of feedback from citizens. As citizens come to know their own minds on issues and priorities, representatives in government can work with greater confidence to develop policies for a sustainable future. With active communication we can achieve the level of mass consensus, cooperation, and coordination needed to adapt our patterns of living to the new global realities.

- **Nurturing a Reflective Perceptual Paradigm**—We need to cultivate a witnessing consciousness that is able to stand back and directly experience the Earth as a tightly interconnected and living system that deserves great care and respect. In seeing the Earth as alive and worthy of reverence, we will cultivate a mind-set that naturally promotes the frugal and judicious use of resources and that safeguards all life on the planet.

- **Reconciliation**—Humanity is profoundly divided between: the rich and the poor, racial groups, ethnic groups, religious groups, men and women, current and future generations, and many other polarities. We need to use face-to-face communication, as well as our tools of electronic communication, to achieve a new level of reconciliation as a human family that gives us a fresh start for moving ahead. The communications revolution will leave no place on the planet to hide from these realities. Nearly every dwelling will have an intelligent and interactive "picture window" that opens with stark clarity onto the world's divisions and suffering billions. If humanity is to work together cooperatively, we must learn to accept our diversity—racial, ethnic, generational, religious, sexual, cultural, geographic, and more. Without reconciliation our efforts to achieve sustainability will be stalemated and stalled.

When we have broken the cultural hypnosis of consumerism and can envision ecological ways of living, and when these modes of living connect with a clear vision of a sustainable future for the Earth that we cocreate with other citizens through the ongoing conversation of a conscious democracy, and when we have the objectivity of a witnessing or reflective consciousness and can achieve reconciliation among the diverse members of the human family, then we have a realistic basis for making the technological and material changes required for building a sustainable future.

SUMMARY

Although the human family is only roughly halfway through the stages of growth required to move from prereflective consciousness to integrated awareness, our initial maturity as a species may be closer than we think. Summarizing our evolutionary journey thus far: Roughly 2.5 million years were required for our earliest ancestors to move from the first glimmerings of self-recognition to decisive awakening in the initial stage of reflective consciousness. It then took about thirty thousand years for physically modern humans to move through the stage of awakening hunter-gatherers; approximately five thousand years to move through the stage of agrarian-based civilizations; and then around three hundred years for a number of nations to move through the stage of industrial civilization. Because the pace of evolution is accelerating enormously, the past is not an accurate guide to the future. If we do not veer off onto some evolutionary detour, then it is conceivable that within a very brief period of time (perhaps five hundred years, or a dozen generations or so) we could build a sustainable and creative planetary civilization that celebrates the many threads that make up the tapestry of its rich character.

We are rapidly approaching one of the most momentous occasions in the evolution of life on any planet—the inevitable "evolutionary inflection" where an arduous process of withdrawing from nature makes a decisive shift toward an equally demanding journey of returning to live in harmony with nature. The inflection represents a unique pivot point in human history where evolution finally becomes decisively conscious of itself as a planetary-scale process, begins to intentionally direct itself, and begins to deliberately shift from a pathway of separation to a pathway of reconciliation.

The period of inflection is reached when our material powers become so great that they progressively destroy the ecological foundations of life on the planet and make it essential for us to work together as a species in a common task of survival. By my reckoning, humanity will likely "hit the wall"—or run into unyielding limits to material growth and be forced to squarely confront the imperative for pervasive change—in roughly the decade of the 2020s.

Figure 21: The Evolutionary Inflection and the Stages of Development

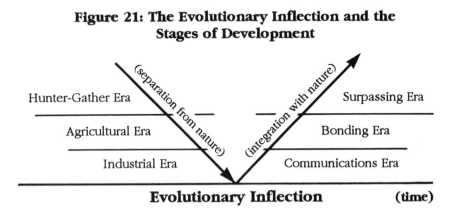

Evolutionary Inflection　　　(time)

How humanity prepares for this unique evolutionary shift will be a real and visible test of our evolutionary intelligence as well as our capacity for compassion and creativity. To move onto a pathway of sustaining and surpassing development will require the enthusiastic involvement of billions of people. Therefore the concerns raised in this broad review of human evolution are ultimately very personal.

Who we become as a planetary civilization will depend directly upon our actions as a global community of individuals. We each have unique talents—and correspondingly unique responsibilities—for participating in the unfolding of life. The awakening of the Earth now depends directly upon the citizens of the Earth acting in concert with one another to build the foundations of a sustainable future. Each individual needs to tithe a significant portion of their time and talent to the healthy coevolution of the planet.

Millions of years lie behind us, bringing us to this moment in human history; and millions of years could lie before us, unfolding a future whose nature may well pivot upon choices we make now. We do not need to belabor the stages of learning and growth that remain. With diligent efforts, a sustainable, compassionate, and creative world civilization could become established within perhaps half a millennium. However, before we reach that stage of dynamic stability, humanity's mastery of the dimensional complexities of the evolutionary process will be challenged repeatedly. What an exciting, demanding, and rewarding journey stretches out before us.

PART II

*D*IMENSIONAL

COSMOLOGY

$\mathcal{T}$HE PERENNIAL WISDOM AND HUMAN EVOLUTION

Individuals are the building blocks of society. No civilization can evolve farther—nor reach any higher—than the citizens who comprise it. By understanding the highest common denominator of individual human experience we can gain insight into where our collective evolution may be headed. This common denominator is often called the perennial wisdom and can be found throughout history, in every part of the world, and in every major spiritual tradition.[1] Although this abiding wisdom has many facets, two aspects are important for understanding the character of a mature human civilization: first, the perception of a deep unity underlying all that exists; and second, the "Golden Rule" as a universally recognized principle for ethical conduct.

A PROFOUND UNITY

Although we live in a world of seeming division and multiplicity, the perennial wisdom is unequivocal in asserting that a profound unity underlies the appearance of separation. Here are a few examples of this affirmation of wholeness, which is found in every spiritual tradition, in every culture, and in every age:

"For those who are awake the cosmos is one."[2]
  —Heraclitus, philosopher who lived in ancient Greece

"The flickering film of the phenomenal world is an illusion which cannot obscure the eternal unity that lies behind it."[3]
  —Arnold Toynbee, scholar of the world's civilizations and religions

"Each element of the cosmos is positively woven from all the others. . . . The universe holds together, and only one way of considering it is really possible, that is, to take it as a whole, in one piece."[4]
  —Teilhard de Chardin, Catholic theologian

"Ultimately, the entire universe . . . has to be understood as a single undivided whole."[5]
  —David Bohm, physicist

"Heaven and earth and I are of the same root . . . are of one substance."[6]
  —Sojo, a monk and scholar from the Zen tradition

"I am in some sense boundless, my being encompassing the farthest limits of the universe, touching and moving every atom of existence. The same is true of everything else. . . . It is

not just that 'we are all in it' together. We all *are* it, rising and falling as one living body."[7]
— Francis Cook, a Buddhist scholar, describing how reality is portrayed in Hua-yen Buddhism

"That which is the finest essence—this whole world has that as its soul. That is Reality. That is Atman [the individual self]. That art thou.[8]
— Hindu tradition, Chandogya Upanishad

When Jesus was asked, "When will the kingdom come?" He replied: "It will not come by waiting for it. . . . Rather, the Kingdom of the Father is spread out upon the earth, and men do not see it."[9] Jesus also said, ". . . the Kingdom is inside of you, and it is outside of you."[10]
— Gospel of Thomas, Gnostic Gospels

"The Self is not reached. You *are* the Self; you are already That."[11]
— Ramana Maharishi, Hindu sage

"God is nearer to me than I am to myself; He is just as near to wood and stone, but they do not know it."[12]
— Meister Eckhart, Christian mystic

"The Absolute . . . dwells within the flux of things: stands as it were at the very threshold of consciousness and knocks, awaiting the self's slow discovery of her treasures."[13]
— Evelyn Underhill, from her book *Mysticism*

"We may imagine that the One, since It is absolute, must be distant from us spiritually or even spatially. . . . We forget that the absoluteness of the One includes absolute immanence, or omnipresence. Thus the One is here and now, not a stranger, not even an other, but the very nature of what we are."[14]
— Lex Hixon, from his book *Coming Home*

"Earth's crammed with Heaven, and every common bush afire
with God."
    —Elizabeth Barrett Browning, poet

"Not knowing how near Truth is,
People seek it far away—what a pity!
They are like him who, in the midst of water,
Cries in thirst so imploringly."
    —Hakuin, from the Zen tradition in Japan[15]

"Like the empty sky it has no boundaries,
Yet it is right HERE, ever serene and clear.
When you seek to attain it, you cannot see it.
You cannot take hold of it,
But neither can you lose it."[16]
    —Yung-chia, Zen tradition

"Each being contains in itself the whole intelligible world.
Therefore All is everywhere."[17]
    —Plotinus, Neoplatonic philosopher who lived in
    ancient Greece

A subtle Life-force infuses, sustains, and unifies our cosmos. The
wholeness of our reality is so complete that we are not separate from
"God" or "Nirvana" or "Brahman" or "Tao" or the countless other
names given to the unnameable presence that pervades the undivided
universe. We don't have to do anything to become a part of the
wholeness of reality—we are already completely at one with it. We are
beings that the universe inhabits as much as we are beings that inhabit
the universe. An appreciation of the unity of existence is not an experience to be created; rather it is an always-manifesting condition of
our existence waiting to be welcomed into awareness.

THE UNIVERSALITY OF THE "GOLDEN RULE"

To build a workable world civilization, the human family needs to trust that it can live together peacefully. All spiritual traditions in the world affirm the same basic ground rule for appropriate conduct: Treat others as you would want yourself to be treated. Despite our many differences, all of the major civilizations of the world have arrived at this same ethic for describing appropriate human conduct—a "Golden Rule" that proclaims that the best way to determine how to treat another is to put yourself in his or her place and act accordingly:

As you wish that men would do to you, do so to them.
—Christianity (Luke 6:31)

No one of you is a believer until he desires for his brother that which he desires for himself.
—Islam (Sunan)

Hurt not others in ways that you yourself would find hurtful.
—Buddhism (Udanavarga)

Do naught unto others which would cause you pain if done to you.
—Hinduism (Mahabharata 5:1517)

Do not unto others what you would not have them do unto you.
—Confucianism (Analects 15:23)

Like different facets of a single jewel or different branches of a single tree, the human family shares a common experience at the core of life, and this has fostered a shared wisdom about how to relate to others. This ethic makes good sense in an ecological reality whose fundamental property is a deep unity—for whatever we do to the rest of the world, we literally do to ourselves.

THE CREATIVE TENSION OF THE PERENNIAL PATH

There are two extremes in how we might view the perennial wisdom. On the one hand, we may think this wisdom is unexceptional because it is so commonplace. We may think that because the "Kingdom of heaven is spread out before us," this "wisdom" must not be very profound or transformative. We may think that with only slight effort we can know these insights and therefore they must be inconsequential. On the other hand, we may go to the other extreme and think this wisdom is so elevated that it is unattainable. We may assume these insights are so distant and so removed from ordinary life that they are unreachable by anyone except the most exceptional and heroic human beings.

We need to take a middle path in approaching the perennial wisdom. On the one hand, this wisdom *is* very close at hand: it is at the very center of our moment-to-moment existence. On the other hand, this wisdom *is* truly elevated, and we should not deceive ourselves as to the immensity of the journey—both personal and social—that is involved in discovering and then integrating it into our lives. Either extreme seems ill advised: To dismiss the perennial wisdom as irrelevant because it seems ordinary and of little value is as unwise as to dismiss it because it seems extraordinary and unattainable.

The eminent anthropologist A. L. Kroeber said that the ideal condition for any person or society is "the highest state of tension that the organism can bear creatively."[18] The perennial wisdom reflects this principle: it presents us with a middle path between two extremes—with wisdom neither too close nor too far, neither too easy to obtain nor too difficult to discover. Our path as individuals and societies is one of high tension and great potential—the most that we can bear creatively.

Again, the universe appears to be an elegantly designed and highly purposeful learning system. The cosmos intends our awakening. Nothing is withheld or hidden—all is present for our learning. The universe does not impose upon us. We have immeasurable freedom to learn as we choose. The universe presents its miracles with an open hand and infinite patience.

Democratizing the Natural Heritage of Mysticism

The initial awakening to the unity of the universe is often accompanied by feelings of great joy, boundless love, and the sense that objects are somehow infused with a subtle, radiant light. For example, here is how a student, F. C. Happold, described a transformative mystical experience he had in 1913:

> There was just the room, with its shabby furniture and the fire burning in the grate and the red-shaded lamp on the table. But the room was filled by a Presence, which in a strange way was both about me and within me, like light or warmth. I was overwhelmingly possessed by Someone who was not myself, and yet I felt I was more myself than I had ever been before. I was filled with an intense happiness, and almost unbearable joy, such as I had never known before and have never known since. And over all was a deep sense of peace and security and certainty.[19]

Harvard psychiatrist John Mack writes, "What we call mystical experiences occur when there is a sense of oneness or harmony between the energy or power in our bodies, minds and spirits and the energy of other beings and the universe itself."[20] A survey conducted by the National Opinion Research Center at the University of Chicago asked a sampling of persons in the United States whether they had ever had experiences that could be interpreted as "mystical." They discovered that among the random sample, 55 percent said they had experienced "a feeling of deep and profound peace," 43 percent said they felt "love is at the center of everything," 29 percent described an experience "of the unity of everything and my own part in it," and 25 percent had the "sense that all the universe is alive."[21] This poll indicates that the experience of intimate union with all of creation is far more widespread than commonly acknowledged. Other national surveys have shown that roughly 40 percent of the public have had the experience of being unified with "God" or the Metauniverse.[22]

These polls suggest that the unitive experience is becoming democratized. For example, they indicate that in the United States in the early 1990s roughly eighty million adults have experienced some degree of integrative or mystical awareness. These experiences of profound union are strongly connected with high levels of mental health. Studies have shown that no other factor is so highly correlated with psychological balance as previously having had a mystical experience.[23] For good reason, then, Western psychiatry is beginning to recognize the validity and value of mystical experiences.

The Spiritual Foundations of Advanced Civilization

In 1901 the physician Richard M. Bucke published his classic study of enlightening experiences, *Cosmic Consciousness*. Bucke wrote that just as, long ago, self-consciousness appeared for the first time and gradually became universal, so, too, will "cosmic-consciousness" continue to develop and become ever more common. He reasoned that because self-consciousness now appears at the average age of three years, so, too, will cosmic consciousness "become more and more common and show itself earlier in life, until after many generations it will appear in each normal individual at the age of puberty or even earlier; then go on becoming still more universal, and appearing at a still earlier age, until, after many thousands of generations, it shows itself immediately after infancy in nearly every member of the race."[24] Bucke's positive outlook was influenced by his own experience of cosmic consciousness, in which he "saw and knew that the Cosmos is not dead matter but a living Presence, that the soul of man is immortal, that the universe is so built and ordered that . . . all things work together for the good of each and all, that the foundation principle of the world is what we call love and that the happiness of every one is in the long run absolutely certain."[25]

Bucke was not alone in his views. His contemporary, the poet Walt Whitman, foresaw that an appreciation of the aliveness of our universe would become more and more widespread until a time would come when hundreds of millions of "superb persons" would live in this consciousness.[26] From Whitman's perspective, the awakening and spread of cosmic consciousness is entirely normal. Just as self-reflective consciousness emerged as an extraordinary faculty roughly 35,000 years ago and has gradually become the norm for humanity, so, too, will an integrative awareness become more and more prevalent, accessible, and perfected with each passing generation until it becomes the norm for our species.

However described—as an experience of subtle radiance infusing the world, as a feeling of deep peace and connection with all life, as the exhilarating experience of riding in the center of time's flow, as the direct intuition of the aliveness of the universe, as a feeling of being reborn into new dimensions of existence, and so on—enlightening experiences tend to produce day-to-day behaviors that are immensely beneficial to an evolving planetary civilization. Here is how two religious scholars describe the worldly expression of what some call cosmic consciousness:

> It is not rare to meet people who appear to have attained . . . cosmic consciousness. . . . One will observe a certain detachment . . . an absence of "grasping"; a scrupulous attention to any task in hand; a capacity for listening, and a talent for answering sensibly and objectively; a liking for silence . . . and above all, an absolute reliability, a consistency from day to day which is lacking in people at large, who are swayed by a succession of moods and desires."[27]

While the awakening of unitive consciousness does not produce flawless beings, it does enhance our ability to participate in life with a more open mind and open heart—both immensely valuable qualities for nurturing the genuine flowering of world civilization. In addition the perennial wisdom provides an anchor for aligning human evolution, both personal and social. This wisdom affirms that human evolution is going somewhere—that we are growing toward ever higher levels of integrative awareness that will enable us to express our appreciation for, and participation in, the unity and creative aliveness of the universe. This wisdom is profoundly relevant, not only for individual growth but also for social evolution.

While some may view the perennial wisdom as so esoteric that it is not relevant to society at large, others see this wisdom as fundamental to human evolution. Indeed, some of the most esteemed historians and social philosophers of our age see humanity growing toward a unitive awareness. Few persons have studied the long sweep of human history so thoroughly as Arnold Toynbee, Lewis Mumford, and Joseph Campbell. Each has concluded in his own way that the perennial wisdom is central to understanding the human journey.

Arnold Toynbee

A distinguished historian who made a thorough study of twenty-one civilizations covering the bulk of recorded human history, Arnold Toynbee was unequivocal in describing the relevance of the perennial wisdom to human evolution. He said that the cause of "suffering and sorrow is the separation of sentient beings . . . from the timeless reality behind the phenomena, and a reunion with this reality is the sole but sovereign cure for our ailing world's ills."[28] Toynbee described the need for "higher religions" that would enable humans "to find a direct personal relation with the transcendent reality in and behind and beyond the Universe."[29] After reviewing the world's major religions, he concluded they all agree that humanity's goal is "to seek communion with the presence behind the phenomena, and to seek it with the aim of bringing the self into harmony with this absolute spiritual reality."[30] For Toynbee the ultimate function of civilizational development was to serve the unfolding of ever deeper spiritual insights and understanding. He said that "civilizations are the handmaids of religion," and that civilizations will have "fulfilled their function when they have brought a mature higher religion to birth."[31] In describing the central role of spiritual growth in the journey to a mature civilization, Toynbee made it clear that he was not forsaking the needs of the world. The goal, he said, "is the kingdom of God; and this omnipresent Kingdom calls for service from its citizens on Earth here and now."[32]

Lewis Mumford

Mumford, a world-renowned historian and social theorist, wrote on a wide range of topics concerning human evolution. In his book exploring the underpinnings of human civilization *The Transformations of Man,* he stated, "No theory of human development is adequate that does not include this widening of the province of love; it is this, rather than intelligence and the division of labor . . . that marks man's full emergence into the human estate."[33] Consistent with the perennial wisdom, he declared, "If life, in its fullness and wholeness, is to furnish our criterion for all development, then our philosophy must respect . . . above all, the tendency to self-actualization and self-transcendance."[34] Like Toynbee, Mumford saw the great need for developing our capacity to love: "Without a positive concentration upon love in all its phases, we can hardly hope to rescue the earth and all the creatures that inhabit it from the insensate forces of hate, violence, and destruction that now threaten it."[35]

Joseph Campbell

The scholar and teacher Joseph Campbell is recognized around the world for his study of the stories, myths, and ideas that have shaped the human interpretation of life. After spending a lifetime looking at the basic stories of humanity throughout history and across cultures, he concluded they all focused on a single, dominant theme: discovery of the underlying ground of being, the perennial wisdom. When asked what was being sought through the vehicle of mythology, Campbell stated, "I think what we are looking for is a way of experiencing the world that will open to us the transcendent that informs it, and at the same time forms ourselves within it . . . to find [the transcendent] actually in our environment, in our world—to recognize it.

To have some kind of instruction that will enable us to experience the divine presence."[36] Understandably, for Campbell, the first function of mythology was to "waken and maintain in the individual a sense of wonder and participation in the mystery of this finally inscrutable universe."[37]

Some will argue that to align human evolution with the perennial wisdom represents a return to an earlier age of superstition and wishful fantasy. In my view—and that of respected scholars such as Toynbee, Mumford, and Campbell—this wisdom represents our highest knowledge as a human family and is the strongest foundation we have upon which to build a planetary civilization.

COMMON GROUND FOR A PLANETARY CIVILIZATION

Fundamental to building a sustainable future is finding a common ground of human experience and a shared vision of evolutionary potential that transcends the differences that now divide humanity. If we cannot find a universal and familiar ground of experience, we will not be able to develop a vision of healthy social evolution that draws out our energy and enthusiasm. Importantly, the perennial wisdom affirms that beyond all of our political, social, and cultural differences there is a unifying experience.

We don't need to be forever divided as a species. The reason we can understand one another—despite differences of language, culture, custom, geography, race, ideology, theology, and history—is that we all share a sense of reality that is much deeper than those things that divide us. After his sweeping review of the world's major religions, Huston Smith concluded that, "in religion all the peoples of the world are fundamentally alike. The differences are but dialects of a single spiritual language that employs different words but expresses the same ideas."[38] The common core of human experience derives from the fact that we all share equally in the aliveness and unity of the universe. Our differences are many and to be celebrated, but our shared wisdom is profound and offers the hope that humanity can become united in a common evolutionary enterprise.

SUMMARY

There is a perennial wisdom—a highest common denominator—found across cultures, across history, and in every major spiritual tradition of the world. This wisdom tells us that the universe is profoundly unified and that we are an integral part of its subtle and vast body of being. As we come to see the living cosmos as a unified organism, we recognize that whatever we do to the world we do to ourselves.

Across the span of history, subtle though profound changes have been occurring as humanity has developed its capacity for self-reflective consciousness. Just as the awakening of a witnessing consciousness was remarkable some 35,000 years ago but is becoming the norm, so, too, will the development of cosmic consciousness eventually be considered normal for the human species.

CONTINUOUS CREATION OF THE COSMOS

To understand the highest levels to which we might evolve, we need to ask basic questions about the cosmos within which we live. How can each of us be intimately connected with the totality of existence at each moment? How can, as Jesus stated, the "Kingdom of Heaven" be continuously present within and around us? How can our vast cosmos function as a unified system? How can the gift of eternity already be present in our lives? The singular answer given to these questions by sages over the centuries is so remarkable, so breathtaking, and so astonishing that it is nearly impossible to conceive: Our vast cosmos is a unified organism that—in its totality of matter-energy, space-time, and consciousness—is being re-created anew at each moment. We cannot take our existence for granted. Our cosmos is a dynamically maintained system of matter and consciousness that lives within and is sustained by an unbounded field of Life-energy—an infinitely deep ecology that I have called the Meta-universe or the generative ground.

Continuous-creation cosmology contrasts sharply with the dominant cosmology in contemporary physics, which assumes that creation ended with the Big Bang some fifteen billion years ago and that since then only the cosmic furniture has been rearranged. Because we are many billions of years removed from what traditional science views as the original, one-time miracle of creation from "nothing," the surrounding trees, rocks, people, and so on are regarded as being constituted from ancient matter. Overall, our universe is viewed as being billions of years from the generative explosion that spewed out lifeless material debris into equally lifeless space and that has, by random processes, organized itself into life-forms on the remote planet-island called Earth.

In striking contrast, continuous-creation theory views our cosmos as a unified system—a living organism—that is being completely re-created at each moment. Instead of creation ending with the miraculous birth of our cosmos from a pinpoint some fifteen billion years ago, the cosmos continues to be maintained—moment by moment—by an unbroken flow-through of energy from the Meta-universe.[1] Like the vortex of a tornado or whirlpool, our cosmos is a completely dynamic structure maintained by the continuous flow-through of energy.* Being thoroughly dynamic, our cosmos has no freestanding material existence of its own but depends entirely on the continuing flow-through of energy. Continuous creation is even more remarkable when we consider that it includes not only matter but also the fabric of seemingly "empty" space.

Like a cloud that is drawn from and exists within the atmosphere, our cosmos is drawn from and exists within the Meta-universe of unbounded dimensionality. Our cosmos is a self-bounding system—a "cloud" of matter-energy-space-time that continually coalesces from the "atmosphere" of the dimensionally unbounded Meta-universe.

---

*It is important to differentiate this theory of "continuous creation of the entire cosmos" from another theory describing the "continual creation of atomic matter." The latter theory was developed by astrophysicist Fred Hoyle and describes a steady-state cosmos where atoms are generated at a rate just sufficient to offset the dispersion produced by the expansion of the universe, thereby producing a cosmos with a relatively even density of matter throughout. In contrast, the theory of continuous creation of the cosmos refers to a process whereby the totality of the universe is continuously regenerated at a rate that is assumed to be revealed by the constancy of the speed of light.

Because every aspect of our cosmos is immersed within and made from the Meta-universe, it means that all things share fully in the deep ocean of creative Life-energy. The Meta-universe is the source from which everything originates and is the unimaginably powerful, creative intelligence that is able, moment by moment, to sustain, with unerring precision and patience, our seemingly "ordinary" life world.

The Meta-universe is profoundly democratic. All things in the cosmos are lifted into existence at each instant in a single symphony of expression that unfolds from the most minute aspects of the subatomic realm, through the middle ground of human existence, then on to the vast reaches of the larger cosmos with its billions of galactic systems. The entire cosmos, all at once, is the basic unit of creation.

When we consider the size and complexity of our cosmos with its billions of galaxies and trillions of planetary systems, we see a flow of creation of such awesome scope, subtlety, precision, and power that it overwhelms the imagination. It is this astounding image—of the whole cosmos being continuously re-created, moment by moment—that awakens an entirely new level of appreciation for the world around us. Our very bodies are a continuing miracle of creation—and by settling into our immediate experience of "self" we are automatically immersing ourselves in the miracle of cosmic-scale creation.

The popular television series *Star Trek* provides a useful analogy for visualizing continuous creation. In nearly every episode people are shown being dematerialized and then "beamed aboard" the spaceship *Enterprise*. The image of a person being materialized—where a vague, shimmering presence coalesces into a solid entity—is very suggestive of the process of continuous creation. However, continuous creation occurs at an entirely different scale—the Meta-universe is beaming the entire cosmos into existence at every instant. Again, this is not a new insight: the theme of continuous creation can be found in all of the world's major spiritual traditions. Yet this view is so astounding in its scope that it has often been dismissed as a flight of the mystic imagination. Recent findings from the frontiers of modern science appear consistent, however, with this process view of reality.

CONTINUOUS CREATION AND
THE NEW PHYSICS

The eminent mathematician Norbert Wiener writes, "We are not stuff that abides, but patterns that perpetuate themselves; whirlpools of water in an ever-flowing river."[2] The view that all existence is pervasively in motion has deep roots in modern science. Although continuous-creation cosmology is consistent with a number of findings from modern science, consistency does not constitute proof. So, without claiming scientific validation, I will consider: (a) the dynamism of matter in the subatomic realm; (b) the dynamism of space at the microscopic scale; and (c) evidence that the dynamism of matter and space are fully unified into one grand system or "uni-verse."

Beneath the solid surface of material objects an extraordinary flow of activity is occurring that is almost beyond comprehension: "Should you glance for just one second, for example, upon an ordinary yellow dress, the electrons in the retinas of your eyes must vibrate about 500,000,000,000,000 times during the interval, registering more oscillations in that second than all the waves that have beat upon all the shores of all the earthly oceans in ten million years."[3] Physicist Max Born writes, "We have sought for firm ground and found none. The deeper we penetrate, the more restless becomes the universe; all is rushing about and vibrating in a wild dance."[4] The farther we look into the heart of matter, the less substantial it seems. Matter appears to be nothing more than ephemeral energy that flows together with exquisite coherence to produce waveforms with a dynamic stability and the appearance of solidity.

Intriguing evidence that material reality is being continuously coalesced from, and sustained by, a deep energy field comes from the work of physicist Harold Puthoff.[5] He has tried to understand why the electrons spinning around atoms don't radiate away their energy and collapse into the nucleus. He concluded that atoms are sustained by constantly drawing energy from the background "vacuum" so as to compensate exactly for the energy that radiates from the electron. Basic to Puthoff's theory (and quantum theory) is the idea that even a small area of empty space contains a uniform sea of enormously powerful background energy. Puthoff suggests that as the electron radiates away energy, it absorbs a compensating amount of energy from the background field so as to exactly balance the loss and thereby maintain dynamic stability. He concludes that the dynamic stability of matter verifies the presence of an underlying sea of immensely powerful energy that is universally present.

Continuous-creation cosmology suggests that seemingly static material objects are actually dynamically constructed resonance patterns that exist within the larger resonance pattern or "standing wave" that is our cosmos. All material forms are dynamically stable, flowing processes. At the atomic scale, matter is almost entirely empty space in ceaseless motion. If a typical atom were expanded to the size of a football field, the seemingly "solid" portion (the nucleus) would be no larger than a baseball. Then, if we were to probe into the heart of the nucleus, we would find quarks, which are unimaginably tiny knots of energy. Despite being almost entirely empty, at the human scale, matter has the appearance and feel of solidity because of its precise, dynamic consistency. The precision and speed with which the cosmos coalesces produces the appearance of persisting and solid structures. When two objects meet—as precisely matched wave-forms—they interact as if they were "hard." We interpret the dynamic consistency of energy as the static solidity of matter.

The analogy of an airplane propeller roughly illustrates this principle: When a propeller is spinning, it creates a circular area that appears to be a nearly solid surface.[6] If we try to put something in its path, it gives us dramatic feedback that seems to confirm its apparent density, even though the propeller actually occupies only a small percentage of the overall space. In a similar way, matter is mostly space, but the energy that comprises it is so highly orchestrated that it functions as if it were solid. Given the high speed of continuous creation, it is easy to see why we think we live in a world of solid objects. However, to view matter as solid and motionless is an illusion. This is not to say that material reality is an "illusion"; rather, if we think matter is static, we are allowing the swift flow of manifestation to fuse into an illusory concreteness.

The fabric of space-time is also involved in this dance of creation. So-called empty space is no longer viewed as a featureless vacuum, as it was in classical physics. Space is not the simple absence of form, waiting to be filled out by matter; instead space is a dynamic presence that is filled with an incredibly complex architecture. In his book *Patterns in Nature* Peter Stevens makes the following observations about the modern view of space:

> The idea that space has structure may sound strange, since we usually think of space as a kind of nothingness that is the absence of structure. We think of space as the . . . passive backdrop for the lively play of material things. It turns out, however, that the backdrop, the all-pervading nothingness, is not so passive. The nothingness has an architecture that makes real demands on things. Every form, every pattern, every existing thing pays a price for its existence by conforming to the structural dictates of space.[7]

Not only does space have structure, it is also infused with intense dynamism. Quantum physicists now theorize that, at an extremely small scale, the relatively smooth structure of space-time becomes an intensely turbulent field that is continually undergoing violent fluctuations and may contain "wormholes" that connect together distant portions of the universe.[8] Space is not static emptiness, but a continuous opening process that provides the context for matter to manifest. Because space-time is inseparable from motion, and motion is another way of describing energy, it follows that vast amounts of energy must be required to generate the openness of the enormous volume of space-time that exists in our cosmos. Physicist David Bohm estimated the power of this underlying sea of energy and concluded that a single cubic centimeter of so-called empty space contains the energy equivalent of many atomic bombs![9]

The pervasive dynamism of reality is a view increasingly confirmed by modern physics. Physicist Fritjof Capra explains, "Relativity theory . . . has made the cosmic web come alive by revealing its intrinsically dynamic character, and by showing that activity is the very essence of its being. . . . The universe is seen as a dynamic web of interrelated events. None of the properties of any part of this web is fundamental; they all follow from the properties of the other parts, and the overall consistency of their mutual interrelations determines the structure of the entire web."[10]

Another recent finding in physics indicates that our immense cosmos is unified to a degree previously thought impossible. Bell's theorem is concerned with whether faster-than-light communication is possible. This would be a profound violation of relativity theory, which assumes the speed of light to be the ultimate speed limit in our universe. However, striking results from experiments indicate that faster-than-light communication does occur! This finding is consistent with the hypothesis that our cosmos is being re-created at each instant and that the Meta-universe provides the context within which all relativistic differences are bridged and reconciled into a unified whole.

The deep unity of the universe has been described by physicist David Bohm by using the analogy of a hologram. If a piece is cut off from a hologram and illuminated, it will still show the entire picture encoded in its structure. Analogously, if the universe is holographic in nature, then it means that at each instant every part contains or involves the whole. Bohm has described the cosmos "as a single undivided whole, in which all parts of the universe . . . merge and unite in one totality."[11] Because a hologram is static and the universe is everywhere in motion, he has coined the word *holomovement* to describe our universe as "undivided wholeness in flowing movement." Bohm's view of a holodynamic reality emerging from an unmanifest domain, or "implicate order," is fully congruent with continuous-creation theory.

A dynamic, holographic analogy not only makes the important assertion that every part of the universe is interconnected; it makes the much stronger assertion that at each moment the entirety of the universe is fully involved in and revealed through each part. Erwin Schroedinger, an eminent physicist, stated it this way: "Inconceivable as it seems to ordinary reason, you . . . are all in all. Hence this life of yours which you are living is not merely a piece of the entire existence, but is in a certain sense the whole."[12]

A grand-scale, cosmic "Now" is essential to achieve the precise weaving of reality into a seamless whole—a now that embraces the entire cosmos and is the same now for all entities and all places. While relativity theory rightly dismissed simultaneity in four dimensions, continuous-creation theory reintroduces a cosmic now as a basic property of higher dimensions. A cosmic now serves a vital purpose— it provides the temporal context for orchestrating all changes happening throughout the universe, thereby keeping its dynamic structure in equilibrium and harmony with itself.[13] With simultaneity no interval of material time is required to factor changes into the flow of overall manifestation, thereby enabling the cosmos to maintain its coherence and integrity as an organism.*

To summarize: All is in motion. Matter is not a static substance but is a flowing pattern of energy. Space is not simple emptiness, but is an opening process that contains an exquisite architecture. If everything, including the fabric of space-time, is a dance of motion, then

---

*If the entire universe is being continuously re-created, then what is the pace of this flow? The speed of creation is impossible to determine objectively because we cannot stand outside the cosmos in its process of becoming and measure it coming into existence. Because we are inside and integral to this flow, we can only make inferences regarding the pace of continuous creation; in turn this points toward one of the most fundamental attributes of the cosmos—the constancy of the speed of light. Continuous-creation cosmology suggests that *the constancy of the speed of light is a result of the precise consistency with which the fabric of reality is dynamically woven together.* In other words, the constancy of the speed of light is produced by and is a result of the evenness with which the cosmos is being generated as a unified system. *The precise consistency of continuous creation at the cosmic scale has been interpreted as the constancy of the speed of light at the local scale.* Continuous-creation theory suggests a straightforward reason for the physical compression, time dilation, and increase in mass predicted by relativity theory as an object approaches light speed. Assuming the cosmos is being generated at a pace revealed by the constancy of the speed of light, then when an "object" (as a flow-through, standing wave) approaches the speed of light, it will necessarily run into itself in the process of becoming itself, and this will produce a literal compression of its dynamic structure in its direction of motion. No object (as a standing wave) can move ahead of the flow that continuously regenerates both the object and the surrounding cosmos. *As an object (or flow-through subsystem of the larger standing-wave cosmos) tries to move ahead of the pace at which it is becoming manifest, it will progressively run into itself becoming itself—a self-limiting process that produces the increasing physical compression, time dilation, and mass predicted by relativity theory.* Although these scientific speculations do not constitute proof for continuous-creation cosmology, they do suggest it may be highly congruent with new findings emerging from physics. For a further discussion, see my article, "The Living Cosmos: A Theory of Continuous Creation," *ReVision,* Summer 1988.

all motion must be orchestrated into a unified whole to produce the unbroken consistency and seamless structure of our universe. Because all is flowing movement, the unfailingly precise correlation of all motion—large and small, near and far—is essential to establish and maintain stable material forms with lawful patterns of interaction. From the movements within the smallest atoms to that of the largest galaxies, every aspect of the cosmos must be precisely synchronized and coordinated to achieve the steady manifestation of the world about us. *If all is in motion at every level, and all motion presents itself as a coherent and stable pattern, then all that exists must be profoundly orchestrated. All flows must comprise one grand symphony, a single creative expression—a uni-verse!*

CONTINUOUS CREATION AND THE PERENNIAL WISDOM

As mentioned earlier, the idea of continuous creation is not new. Over the centuries individuals from spiritual traditions from around the world have penetrated deeply into the nature of reality and have described the universe around us as being re-created anew at each instant. Here's a sampling of these insights:

> The teachings of Jesus burst with new meaning when considered from the view of a continually arising cosmos. To say "the Kingdom of Heaven is spread out before us" makes sense if the cosmos is being ceaselessly regenerated from out of the infinite depths and power of the Meta-universe. The great Christian mystic Meister Eckhart gives this striking description of continuous regeneration of the cosmos: "God is creating the entire universe, fully and totally, in this present now. Everything God created . . . God creates now all at once."[14] From the modern Christian tradition we have the related insights of Matthew Fox and his "creation spirituality."

Fox says that creation spirituality considers the ever-moving center of the historical moment—the Eternal Now—as the precise center of an actual, ongoing process of cosmic-scale creation.[15]

The highly respected Zen scholar and teacher D. T. Suzuki writes, "My solemn proclamation is that a new universe is created every moment."[16] Elsewhere he writes the following, "All things come out of an unknown abyss of mystery, and through every one of them we can have a peep into the abyss."[17] Also from the Zen tradition we have this unequivocal statement from Alan Watts: "The beginning of the universe is now, for all things are at this moment being created, and the end of the universe is now, for all things are at this moment passing away."[18]

The acclaimed scholar of the world's mythical traditions, Joseph Campbell, writes, "Things are coming to life around you all the time. There is a life pouring into the world, and it pours from an inexhaustible source."[19]

From the ancient Greek philosopher and mystic Heraclitus we hear, "All things are in a state of flux." "Reality is a condition of unrest."[20] He also states that because one aspect of life is an eternal Becoming, the universe may be viewed as continually "flowering into deity."[21] In addition he says, "This world [is] . . . an ever-living fire, with measures of it kindling, and measures going out."[22]

In her classic study of mystical experiences Evelyn Underhill concludes that "mystics declare, as science does, that the universe is not static but dynamic; a World of Becoming." She also states that "this universe is free, self-creative . . . . divine action floods it"[23]

Buddhism describes the world as a flickering film being generated at a high rate of speed by an underlying Life-force. From the Tibetan Buddhist tradition the teacher, scholar, and artist Lama Govinda writes; "The world is in a continuous state of creation, of becoming, and therefore in a continuous state of destruction of all that has been created."[24] He also states that "this apparently solid and substantial world [is] . . . a whirling nebulous mass of insubstantial, eternally rotating elements of continually arising and disintegrating forms."[25] Namkhai Norbu, another esteemed teacher in the Tibetan Buddhist tradition, states, "All phenomena . . . no matter how solid they may seem, are in fact essentially void, impermanent, only temporarily existing. . . . From the enormously large, to the infinitely small, and everywhere in between, everything that can be seen to exist can be seen to be void."[26]

Islamic spirituality has a view called "occasionalism" that describes the universe as being continuously reborn in a series of unique occasions or events.[27] Al-Ghazzali, the great synthesizer of Muslim thought who lived in the 1100s, did not view our universe as an ancient structure, but rather saw it as being born anew at each moment—created out of nothing in a series of events by the will of Allah.[28] In this view nothing continues to exist unless God constantly re-creates it. This book that you are holding now will, in another instant, not be the same book but will be a new "occasion" of the book that went before it.

From China and Taoism we find that existence is viewed as an unfathomable mystery that is always arising anew. The Tao is the sustaining Life-force and the mother of all things; from it, all "things rise and fall without cease."[29] In Taoism the highest wisdom is to come into harmony with this flow. Alan Watts says, "The general idea behind Tao is that of . . . the perpetual movement of life which never for a moment remains still. . . . The highest form of man is he who adapts himself to and keeps pace with the movement of Tao."[30]

The Aborigines of Australia believe the universe has two aspects. One aspect is ordinary reality and the other aspect is the

"Dreamtime" reality from which the physical world is derived. In Aboriginal cosmology the everyday reality of people, trees, rocks, and animals is "sung into existence" by the power of the Dreamtime—and the Dreamtime needs to continue unabated if the ordinary world is to be upheld and maintained.[31]

In Hinduism reality is viewed as being continuously upheld by a divine Life-force. In the words of Huston Smith, scholar of the world's religions, "All Hindu religious thought denies that the world of nature stands on its own feet. It is grounded in God; if he were removed it would collapse into nothingness."[32] The respected scholar of Indian art and civilization Heinrich Zimmer provides a similar description of the Hindu cosmology: "There is nothing static, nothing abiding, but only the flow of a relentless process, with everything originating, growing, decaying, vanishing."[33] Hindu mythology says the cosmos is born anew at each moment through the cosmic dance of the God Shiva: "All the features and creatures of the living world are interpreted as momentary flashes from the limbs of the Lord of the dance."[34] Shiva is the cosmic dancer who "embodies in himself and simultaneously gives manifestation to Eternal Energy. The forces gathered and projected in his frantic, ever-enduring gyration, are the powers of the evolution, maintenance, and dissolution of the world. Nature and all its creatures are the effects of his eternal dance."[35] Finally, a revered Hindu teacher, Sri Nisargadatta Majaraj, taught, "The entire universe contributes incessantly to your existence. Hence the entire universe is your body."[36]

Christians, Buddhists, Hindus, Muslims, Taoists, mystics, tribal cultures, and Greek philosophers have all given remarkably similar descriptions of the deep and pervasive dynamism of reality. These are more than poetic and metaphorical explanations: *The world's wisdom traditions are clearly describing a literal process of continuous creation.* Because we find this insight across cultures and across the millennia, it provides compelling evidence that humans have the ability to experience directly the continuous regeneration of the cosmos.

FLOW CONSCIOUSNESS AND
REALITY SURFING

Continuous-creation cosmology views enlightening experiences not as an altered psychological state that happens inside our brain but as a flow-experience that involves our whole being and occurs when we come into dynamic alignment with the cosmos in its process of continuous manifestation. When our moment-to-moment flow of awareness comes into dynamic alignment with the flow of the cosmos as it is being created, then we become identical with, and transparent to, that larger process. An enlightening awareness emerges naturally as we settle into our centered self-experience while simultaneously being mindful of the world around us. As we become quiet within ourselves and mindfully synchronized with the subtle flow of creation, we recognize that we are identical with the flow of Life-energy that gives rise to all that exists. *Because we and the cosmos arise together, when both are embraced in awareness, the two are naturally one in experience.*

An analogy suggests the nature of flow consciousness: When a boat is pushing against a river, a pressure wave rises up and stands between the boat and the flowing movement of the river. However, when the boat and the river are moving in the same direction and at the same speed, then there is no pressure wave, no interference pattern to mark out a boundary between the boat and the river. Similarly, when we quiet the pushes and pulls of our thinking mind and come into dynamic alignment with the flowing cosmos, then the pressure wave subsides that marks out a boundary between the experience of the larger cosmos and the experience of ourselves. With no interference pattern to stand between the experience of self and the experience of a flowing cosmos, we experience directly that we are an unbounded flow of awareness of cosmic proportions—hence the phrase *cosmic consciousness.*

The mentally constructed I-sense or ego or "thinking self" is generally so strong that it masks our awareness of the spontaneously given I-sense that is always bubbling up at the center of our experience. Through meditation we can learn the skills of reducing the distance between knower and known so that gradually we become transparent to our true nature as the Meta-universe. We cannot stand back and objectively know the Meta-universe, because that is what we are already. The only way to know it is to BE it. And when we come to the precise center of ourselves in the flow of continuous creation, we discover that our nature is eternal. In the words of Goethe:

> For what the center brings
> Must obviously be
> That which remains to the end
> And was there from eternity.[37]

There is never an end to looking for ourselves "out there." But there is always a middle, "in here" at the very center of our moment-to-moment experience. At the center a knowing presence exists with no need for confirming thoughts or external validation.

IMPLICATIONS OF
CONTINUOUS-CREATION COSMOLOGY

There is no island of stasis where we can stand apart from the flow of creation. We are totally in it and of it. As we awaken to the subtle presence of continuous creation, its all-inclusive nature touches and transforms every facet of life.

A Rebirth of Mystery in Nature

American Indian lore speaks of three miracles: the miracle that anything exists at all, the miracle that living things exist, and the miracle that living things exist that are conscious of their existence. Because we humans are conscious of our existence, we tend to focus on the third miracle and take the other two for granted. However, continuous-creation cosmology invites us freshly to appreciate the first miracle. The wonder that anything exists at all is not a onetime miracle but a continuously renewed gift, forever alive with mystery.

In recognizing the first miracle we can begin to reclaim the wisdom of our ancestors. Luther Standing Bear said that for the Lakota Sioux "there was no such thing as emptiness in the world. Even in the sky there were no vacant places. Everywhere there was life, visible and invisible, and every object gave us a great interest to life. The world teemed with life and wisdom, there was no complete solitude for the Lakota."[38] With a cosmology of continuous creation, nature again comes alive: A shining miracle exists everywhere. There are no empty places in the world. Everywhere there is life, both visible and invisible. All of reality is infused with wisdom and a powerful presence.

We can glimpse the flow of creation in small ways—perhaps in the shimmering radiance of the golden light of a late afternoon or in the luster of an old wooden table that shines with an inexplicable depth and glow. We can also witness the buzzing aliveness of creation in places that may seem far removed from nature—even a room filled only with plastic, chrome steel, and glass can display the flow of creation in the raw. In the gentle contemplation of any part of ordinary reality we can catch glimpses of the great hurricane of energy that blows with silent force through all things. Even empty space will sometimes disclose that it is an ocean of dancing aliveness—a subtle symphony of radiant architecture that has traveled an eternity to provide a context for matter at each moment.

An Expanded Sense of the Spiritual

Instead of seeing "God" as a grandfatherly being, continuous-creation cosmology sees the divine as an exquisitely creative, inexhaustibly intelligent, and infinitely aware Life-energy that is both immanent (manifestly present throughout the cosmos) and transcendent (present in ecologies that extend far beyond our cosmos). To view "God" as the divine Life-force that is manifest in all things brings a sense of the sacred into the immediate circumstances of all life. To also view "God" as the Meta-universe that transcends and sustains our material existence fosters a sense of the deep spiritual ecology from which our world originates and into which it returns, moment by moment. The traditional Western image of God as a separate Being "out there" is transformed into a creative and powerful Life-force that is simultaneously *personal* (upholding the most minute aspects of our physical existence at each instant), *impersonal* (giving all of creation great freedom to learn and grow in ways of its own choosing), and *transpersonal* (simultaneously transcending the dimensional boundaries of the cosmic system we inhabit).

Our spiritual challenge is not to reach beyond this world; rather it is to come into dynamic alignment with the world as it is and thereby to come into a living relationship with the divine Life-force. No matter how mundane the circumstance, no matter how seemingly trivial the situation, we can always become directly aware of the subtle hum of creation happening within and around us. When we discover that all beings are part of the seamless fabric of creation, it naturally awakens a sense of connection with, and compassion for, the rest of life. We automatically broaden our scope of empathy and concern when we realize that we are inseparable from all that exists. We no longer see ourselves as isolated entities whose being stops at the edge of our skin. We see that because we all arise simultaneously from a deep ocean of Life-energy, a vital connection is continuously present among all things.

The Spontaneously Given Self

We are standing on nothing but the flow-through of the Meta-universe. Like a person floating in an ocean that is millions of miles deep, we are dynamically suspended within a living, dimensional space that is infinitely open. If we trust that we will always be actively supported, then we can let go, releasing our mentally constructed self and relaxing into our spontaneously given beingness. We can then be nurtured by the flow of continuous creation rather than cut off from the Life-energy of eternity that is our original nature and true home. In the words of the fourteenth-century English mystic Julian of Norwich, "We have been loved from before the beginning."[39] We are created from love, in freedom, for love.

For each of us there is only one still point in this ever-returning world, and that is the spontaneously given self at the very center of our unfolding existence. By coming to the precise center of our flow of experience, we become the flow of continuous creation and encounter, as direct awareness, the Meta-universe. When the moving center of the self and the moving wholeness of the cosmos become centered in experience, then a window opens to reveal the All.

Our spontaneously given self comprises two, seemingly opposite, but actually complementary, aspects of reality. On the one hand, we and the cosmos are continually arising anew so that one aspect of our nature is a continual flow of *Becoming*. On the other hand, we and the cosmos arise from the perfect wholeness and unconditional love of the transcendent *Being* that is the Meta-universe. It is the paradox of ourselves as embodying both Being and Becoming that makes it impossible for us to limit and concretize our sense of self.

A New Sense of Human Significance

Humanity's powers are put into perspective when we realize that despite all of the technology we have developed, we do not know how to create from nothing a single flower, or a piece of rock, or a cubic inch of space. In contrast the Meta-universe continuously creates not only the structure of space-time, but billions of galaxies and trillions of planetary systems! This is creation on such a vast scale and with such elegance of design that it is utterly beyond our mental comprehension. We are simultaneously exalted and humbled when we see that, far grander than the scope of "Gaia's body" or the Earth as a self-regulating system, is the "Meta-Gaia" of the cosmos as a unified, living organism. To see the entire cosmos as an integrated, living organism brings a new sense of reverence and perspective to human life and civilization. Awakening to the miraculous nature of our universe can help us to overcome the species-arrogance and limited vision that now threaten our survival. There is such a subtle and purposeful intelligence in the design of the universe that it is only natural to think that humanity has an evolutionary purpose that is equally exalted. Our evolutionary potentials as a species are as magnificent and as subtle as the Meta-universe that continuously sustains our cosmos.

A New View of Society

Society mirrors our views of self and reality. On the one hand, if we think we live in a material universe that was set adrift billions of years ago and is governed by impersonal forces and accident, and that we have no higher purpose than physical survival, then it seems logical to view the accumulation of material wealth and power as the primary measures of meaning and success. In viewing ourselves as purely biological beings and the world around us as lifeless matter and empty space, it is only rational that we would be primarily concerned with the material aspects of life. If we don't expect more from life, we won't look for more. And when many people share our expectations, it sets up a self-fulfilling pattern of feedback. Social life then settles into a self-confirming process that overlooks the subtle miracle of continuous creation always pushing at the edges of our perceptions. On the other hand, if we view ourselves as beings of infinite scope that are intimately involved in a flow of cosmic creation, then our behavior will naturally shift to come into accord with this view of reality. We are participants in an unceasing miracle, and as we come to see this, we will tend to view all life as increasingly sacred and worthy of great respect. A new pattern of self-confirming expectations and behaviors will infuse society, and an upward spiral of coevolution will unfold.

SUMMARY

In keeping with the perennial wisdom, I do not believe the miracle of creation ceased the moment our cosmos came into existence. Since the Big Bang our universe has been continuously regenerated. For the entire span of evolution our cosmos has been sustained as a self-consistent and unbroken whole in an unutterably vast and intensely alive process of unimaginable precision and power. The cosmos is a single flowering of spontaneous creation, a gift that is continuously given anew. Awakening naturally occurs when our moment-to-moment flow of knowing comes into dynamic alignment with the flow of the cosmos as it is reborn at each instant.

COEVOLUTION AND THE META-UNIVERSE

The pathways taken by civilizations are profoundly influenced by their views of reality. Western civilizations have generally viewed matter as the primary reality and have tended to pursue material growth, with diminished attention to the nonmaterial side of life. Eastern civilizations have generally viewed consciousness as the primary reality and have tended to pursue spiritual growth, with diminished attention to social and material development. As we approach the turn of the century, it is evident that these two separate streams of development have exhausted their potentials. We now need the synergy and creativity of their combined powers. An integrative approach holds great promise for fostering the development of a mature, planetary civilization.

COEVOLUTION AND SYNERGY

From a coevolutionary perspective, civilizational development involves the simultaneous refinement of the material side of life (learning to do ever more with ever less) and the consciousness side of life (learning to touch life ever more lightly and gently):

- **Material Evolution**—By progressively refining the material side of life we touch the Earth ever more lightly with our material demands; we learn to touch others ever more gently and responsively with our social institutions, thereby promoting self-determination and self-governance; and we learn to live our daily lives with less material complexity and clutter, thereby freeing energy and attention for the cultural and spiritual dimensions of life.

- **Consciousness Evolution**—By progressively refining the consciousness side of life, we learn to release habitual patterns of thinking and behaving that make our passage through the world weighty and cloudy rather than light and spacious; we learn how to "touch and go" and not hold on, allowing each moment to arise with newness and freshness; and we learn to be in the world with a quiet mind and an open heart that appreciates the miracle of existence.

The synergy achieved through the simultaneous development of the material and the consciousness aspects of life is enormous. Material evolution provides the physical necessities of life that support the widespread realization of psychological and spiritual potentials. Consciousness evolution provides the insight, compassion, and creativity needed to orient material development into a sustainable pathway for the future. Coevolution is a balanced, middle path that integrates matter and consciousness into a coevolving spiral of mutual refinement. Rather than competing with each other, the material and the consciousness aspects are mutually enabling.

The coevolution of the material and consciousness sides of life is intensely synergistic. Like the double helix in the DNA molecule, these two aspects spiral around and support each other in their mutual ascent toward an ever-wider scope of integration and differentiation, unity and diversity. Each time the spiral returns to its former position at a higher level, self and world are known and realized more fully. By bringing these two powerful streams of human learning together into a synergistic whole, we can embark on an evolutionary journey that would not have been possible, and could not have been imagined, by focusing on either one in isolation.

From a coevolutionary view the purpose of life is not to dissolve into an undifferentiated unity of consciousness, nor is it to fragment into competing forms of material diversity; rather it is continuously to unfold an ever more diverse and simultaneously unified whole. Unity seeks diversity of expression as much as diversity seeks unity of connection.

MATTER AND CONSCIOUSNESS: A MUTUALLY SUPPORTIVE PARTNERSHIP

Matter and consciousness are the vehicles through which the clear Life-energy of the Meta-universe reveals itself to itself. In the same way that introducing smoke into a room can disclose the presence of otherwise invisible air currents, so, too, does the dynamic interaction of matter and consciousness reveal the otherwise invisible Life-force. Matter and consciousness are mutually supportive of each other. Matter can only know itself through its interaction with consciousness, and conversely consciousness can only know itself through interaction with matter. Just as a mirror reveals the presence of an object and conversely the reflection of the object reveals the existence of the mirror, so, too, do matter and consciousness mutually illuminate each other.

- Without matter to push against, consciousness—or the self-referencing potentials of life—would remain undisturbed and unknown. Matter makes life specific, tangible, and undeniable. The subtle feedback or mirroring qualities of consciousness are anchored by the concrete reality of the material dimensions.

- Without the self-referencing capacity that consciousness provides, matter would remain undisturbed and unknown. Without an observing potential, matter would never know of its own existence and would not have the ability to pull itself together into an organic system and evolve to higher levels of self-referencing and self-organizing functioning.

A meaningful reality requires the interaction of both matter and consciousness. Matter is blind in its evolutionary ascent without the knowingness that consciousness provides, and consciousness is blind in its evolutionary ascent without the grounding and aligning potential that matter provides. Evolution, then, is a mutually supportive process whereby matter seeks reflective affirmation of its presence through consciousness as much as consciousness seeks clarity of expression through matter. *The goal of evolution is not to move from matter to consciousness; rather it is to integrate matter and consciousness into a coevolving spiral of mutual refinement that ultimately reveals the generative ground from which both continuously arise.* Matter and consciousness support each other in their mutual ascent toward an ever-wider scope of integration and differentiation, unity and diversity. At very high levels of mutual refinement and dynamic alignment, the deep Meta-universe from which both continuously arise is directly evident as nondual or unified awareness.*

---

*This cosmology is congruent with philosopher Georg Hegel's view of a dialectical process that culminates in revealing our transcendent nature. In terms of dimensional cosmology, the dialectical interplay of culture and consciousness or of matter and spirit ultimately reveals the generative ground from which both arise. Hegel's view is summarized succinctly by Richard Tarnas: "God is not beyond the creation, but is the creative process itself. Man is not the passive spectator of reality, but its active cocreator. . . . The universal essence, which constitutes and permeates all things, finally comes to consciousness in man. At the climax of his long evolution, man achieves possession of absolute truth and recognizes his unity with the divine spirit that has realized itself within him."[1]

THE META-UNIVERSE

When our cosmos blossomed into existence from an area smaller than a pinpoint some fifteen billion years ago, it emerged out of an infinitely deep domain of vast intelligence, creativity, and energy. Modern physics is beginning to acknowledge and speculate on the nature of this generative ground. For example, the distinguished Princeton astrophysicist John Wheeler views space as the basic building block of reality. He states that material things are "composed of nothing but space itself, pure fluctuating space . . . that is changing, dynamic, altering from moment to moment." He goes on to say, "Of course, what space itself is built out of is the next question. . . . The stage on which the space of the universe moves is certainly not space itself. . . . The arena must be larger: *superspace* . . . [which is endowed] with an infinite number of dimensions."[2] It is this underlying and transcending "superspace" that is termed here the Meta-universe.*

The idea of a "superspace" has ancient roots. More than twenty centuries ago the Taoist sage Lao-tzu described it this way:

> There was something formless and perfect
> before the universe was born.
> It is serene. Empty.
> Solitary. Unchanging.
> Infinite. Eternally present.
> It is the mother of the universe.
> For lack of a better name,
> I call it the Tao.[4]

The perennial wisdom agrees that the nature of the Meta-universe is ultimately beyond description. Still, attempts have been made to

---

*In philosophical terms this is a *panentheistic* view, which holds that the being of "God" includes and penetrates the whole universe but also transcends or extends beyond our cosmos.[3]

describe its paradoxical qualities, for example, by Zen Buddhists who have penetrated deeply into the nature of reality through meditation.[5] Interestingly, their descriptions are surprisingly similar to those of Western physicists of the late 1800s, who were trying to articulate the nature of what was then called the ether, or the underlying structure of material reality.* Following are some of the key properties of the Meta-universe that seem congruent with insights from both East and West:

- **Profoundly creative**—Compared with that of humans, who do not know how to create a single flower or cubic inch of space, the creative power of the Meta-universe is of incomprehensible magnitude, depth, and subtlety.

- **Everywhere present**—The clear, unbounded Life-energy of the Meta-universe is present in all material forms as well as in seemingly empty space.

- **Nonobstructing**—The Meta-universe is a living presence out of which all things emerge, but it is not itself filled in or limited by these things. Not only are all things in it, it is in all things—mutual interpenetration without obstruction.

- **Utterly impartial**—The Meta-universe allows all things to be exactly what they are without interference. We have immense freedom to create either suffering or joy.

- **Ultimately ungraspable**—The power and reach of the Meta-universe is so vast that it cannot be grasped by our thinking mind. As the source of our physical existence, thinking process, and reflective consciousness, it is beyond the ability of our limited faculties to capture and concretize conceptually.

- **Beyond form**—The Meta-universe is the source of both material forms and the space-time within which those forms present themselves. Being the source and the context of all forms, the Meta-universe transcends the world of form.

- **No objective measurement**—It is impossible to prove the existence of the Meta-universe through objective measurements,

---

*Although the famous Michelson and Morley experiment in physics disproved the existence of ether as a *static and external* ocean that matter could push against, there are a number of attributes of ether theory that are highly dynamic and strikingly similar to the all-sustaining "void" of Eastern spiritual traditions.[6]

since it is the source and basis for all objective phenomena. The Meta-universe is of infinite dimensionality, so we cannot limit it to the few dimensions that we inhabit so as to measure "it."

- **More than nothing**—Because the Meta-universe can generate an entire cosmos with billions of galactic systems and life-forms, it is much more than simple emptiness.

- **Immanent**—The Meta-universe is not separate from us, nor is it other than the "ordinary" reality continuously present around us.

- **Transcendent**—The Meta-universe is of infinite dimensionality and reaches far beyond our dimensionally bounded cosmos.

- **Compassionate**—To experience the subtle and refined resonance of the Meta-universe is to experience unconditional love. Boundless compassion is the essence of the underlying generative ground.

These extraordinary characteristics of the Meta-universe are useful in awakening our everyday thinking to the profound miracle in which we are immersed. Here is an evocative portion of what the Chinese monk Shao said in describing what is called here the Meta-universe:

If you say that It is small,
It embraces the entire universe.
If you say It is large,
It penetrates the realm of atoms.
Call It one; It bears all qualities.
Call It many; Its body is all void.
Say It arises; It has no body and no form.
Say It becomes extinct; It glows for all eternity.
Call It empty; It has thousands of functions.
Say It exists; It is silent without shape.
Call It high; It is level without form.
. Call It low; nothing is equal to It.[7]

Because we tend to concentrate our attention on a very thin slice of social and physical reality, it is helpful to contemplate the ineffable nature of the Life-force that infuses every aspect of our existence as a way of expanding our appreciation of the extraordinary reality that is our home.

DISCOVERING OUR
TRANSMATERIAL NATURE

Our existence at each moment is a priceless gift spontaneously given by the Meta-universe. Because we are continuously created from the unbounded Life-energy of the Meta-universe, our essence is invisible—or more accurately, "transmaterial"—not because we are of lesser significance than matter but because we are much greater. To repeat an important analogy, just as clear light can be divided with a prism to reveal a rainbow of colors hidden within its transparent nature, so, too, can the clear light of the Meta-universe be divided into matter and consciousness so as to produce the rainbow of material expressions that is our manifest existence.

Because our core nature is infinite and eternal, it is very helpful to have a limited and firm environment to push up against to obtain impartial and clarifying feedback about who and what we are. Our hard material world is an unfailing friend in our process of self-discovery. Imagine living in a world where the ground and all footing was made of sand. Because of its soft and yielding qualities, walking on sand requires enormous energy. Instead of pushing against firm ground to jump and run, we would forever have to slog along, always slipping back and digging in, moving unproductively, and tiring easily. In a similar way, if all of life's surfaces were equally soft and yielding, then existence would be an endlessly frustrating, ambiguous, and toilsome struggle. We should celebrate the fact that we can stand on hard ground and interact with the firm surfaces of life—emotional and mental as well as physical. The "solidity" and hard edges of life provide us with clarity of interaction and learning. Assuming we are here to discover our basic nature as beings made from eternity, the material world provides an efficient and liberating environment where we can develop our ability to "know that we know."

The Meta-universe seems fiercely dedicated to the evolution of self-referencing beings that achieve self-knowing in their own time and manner. Because we must each live with ourselves for eternity, it is important that we discover and develop ourselves in true freedom. If we did not freely choose our own character and resonant identity, we could forever be at war with the being that "God" chose for us.

From a dimensional perspective there is a natural sequence to the awakening of our core identity. Initially we tend to identify ourselves with the physical and feeling aspects of existence. When we deplete the learning potentials of these, we move on to mentally oriented foundations for identity formation. In experiencing the limitations of an intellectual basis for our identity, we then move on to discover our capacity for reflective consciousness. We then identify ourselves with both the material and the consciousness aspects of existence, and our sense of self evolves into the back-and-forth dynamic between observer and observed, knower and known. As we come to the precise center of the polarity of knower and known, we discover that ultimately we are created from the Meta-universe, whose nature is infinite and eternal.

LIVING IN ETERNITY

Everything we do is unavoidably woven into the living field of resonance that is the Meta-universe. We each learn and act on behalf of the totality. What we learn is kneaded into the fabric of the infinite ecology of the Meta-universe. In the long sweep of cosmic evolution everything material will eventually vanish. However, the intensity, character, and texture of knowing-resonance that we experience and nurture within ourselves feeds into the deep fabric of the Meta-universe and thereby lives in eternity.

Because life can only proceed from life, the Life-force that animates us has existed since the beginning of all beginnings. This Life-force is inconceivably ancient—we have existed forever as a spark of life handed down through an unbroken and unutterably vast chain of evolution. Although material forms pass through their cycles of growth and decay, the animating Life-energy is passed along, without any break, from its unimaginably remote beginnings. Because we are, moment by moment, generated by the Life-force of the Meta-universe, our core nature is already eternal. It is our responsibility to nurture the glowing ember of life inside each of us into a flame of loving and creative expression. Eternal life cannot be earned—it is a priceless gift that has already been given. Our work is to grow in recognition of who and what we already are.

When we achieve self-referencing knowing—when we "know that we know"—we no longer require the density of our material world and physical body to center our knowing process upon itself. The body that provided the aligning structure to awaken self-referencing knowing can then die, and "we" will then endure as a subtle body of light and knowing. Because physicists describe matter as frozen light, it means that we are already living in a world, and a body, of light. Research into near-death experiences and the perennial wisdom both affirm that there are many domains or "ecologies of light" beyond our material cosmos where we can live.[8] As Jesus said, "There are many rooms in my Father's house." In the infinite ecologies of the Meta-universe there presumably exist many living and learning environments with a vastly enlarged opportunity for creative expression and loving communion. When we "know that we know," we are connecting with the deathless part of ourselves. When we acquire the capacity for double-wisdom, we can move into these more subtle realms of being and becoming, confident that we exist as a thread of knowing that provides the core resonance around which an appropriate body of light will coalesce.

If we don't recognize ourselves as knowing-resonance while we live in a physical body, we can overlook ourselves when our body dies. In the words of Jesus, "Take heed of the Living One while you are alive, lest you die and seek to see Him and be unable to do so."[9] In Buddhist terms, it is precisely while we have a physical body that we need to recognize our core nature as pure awareness or as the "ground luminosity."[10] In the words of the fifteenth-century Hindu and Sufi master Kabir:

The idea that the soul will join with the ecstatic
just because the body is rotten—

that is all fantasy.
What is found now is found then.
If you find nothing now,
you will simply end up with an apartment in the City of Death.
If you make love with the divine now,
in the next life you will have the face of satisfied desire.[11]

If we don't use this physical body and world to discover our capacity for self-luminous knowing, when we die we may look out from our subtle body of light and awareness and not recognize our refined existence. If we use our time in this precious body and physical world to come to self-referencing awareness, we anchor the gift of eternity in direct knowing. We can then evolve through the ever more subtle realms of the Meta-universe without forgetting ourselves.[12]

The perennial wisdom—the deepest human insights across the generations, across spiritual traditions, and across cultures—declares that we are here to learn of our unity with all of creation and of the profound aliveness at the core of our being. We are free beings whose purpose is to appreciate the miracle of life that has been spontaneously given and to contribute to its creative expression. The Meta-universe does not subject beings to great suffering to become self-aware only to have them dissolve into the great All. Instead we are learning the skills needed to function as ethical, self-referencing beings in the infinite ecologies beyond our material cosmos.

Having used the material world to encounter and develop ourselves, our bodies (as aligning structures of matter and consciousness) can then die, enabling our nonmaterial essence (as a body of light) to move into ever more subtle ecologies beyond this realm.* Once

---

*In his encyclopedic book on the further evolution of human potentials, *The Future of the Body*, Michael Murphy discusses the possible nature of postmortem existence. He says that if there is indeed an afterlife, it must involve more than undifferentiated awareness and that a wide range of capacities might continue to develop after bodily death. Among the "metanormal" perceptual abilities he describes that do not appear to depend upon our physical existence and therefore could continue to function in postmortem realms are: nonphysical tactile impressions and hearing; direct awareness of luminous beings; the telepathic exchange of emotions, thoughts, and intentions; the telepathic transmission of spiritual illumination; and communal ecstasies.[13] These few examples suggest a postbodily existence of great richness of

grounded in the double-wisdom of unconditional awareness, we can be self-knowing in these subtle ecologies without fear of forgetting ourselves. There is no more elevated task than to learn, of our own free will, to live in eternity.

Assuming we live in an ecology of life of infinite variety and depth, then our time in these physical bodies and this material world is brief and precious. Regardless of the specific potentials that might emerge in the further realms of existence, it is useful to remember what we might miss if we never again encounter the precise and vivid experiences offered by this world: the rough bark of a tree; the squeaking aliveness of grass directly underfoot; music made from instruments of wood and metal; ocean waves crashing against rocks; the taste and crunchy texture of an apple; the unwavering presence of a mountain landscape; the smell of freshly mown hay; and the sensitivity and yielding softness of human bodies. A countless number of ordinary miracles surround us. Often we take these miracles of clarity, texture, taste, smell, and sound for granted. Before seeking dimensional realms of greater ephemerality, freedom, and subtlety, it seems wise to appreciate, and learn from, the unambiguous qualities of the domain within which we now exist.

SUMMARY

When the knower and the known become a unified flow, we know that we are identical with the deep Meta-universe from which we continuously arise. Upon realizing that we and the cosmos arise together from the Meta-universe, we know that we share the same "body." We become aware of life as an ever-renewing wonder. No longer seeking escape from or domination over the world, but more conscious and direct participation within it, we move in gratitude through the vast body of Being that is the Meta-universe.

---

experience and evolutionary potential. Importantly, Murphy suggests that by cultivating these metanormal capacities in this life, we may be able to enrich and enhance our spirit-body's postmortem journey.

SACRED GEOMETRY AND STAGES OF GROWTH

Imagine that you are well known for your skilled and creative designs. The Meta-universe comes to you and says, "I really appreciate your work. Would you like to bid on a project to build a cosmos? Think about it." Then the Meta-universe hands you these ten construction and design requirements:

- First, you must create a transparent field within which to place the cosmos; fill it with an invisible structure or "geometry" that will keep everything in its proper place and proper time over billions of years.

- Second, you are required to construct the cosmos from nothing visible. You must build everything from what seems to be nothing as a testament to the miracle that anything exists at all.

- Third, instead of allowing the cosmos to emerge fully developed, you must engineer it so that it inflates from the size of a pinpoint and then grows quickly to contain a trillion galaxies, each with a billion or more stars.

- Fourth, design a field called "space-time" within which to place these vast, swirling clouds of billions of galaxies with their billions of stars and planets. Simple emptiness or the absence of matter won't do; the invisible fabric of space-time must be an "opening process" that continually provides the space and time within which matter can present itself. Guarantee the immense field of space-time will work flawlessly for billions of years.

- Fifth, design "matter." Take clouds of energy that are almost entirely empty space and have them flow through and around themselves in order to become stable, self-referencing forms. Despite their totally dynamic nature, give these whirlwinds of spacious energy the appearance and feel of "solid" matter.

- Sixth, design a cosmic information system that connects across trillions of miles, instantaneously. Anything that happens anywhere must be knowable everywhere, instantly.

- Seventh, design "life." Once you set it free, ensure that life-forms will tend to evolve towards ever more complex and conscious entities.

- Eighth, design planetary-scale ecosystems with billions of unique living organisms that can feed off each other in a process that can be sustained for billions of years.

- Ninth, design the cosmos with a pervasive capacity for reflective consciousness that ultimately enables organisms to achieve full self-referencing knowing. Connect this observing capacity directly into the functioning of the Meta-universe so that it produces a capacity for instantaneous, translocal knowing.

- Tenth, design a process that enables the cosmos to be re-created in its entirety, at every single moment. This flow of continuous creation must include the fabric of space-time, the capacity for thought, feeling, as well as reflective consciousness, and all forms of matter.

Contemplating these design requirements deepens our appreciation of the extraordinary power, wisdom, and subtlety embodied in our cosmos. We live in the midst of great and purposeful wonder. Our cosmos is a supremely elegant masterwork of continuous creation. In recognizing the magnificent feat of design and engineering represented by our cosmos, we are invited to look at the world around us with new wonder, awe, and appreciation.

SACRED GEOMETRY

The theory of dimensional evolution assumes that the universe is a living system held together through the cohering influence of a sacred geometry that pervades the cosmos and provides the organizing framework for the orderly manifestation of our "material" universe, as well as the organizing context through which life evolves. We live in a highly efficient universe of elegant design that performs multiple functions simultaneously: *The same geometry that structures physical reality also provides a series of perceptual environments that people and civilizations move through in a systematic learning process.* Each dimension represents a unique perceptual space and learning context for personal and social evolution. Each new dimension awakens a new set of perceptions and potentials that we are free to recognize and actualize—or not. By understanding the dimensional structure within which we are immersed, we can understand more clearly the direction and pattern of personal and social evolution.

Although modern science generally assumes there is no deeper significance to the dimensional geometry of the universe beyond its physical aspects, a contrasting view has ancient roots in human thought. In roughly 500 B.C. the Greek philosopher and mystic Pythagoras taught that the discoverable mathematical patterns in the universe were expressions of divine intelligence and intention.[1] He wrote that we are infused with, and surrounded by, an organizing intelligence that is expressed most purely in mathematical regularities and musical harmonies. He felt that by going to the center of our experience, we could know the organizing patterns and principles that permeate the universe. Pythagoras was apparently the first person to use the word *cosmos* to refer to the universe as a place of "harmonious and beautiful order."[2] Plato (who taught roughly a century later) was familiar with Pythagorean thought, and he, too, viewed the universe as being organized in accordance with transcendent "ideas" and mathematical principles: Above the door to his Academy he placed the words "Let no one unacquainted with geometry enter here."

In many other early civilizations around the world there was assumed to be an intimate connection between everyday life and the mathematical orderliness of the universe. Therefore the view that a highly purposeful field of geometry infuses the universe and structures our perceptions is an idea with ancient roots in human intuitions regarding the divine underpinnings of reality.

DEEP SYMMETRY

Although "dimensions" are generally viewed as referring to spatial extension (or the height, breadth, and depth of the world around us), dimensionality includes additional properties. For example, relativity theory has shown that there are unique time properties associated with each spatial point, so dimensions must contain temporal as well as spatial properties. Furthermore, when we go beyond purely physical systems to living systems that have a capacity for reflective consciousness, then added dimensions are required. Psychic research indicates that consciousness is not localized within the brain but can extend beyond the body.[3] Therefore additional dimensions beyond the four of relativity theory are required to provide the contexts within which the translocal properties of consciousness can exist and function.

I assume the reflective properties of consciousness both transcend and mirror the expressive properties of matter; in other words, the fact, depth, and dynamism of the material realm are mirrored by a corresponding fact, depth, and dynamism of consciousness. Because these two aspects are symmetrical, a conscious organism has the capacity to become fully self-referencing and self-organizing. If the consciousness dimensions did not precisely mirror the material dimensions, then the overall system of matter-consciousness would not be able to know itself reliably and would not be able to pull itself together into a coherent, self-referencing, and self-organizing system with the ability to sustain itself—presumably a primary evolutionary drive.

Because one dimension represents the collapse of the material and consciousness aspects of reality into a point, at least two dimensions are required for matter to "open up" and become explicitly manifest. Therefore this typology begins with the second dimension as the first "manifest" dimension. Given symmetry principles, three consciousness dimensions are assumed to reflect and connect the activity occurring in the three material dimensions, and together they work to create dynamically stable, self-referencing systems. Given a coequal and symmetrical relationship between matter and consciousness, a "division of labor" can be inferred between their respective functions:

Symmetry of Matter and Consciousness

Matter:	Consciousness:
2nd D: **Fact** of material existence	5th D: **Fact** of knowing
3rd D: **Depth** of material existence	6th D: **Depth** of knowing
4th D: **Dynamism** of material existence	7th D: **Dynamism** of knowing

The geometry infusing the universe appears to be neither arbitrary nor superficial—it is a sacred geometry of exquisite subtlety, depth of design, and elegance of purpose. A dimensional geometry is extraordinarily democratic. It has no political or religious bias, it overtly favors no one, and it is easily disclosed to all. Geometry is impartial: it is not swayed by whether a person is a Buddhist, Christian, or Muslim. Dimensionality simply creates a spatial, temporal, and reflective structure and allows individuals and civilizations to fill it out as they choose.

DIMENSIONAL EVOLUTION

The theory of dimensional evolution suggests that our primary task is to move through a series of expanding dimensional contexts that enable us to develop our capacity for self-referencing knowing, both personal and social. Each dimensional stage represents an integrated pattern of technology, culture, politics, perceptions, motivations, and values. All the major elements of each stage tend to be internally consistent with and supportive of one another. A dimensional stage can endure as a stable, self-reinforcing system for hundreds or thousands of years before its success creates conditions of crisis that push both individuals and societies to a more inclusive level of perception and action. Problems arise at one dimensional level that can only be resolved at a more comprehensive level, and there is a strong push to shift upward to a more embracing perceptual paradigm. A culture is not allowed rest with the completion of a given stage of dimensional development; it is compelled by the crises generated by its success to move to the next dimensional stage in order to cope with its untenable predicament. A higher dimensional context then provides a new way of seeing how to cope with the stresses created by the exhaustion of the previous dimension's evolutionary potentials. Evolution is a self-driving process.

There is an intimate connection between the personal and the social aspects of dimensional evolution. As individuals we are seldom encouraged to advance in our levels of dimensional understanding beyond that which is the norm for the civilization in which we live. For example, in an agrarian civilization a three-dimensional perceptual outlook would be required, but no more would be expected—and a majority of persons would easily settle into this dimensional norm. When a more inclusive perceptual context becomes the common sense of the culture, then a majority of persons will work diligently to become educated into the perceptions and assumptions common to this new frame of reference. As civilizations advance dimensionally, they carry entire populations along in a massive learning process. The civilizational context invisibly and naturally draws out learning that individuals may not have been motivated to accomplish on their own.

Evolution moves through a nested set of dimensions that are mutually interpenetrating yet noninterfering with one another. Each smaller or interior dimension fits precisely within more embracing dimensions. The interrelation of dimensions is analogous to a flat, two-dimensional circle nested exactly within the center of a three-dimensional sphere, giving the circle total freedom to move within the context of the sphere. Similarly, each dimension provides freedom of expression for the unique qualities and potentials of other dimensions.

The limited scope of each dimension or perceptual paradigm produces graspable chunks of experience and learning. We are not given everything to learn all at once, but can instead acquire knowledge in useful stages and in environments that are appropriate to what we can reasonably assimilate. The Meta-universe seems to have designed the series of dimensional stages in order to create an optimal flow of learning for achieving self-referencing beings and civilizations. By growing into each new dimensional context, we come to an increasingly more inclusive sense of ourselves and reality. As each dimensional stage builds upon and internalizes the learning of the preceding stage, it creates an ever more integrated system in which a person or society is able to function ever more fully in a self-determining and self-aware manner.

The theory of dimensional evolution can be thought of as a "paradigm of paradigms" or as a *meta-paradigm,* containing seven paradigms of perception. Despite its scope, this is not a comprehensive view of evolution. For example, this theory does not address biological transformations achieved through natural selection or directed mutation.

FREEDOM TO EVOLVE

The freedom to make mistakes and to learn from our actions is fundamental to dimensional cosmology. The Meta-universe does not interfere with our actions and learning. We humans can devastate the
ecology of the planet, drive into extinction millions of life-forms, and
doom a billion or more humans to lives of utter poverty and desperation—and still the Meta-universe will not intrude. The fierce and un-
compromising liberty we have to make mistakes demonstrates how
much our actions do in fact matter. With no benevolent deity to intervene and soften the suffering of life, or to reduce the destruction of
the environment, or to incline humanity in a more altruistic direction,
we are obliged to recognize the immense gift of freedom that is given
to us.

It is important that we grow in freedom. If we did not freely
choose our unique self and societal existence, then we could forever
be in conflict with the Life-force that selected our identity for us. As
we evolve through the infinite ecologies of the Meta-universe, it is
important for us to know that our journey began in freedom. From
our first awakening as self-reflective beings, it is vital that we know we
have woven our lives together in a manner, and with a character, that
is of our own choosing.

Because we have been given the immeasurable gift of an un-
formed life in the context of great freedom, it is unavoidable that
hardship will result from the unconscious desires and fears that initially motivate many of our actions. Suffering is the intimate partner
of immense freedom combined with limited awareness. Life is a pack-
age bargain. If we celebrate our freedom, then we should not curse
the pain and distress of our world. We are here to grow in compassion
and respond to that suffering. Reality is not an illusion or a game. It is
a process that grinds through living systems in a fierce and unrelenting flow of learning. The undeniable reality of needless suffering
teaches us compassion and responsibility, awakening these qualities
within free individuals.

In describing the nature of our freedom, it is important to distinguish between the *impartial* universe described by dimensional evolution and the *indifferent* universe described by contemporary science:

- **Traditional scientific cosmology**—Mainstream science generally assumes that our universe is indifferent to the human agenda. Fifteen billion years after its apparent birth, the universe is now viewed as a cold and violent place that is blind and deaf to subjective human existence and needs—a platform for our physical existence and little more. Our implied agenda, then, is to "do the best we can" to cope within a cosmos indifferent to our existence and evolution.

- **Continuous-creation cosmology**—Where traditional science sees a universe that is indifferent and uncaring, continuous-creation cosmology sees a universe that is impartial and noninterfering. Our universe is deeply caring but intent upon giving us the precious freedom we need to develop our unique capacity for reflective self-determination. The universe exemplifies a masterful and elegant design throughout that seems entirely intent on supporting our process of becoming self-referencing beings and civilizations.

After giving us the priceless gift of existence, the Meta-universe demonstrates its great compassion by not interfering in our choices, whether personal or planetary.

SUMMARIZING THE THEORY OF DIMENSIONAL EVOLUTION

Dimensional evolution is not a single theory but an intertwined pattern or system of theories. Summarized below are a dozen elements that are at the heart of this theory:

1. **Meta-universe**—Before the Big Bang that gave birth to our cosmos there existed an unimaginably vast, incomprehensibly intel-

ligent, and infinitely creative Life-force that chose to bring our cosmos into manifest existence. It is the Meta-universe that created, and now continuously sustains, our cosmos as a unified organism. It is quite conceivable that the Meta-universe has created an array of cosmic systems of which ours may be only one.

2. **Sacred geometry**—An invisible geometry provides the organizing framework for physical reality and also forms a nested series of perceptual environments through which people and civilizations move in a learning process. Each succeeding dimension presents a new perceptual space and learning context for personal and social development. Because we live in and are constructed from a multidimensional reality, it is natural that we can experience directly many more dimensions than we can describe conceptually.

3. **Double-wisdom**—Our highest potential as a species is embodied in our name *Homo sapiens sapiens*. Humans have the potential for double-wisdom or "knowing that we know" (which is pure, self-validating awareness).

4. **Trinity**—Reality is composed of three aspects: matter, consciousness, and pure awareness. Matter and consciousness are coequal and always arise together in a way that is mutually revealing of one another. At high levels of mutual refinement the matter-consciousness system reveals the Meta-universe, or the generative ground of pure awareness from which both arise.

5. **Coevolution**—Matter always arises with the mirroring potential of consciousness, and consciousness always arises with the expressive potential of matter. Being coequal, matter and consciousness naturally coevolve. Our challenge is to unfold both in concert with each other and to move through a series of perceptual paradigms that develop our unique character and ultimately disclose that we are continuously created from—and therefore identical with—the Meta-universe.

6. **Ephemeralization**—As evolution proceeds, both the material and the nonmaterial aspects of life grow in refinement and complexity. The material side of life becomes lighter, more aesthetic, more articulate, and more refined, and simultaneously the nonmaterial side of life (the capacity for love, musical and artistic expression, and so on) also becomes more refined, cultivated,

and expressive of subtlety. The progressive simplification of the material side of life enables societies to shift an increasing proportion of attention to the nonmaterial side of life (the domain of psyche, culture, and spirit). With progressive ephemeralization, basic needs (such as ensuring security and survival) can be met with proportionately smaller increments of energy and resources, thereby freeing time, energy, and creativity for higher pursuits (such as self-actualization and cultural advancement).

7. **Symmetry**—Given a coevolving reality, we should expect to find an intimate reciprocal relationship between the material and the consciousness aspects. If the consciousness dimensions did not precisely mirror the material dimensions, then the overall system of matter-consciousness would not be able to know itself fully and therefore would be unable to pull itself together into a coherent, self-referencing, and self-organizing system.

8. **Continuous creation**—The entire cosmos is a unified system—a living organism—that is being continuously re-created in its entirety by the flow-through of an unimaginable amount of energy in a process of extraordinary precision, patience, and power. The fact that anything exists at all is an ongoing miracle of creation. Because all is energy in motion, for the world to appear stable and solid, the completely flowing nature of the universe must be profoundly orchestrated and coordinated. All flows must comprise one grand symphony, a single creative expression—a uni-verse.

9. **Holographic interpenetration**—In a holographic cosmos a change anywhere results in a change everywhere. With holographic interpenetration, all is within all. At each instant the totality is fully present within and expressed through each part, and each part is fully connected with the whole. Beyond the local causality of physical systems, an instantaneous, nonlocal causality functions to connect the immensely vast cosmic system into a single, living organism.

10. **Self-organizing systems**—The torus is the simplest geometry of a self-referencing system and suggests how the material and consciousness dimensions work together to create a stable system from flowing processes. The torus also symbolizes our paradoxical nature: On the one hand, at the center we are

completely open to and connected with the flow-through of infinite Life-energy. On the other hand, we are each differentiated, self-referencing systems that uniquely reveal and express that Life-energy.

11. **Radical freedom**—The universe does not interfere with the choices we make. Within broad limits of human psychology and planetary ecology, we can evolve in whatever way, and with whatever timing, we want. We learn through our mistakes, and we are free to make mistakes of planetary proportions. Suffering is the inevitable result of our great powers combined with limited experience and a still-maturing consciousness. We are here to learn how to live ethically in the infinitely deep ecology of eternity.

12. **Stages of development**—Just as there are stages in the development of a child into adulthood, so, too, are there stages along the way as we progress toward our maturity as a planetary civilization: (1) For several million years our humanlike ancestors lived in the twilight of awakening. (2) Then, roughly 35,000 years ago, we became decisively aware of the fact of our bodily existence and, with a *sensing consciousness,* we made a dramatic leap forward in our ability consciously to appreciate our existence and in turn to develop advanced tools, artistic expressions, trading networks, and so on. (3) Roughly 10,000 years ago we moved into the agrarian era and, with an agricultural surplus and a *feeling consciousness,* we eventually began to build city-state civilizations. In this era we developed astronomy, writing, the priesthood, kings, warfare, mathematics, and so on. (4) Approximately 300 years ago advances in science and a *thinking consciousness* enabled humanity to achieve unprecedented understanding and control of nature and thereby the ability to build urban-industrial civilizations that are currently devastating the biosphere of the planet. (5) In the present time we are seeing the awakening of a *reflective consciousness* that is able to observe with detachment the crises created by the industrial era and then to work for an entirely new level of human communication and reconciliation around a sustainable pathway into the future. (6) Once we develop a shared vision of, and commitment to, a sustainable future, we must then actually build that future, and this will foster an *oceanic consciousness*

and deep bonding among the human family. (7) Once we are secure in knowing that we can maintain ourselves into the indefinite future, we will then be challenged to move beyond maintaining ourselves to continuously surpassing ourselves by learning how to liberate our creative potentials as a human family. In this stage we will develop our capacity for *flow consciousness*, which is able to balance creative diversity with a sustainable unity. (8) With our creativity harnessed as a force for synergistic evolution, a wisdom-culture will emerge with *integrative awareness* and the perspective, compassion, and creativity to endure, perhaps for millions of years into the future. By becoming established in the spaciousness and harmonious flow of the eighth stage our evolutionary journey can begin again, with new dimensions of learning to explore with potentials we can scarcely imagine.

PERSONAL AND PLANETARY AWAKENING

Throughout history human evolution has enjoyed long periods of stability followed by accelerated transitions that lead to new levels of perception and social organization. Now, at the close of the twentieth century, we are in the midst of a quantum leap in the coevolution of humanity's culture and consciousness. We have reached a choice-point, and the decisions we make during this extraordinary time of transition will reverberate into the distant future.

The human family will not reach its maturity automatically. There are no free gifts in evolution. Although this book has emphasized the unfolding of entire civilizations, I believe the basic agent of evolution is at every step the individual. Humanity can reach no higher than the social fabric that can be woven together from the synergy of our individual lives. Each person is a vitally important and unique agent in the process of planetary evolution. Now is the time to invest our enthusiasm in the conscious coevolution of life on Earth, for it is only through our individual awakening and creative action that the Earth will awaken as well.

PART III

APPENDICES

$\mathcal{A}$PPENDIX I:
CORRELATIONS WITH
PSYCHOLOGICAL THEORIES
AND SPIRITUAL TRADITIONS

Although the theory of dimensional evolution is grounded in a sacred-geometry and process-view of reality, it is highly congruent with the stages of human development described by Western psychology and Eastern meditative traditions. Because these embody an enormous literature with subtle and wide-ranging theories, it is not my intention to describe the correlations between them and dimensional theory in any depth. However, it is important to describe briefly how the theory of dimensional evolution is compatible with and informed by major psychological theories and spiritual traditions.

For this brief overview I will draw upon: the Western psychology of Mihaly Csikszentmihalyi; the spectrum psychology of Ken Wilber;[1] the philosophy and history of human consciousness of Jean Gebser;[2] the humanistic psychology of Abraham Maslow;[3] the Hindu philosophy and meditative insights of Sri Aurobindo;[4] the Christian tradition, and a range of Buddhist traditions.[5] These will be sufficient to illustrate how the stages of dimensional evolution are not arbitrary but are in accord with well-established views from both Western psychology and the perennial wisdom of the world's spiritual traditions. Generalizing, the initial stages (second through fourth dimensions) seem consistent with the views of Western psychology and the later stages (fifth through eighth dimensions) seem congruent with insights from major meditative traditions.

Mihaly Csikszentmihalyi is the former chairman of the Department of Psychology at the University of Chicago and has done extensive research on what he calls the psychology of optimal experience. He writes, "There is a consensus among psychologists . . . that people develop their concept of who they are . . . according to a sequence of steps."[6] Because this sequence so closely parallels the first five stages described by dimensional theory, it is useful to quote his conclusions directly:

> Each man or woman starts with a need to preserve the self, to keep the body and its basic goals from disintegrating. At this point the meaning of life is simple: it is tantamount to survival, comfort, and pleasure. When the safety of the physical self is no longer in doubt, the person may expand the horizon of his or her meaning system to embrace the values of a community— the family, the neighborhood, a religious or ethnic group. This step leads to a greater complexity of the self, even though it usually implies conformity to conventional norms and standards. The next step in development involves reflective individualism. The person again turns inward, finding new grounds for authority and value within the self. He or she is no longer blindly conforming, but develops an autonomous conscience. At this point the main goal in life becomes the desire for growth, improvement, the actualization of potential. The fourth step, which builds on all the previous ones, is a final turning away from the self, back toward an integration with other people and with universal values.

The stages of growth outlined in this book follow this pattern closely, but expand the description of later stages in ways that are consistent with insights from meditative and contemplative traditions. With this as background, here are the correlations between the dimensional stages of development and those described by respected psychologists, contemplatives, and philosophers:

- The first stage is that of a **contracted or embedded consciousness** and is characteristic of the prereflective consciousness of our human ancestors. This does not mean that our early human ancestors were completely lacking in a sense of self (animal research shows that even chimpanzees have a basic capacity for self-recognition); rather the dominant mode of being and behaving was characterized by a largely unconscious fusion of self and world. In Gebser's terms this is the stage of "archaic consciousness," where the reflective capacity is latent but has not yet emerged as a distinct psychological structure. Archaic psychology seems characteristic of the consciousness of presapient humans, such as *Australopithecus africanus*. In Wilber's typology this is the stage of an "uroboric" consciousness that is embedded within nature and dominated by animal impulses. Overall, a sense of self has not yet emerged that is clearly differentiated from the rest of nature.

- The second stage is characterized by the **surface consciousness** of an awakening hunter-gatherer who is flat up against the world. This is the first stage in the awakening of reflective consciousness and represents what Gebser calls magical consciousness where a rudimentary and childlike self-sense predominates. With no distinct sense of time or causality, there is a feeling of intense immediacy to life-experience—and this adds to its magical quality. In Wilber's typology the second stage corresponds with what he calls the "typhonic" self, whose identity is associated with one's body and physical existence. With this stage there is a breakthrough that enables the body-self to stand back from immersion within nature and to begin to identify itself as a differentiated or separate being. Wilber generally associates the typhon with the period of the earliest *Homo sapiens* (Neanderthal and Cro-Magnon). In Abraham Maslow's hierarchy of needs, this stage would correspond to the person whose needs are dominated by the search for physical security and survival.

- The third stage is that of the **depth consciousness** of the agrarian-based civilizations and seems to correspond to what Gebser calls the "mythic consciousness" and what Wilber terms the "membership self." In the mythic-membership stage there is a growing capacity for imagination, empathy, and an emotional life with a language to represent it. In

being able to describe emotional qualities and distinctions, there is growing depth of conscious experience and a deepening sense of self and community. With an expanding verbal representation of the world, reality
increasingly acquires spatial and temporal structure and extension. A se-
quential and cyclical time sense emerges gradually in both language and
consciousness, thereby enabling humanity to farm nature and to develop
agrarian-based civilizations. In terms of Maslow's hierarchy, this stage
corresponds to the meeting of needs for "belonging" through a stable
pattern of relationships, particularly with one's extended family and local
community.

• The fourth stage is that of a **dynamic consciousness** characteristic
of the industrial era and involves the development of a thinking-based
sense of self. This stage seems to correspond to what Gebser calls "mental consciousness." Time expands beyond a sense of duration and natural
rhythm to embrace an open and progressing spiral—a view of time that
supports the perception of the potential for material progress. This is the
stage that Wilber calls the "mental-egoic realm" and is characterized by
a strong ego with mental and intellectual abilities for describing oneself
and the world in a logical manner. Strengthened conceptual and mental
abilities support a strong self-concept that is verbally defined. In terms of
Maslow's hierarchy, this is the stage where needs for self-esteem and
self-recognition are met. Through the power of the intellect and personal will, people achieve recognition for their worldly accomplishments
and thereby are able to differentiate themselves from others. Gradually
people will move beyond self-recognition needs to self-actualization
needs and seek to realize their unique capacities and potentials (in what
Wilber terms the "centauric realm").

• The fifth stage is that of **reflective consciousness** and is associated
with an era of global reconciliation and mass communication. In this
stage an observer-self stands distinctly apart from the integrated ego,
thereby establishing the polarity of knower and known or watcher and
watched. In the Christian tradition this stage seems to correspond to a
"witnessing" consciousness. Gebser has collapsed the next three dimensional stages into one stage and called it "integral consciousness."
Wilber, however, continues his spectrum, and reflective consciousness
seems to correspond to what he calls the "low subtle realm." This realm
marks the beginning of transpersonal consciousness, as the individual

now has the psychic tools to begin to stand back from complete identification with bodily based desires, emotions, and thoughts. Because an observer or witness is consciously present, it is experientially self-evident that the scope of one's true self extends beyond bodily desires, feelings, and mental activity. In Buddhist terms this seems to correspond to the conscious witness or observing self that is characteristic of Theravada teachings. This stage also seems to correspond to what Aurobindo calls an "illumined mind" that is able to transcend identification with thought through the penetrating clarity of consciousness.

• The sixth stage is that of **oceanic consciousness** and is associated with an era of global human bonding and building a future of mutually supportive development. In this stage consciousness seeks to know its origins and we dive into the very center and heart of the Meta-universe. As consciousness becomes the object of consciousness and seeks to know its own source, the infinitely deep ocean of Life-energy that infuses and sustains all that exists becomes self-evident. When we allow the arising of ordinary knowing to relax into itself, then knowing becomes self-appreciative. Given its infinite basis, knowingness is naturally experienced as "oceanic" or boundless. In Wilber's typology this stage seems to correspond to what he calls the "high subtle realm," where the experience of self dissolves into the divine Life-force and is permeated with feelings of great compassion. He also describes this as a domain of transcendent insight and absorption. In Christian terms this corresponds to the teachings of Jesus, whose highest commandment was that we should love God, others, and ourselves with all our heart and soul. In Buddhist terms this corresponds to the boundless compassion and loving-kindness of the Bodhisattva emphasized in the Mahayana tradition. This stage also seems congruent with what Aurobindo calls the "intuitive mind," which experiences the transcendent realms and the rapture of unbounded knowing.

• The seventh stage is that of **flow consciousness** and is associated with the surpassing era where human creativity is liberated. This stage seems to correspond to what Wilber calls the "causal realm," where the entire cosmic process is experienced as continuously arising. The eternal now is experienced as always fresh and alive with an abundance of time flowing through it and from it. In experiencing the self that exists prior to the world of forms, there is an experience of the unbroken continuity and eternal nature of one's being. In Buddhist terms this seems to correspond to the thread of knowing or continuity of connection that is emphasized in the Tantric tradition. The seventh stage also seems to correspond to what Aurobindo calls the "overmind," with its capacity for direct and unobstructed spiritual awareness.

• The eighth stage is that of **integral awareness** and is associated with a mature species-civilization that has become established in its capacity for double-wisdom, or self-organizing and self-referencing knowing. This stage seems to correspond to what Gebser calls realization of the "ever-present Origin," where a divine Life-force is seen to shine continuously throughout this world. In Wilber's typology this is the "ultimate realm" and emerges when a being awakens to the fact that he or she has always been the absolute Spirit whose radiance pervades all existence. One's being is experienced as existing beyond the world of forms and, at the same time, not being other than the entire world in its process of continual becoming. In Christian terms this stage recalls the statement made by Jesus that "heaven is spread out before us and we are not seeing it." The unity of this stage is so complete that it effortlessly embraces the seeming paradoxes of being and becoming, transcendence and immanence. In Buddhist terms this stage corresponds to the insight of the Dzogchen teachings that all existence is a shining manifestation of the spiritual radiance of the Meta-universe, whose original nature is pure awareness; in turn we know that we are continuously created from, and will live within, the enlightened, primordial Life-force forever. From the Hindu perspective this stage corresponds to what Aurobindo calls the "supermind," where "the divine unity is expressed through diversity, individuals are harmonized with their universal Ground, and personal will is joined with the cosmic action."[7] The supermind is not a different level but the foundation and ground for all levels.

Although dimensional theory is not derived from psychospiritual theory, this brief survey shows there is a very strong correlation between dimensional cosmology and Western psychology as well as Christian, Buddhist, and Hindu spiritual traditions. In exploring these correlations, it is important to demystify the mystical and remember that these seemingly elevated realms are within our immediate experience—they are not impossibly distant or remote but represent a heightened wakefulness to the miracle of life as it already is at the center of our "ordinary" awareness.* The fact that relatively few make a sustained effort to reach beyond the perceptual paradigm of their culture to discover these experiences should not blind us to the immediacy of their presence.

Different psychological and spiritual traditions reveal different facets of our existence and have different strengths. Each is valid for what it reveals. The theory of dimensional evolution offers a useful window onto the process of human development, both personal and social, but it is only one among many models of reality.

Although the theory of dimensional evolution is in accord with insights from both Western psychology and Eastern meditative traditions, there are significant differences that should not be ignored. In particular:

- **Potential for social change**—Eastern spiritual traditions (for example, Hinduism, Buddhism, Taoism, Zen) have arisen and matured within an agrarian context and have naturally assumed an unchanging material and social existence for the majority of people. Therefore they tend to be socially passive and place their emphasis on supporting a relatively few individuals in getting off the wheel of material existence through enlightenment. In contrast, dimensional cosmology assumes that development of the material and social aspects of life is integral to the unfolding of consciousness. It is a socially engaged cosmology that emphasizes the co-evolution of culture and consciousness in a mutually supportive spiral.

- **Consciousness/awareness differentiation**—Dimensional cosmology makes a crucial distinction between consciousness and awareness. *Consciousness* is assumed to arise in coequal partnership

---

*To illustrate the unpretentious nature of ultimate knowing, consider the teachings of Tibetan Buddhists, who are widely recognized for the sophistication of their insights, nurtured by many centuries of physical isolation and undistracted devotion to meditative traditions and practice. For example, in the Dzogchen tradition, the "supreme method" for recognizing our radiant and luminous nature is to concentrate continuously on "the ultimate nature of ordinary mind."[8] If we cut through the complexities of language to the core teachings, we find nothing more is necessary than to not interfere with our knowing capacity and to not stray from that knowing. The essence of even the most sophisticated path is of utmost simplicity.

with matter and to have an instrumental role—that of providing an appropriate reflective capacity for material systems at every scale. *Awareness* is assumed to be identical with the Life-force of the underlying Meta-universe and is characterized by unconditional knowing. At high levels of mutual refinement of matter and consciousness (as the experienced distance between observer and observed is progressively diminished), the Meta-universe is ultimately disclosed. These clarifying distinctions regarding the nature and role of matter, consciousness, and awareness are not always made; instead consciousness is sometimes described as being primary or more fundamental than matter and then equated with awareness, thereby leading to confusion about the nature of the evolutionary journey.*

- **Continuous creation**—Although the deepest teachings of each of the world's major spiritual traditions affirm the insight that all existence is regenerated anew at each moment, the idea that enlightening experiences emerge as a result of a literal process of bringing oneself into dynamic alignment with the cosmos in its flow of continuous creation is not emphasized in many spiritual teachings. Instead there has been a tendency to assume we are biological beings who evolve through different mental and psychological states of consciousness to reach interior insights about our connection with the All.

- **Cosmic purpose**—Dimensional cosmology views each being as a precious flowering of awareness through which the infinite achieves creative and knowing expression in the moment. In this

---

*For examples of persons who do not seem to differentiate between consciousness with an object and awareness (or consciousness without an object) see, for example: Larry Dossey, *Recovering the Soul* (New York: Bantam Books, 1989). Dossey states that "it is not possible to separate the concepts" of mind, soul, and consciousness (pp. 2–3). Another person who seems to equate the "ground of being" with "consciousness" is David B. Griffin (ed., *The Reenchantment of Science* (New York: SUNY Press, 1988), see pp. 126–127. Illustrative of persons who differentiate between matter, consciousness, and a deeper generative ground of pure awareness is the work of philosopher Renee Weber in her book *Dialogues with Scientists and Sages* (London: Routledge & Kegan Paul, 1986). Weber searched for the underlying unity of the universe in conversations with both scientists and mystics and concluded, "Neither matter nor consciousness are ultimate. Both have their source in something beyond themselves of which they are the outcome and expression, in which they are rooted and reconciled" (p. 15). Recall also the clear distinction between consciousness and awareness made by Stephen Levine in *Who Dies?* (New York: Anchor Books, 1982), p. 104.

view we are here to learn, in freedom, how to live ethically and creatively in the deep ecology of the Meta-universe. There are an infinite number of dimensions and self-organizing ecologies, each with increasing levels of freedom and potential for creative expression and learning. It seems natural that once we acquire the capacity for integrative awareness, we could evolve forever through ever more ephemeral bodies and ecologies in realms that extend beyond our cosmos. In contrast to this creative and open-ended view of purposeful evolution, some Eastern traditions tend to view the Meta-universe as being engaged in a great game of hide-and-seek where nothing evolves or changes in a fundamental way; instead the Spirit deliberately loses and forgets itself only to eventually return to itself by dissolving all distinct awareness in complete, undifferentiated wholeness after an immensity of time and play.[9] The purpose of human existence—both in its joys and in its suffering—is to provide the Spirit with endless cycles of divine fun and sport in an otherwise changeless universe.

- **Time frames for stages**—There are significant differences in how various people describe the stages of development. For example, Ken Wilber describes the "mental-egoic" stage as extending from roughly 1500 B.C. up to the present and then a hundred years or more into the future.[10] In contrast, I have described the stage of emotional/depth consciousness (third dimension) emerging around 3500 B.C., followed by the transition into the mental/dynamic stage of consciousness (fourth dimension) around A.D. 1500, which, in turn, is now being surpassed by the emergence of a witnessing/reflective stage of consciousness (fifth dimension) in the time frame beginning roughly 1970 to 2000. Clearly there are major differences in how the dimensional model and, for example, Wilber's model are anchored in historical experience. Major differences also exist between the historical stages described by Gebser and those that seem consistent with dimensional theory.[11]

In conclusion, while there are strong correlations between dimensional evolution and Western psychology and Eastern meditative traditions, there are a number of significant differences that should not be overlooked. A widely shared consensus about the specifics of an evolutionary cosmology for the species is still in the process of being discovered.

$\mathcal{A}$PPENDIX II:
MEDITATIVE ORIGINS OF
DIMENSIONAL COSMOLOGY

This cosmology has its origins in both extensive research and intensive meditation. I began research for this book in earnest in 1973 when I worked with Joseph Campbell and other scholars to describe the deep, archetypal levels of social evolution, both past and future.[1] This year-long project was a catalyst for twenty years of personal and professional exploration spanning a wide range of disciplines: anthropology, history, psychology, comparative religion, systems theory, philosophy, physics, economics, future studies, sociology, and more. My consuming interest was to understand the nature and direction of human evolution, both personal and planetary.

Despite years of research, no matter where I turned, I found only partial answers. I could find no satisfying vision of human evolution that embraced both the material and the spiritual aspects of existence. Although these years of scholarly inquiry provided a great deal of specific information to flesh out the view of evolution described here, the sacred geometry that constitutes the skeleton or organizing framework was a gift from the universe that emerged in May 1978 as the culmination of six months of self-directed meditation. Because this coevolutionary view of reality, identity, and society was born from an intensive meditative experience, and because I believe we all have access to comparable experiences, I've decided to share the origins of the organizing pattern at the heart of this book.

In late 1977 I had reached a crisis in my life and I decided to take a half-year retreat from the work I had been doing (primarily strategic planning, futures research, and policy studies for government agencies) and devote myself wholeheartedly to self-directed study and meditation. My goal was to come to a deeper understanding of age-old questions: What are we doing here? What are our highest potentials? Where is evolution headed?

Intensive mediation over the previous ten years had given me glimpses of insight into these questions. This meditation practice was based primarily on Buddhist approaches but included study of a number of other spiritual traditions—in particular, contemplative Christianity, Zen, Hinduism, and Taoism. In addition, for several years I had been a subject in a range of parapsychology experiments at a major think tank (SRI International) and had the opportunity to learn firsthand about the nature of our energetic connections with the universe. Finally, I accepted the Pythagorean premise that the aesthetic structure of the universe becomes self-evident when we come into authentic union with it. As I entered this self-directed retreat, I was confident that if I approached the cosmos with purity of intent and a one-pointed desire "to know," the universe would meet me halfway with insights commensurate with my intention—and intensity—to know.

Throughout the winter and spring of 1978 I spent weeks at a time alone in my home. Approximately half of this time was invested in formal meditation and quiet contemplation. The remainder of the time was spent reading dozens of books on subjects ranging from the world's spiritual traditions, physics, history, anthropology, psychology, and systems theory. Over a period of months I put up notes, charts, lists, diagrams, poetry, and pictures on the walls of my kitchen, living room, and bedroom. Gradually my entire home was transformed into a single quest and question.

By late spring the coherent picture of reality, identity, and social evolution that I was seeking had not emerged. Instead of finding clarity, I was more confused than ever. I felt overwhelmed with the mountain of ultimately disconnected information and ideas that had accumulated over the years. Missing was the wisdom and insight that could bring all the disorganized knowledge into an organic and living whole. Day by day and week by week I searched for resolution. Increasingly I felt that I was wasting precious time in a fruitless, idealistic pursuit.

With my allotted time running out, I finally made a decision based on roughly equal measures of unshakable confidence and utter desperation. I resolved to go to the end of this path by holding in consciousness the felt experience of all the questions now burning in my mind, body, and soul regarding the nature of reality, life, and evolution. I decided to hold fast to the experience of these questions until genuine insight and unifying awareness emerged, no matter what.

Physically rested and psychologically settled, on the morning of the first day of May, I proceeded with irrevocable determination and concentration. Moment by moment by moment I nurtured the felt experience of knowing (and intending to know) until it became a continuous thread of resonant experience that filled every aspect of my consciousness. With immense difficulty—second by second, minute by minute, and hour by hour—the pressure and sensation of this conscious intention "to know" was nurtured and focused.

Toward the end of the first day my experience was analogous to being inside a lighted hollow ball with fragments of mirrors covering the entire inner surface. Everywhere I looked, there was a mirror of consciousness to reflect back every aspect of my life and existence. Mundane and profane, loving and indifferent, caring and cruel, intellectual and emotional—everything was equally suitable for reflection in the mirror of consciousness. Only with utmost determination and unconditional self-acceptance could "I" stay with my self-experience and avoid endless distractions of judgment and imagination. Gradually the pressure of conscious intention began to penetrate through layer after layer of my mentally constructed being. That night I slept lightly and arose early to continue with meditation.

With single-minded concentration I moved ever deeper into this raw process of self-inquiry. As I stripped away uncountable layers of self-pretense and returned, again and again, to the core intention, a humbled being gradually emerged. By the evening of the second day all was constantly dissolving—even the mirror of consciousness that reflected my experience was dissolving and reconstructing itself second by second. All that existed was an ocean of living process in constant change. Nowhere was there anything that I could hold on to, or rely upon, or build upon. There was no fixed meaning, no fixed self, and no fixed reality to be found anywhere. Again and again and again I was forced to abandon everything I had formerly known and simply trust the purity of my intention to carry "me" through the constantly disassembling reality. The unbroken silence of these seconds, minutes, hours, and days now penetrated ever deeper, asking me to yield ever more until it felt as if nothing more could be surrendered. The second night seemed as if it could be the last of my life.

By the third day the thread of intention had grown into a living field of awareness with a distinct and palpable presence and texture. With growing ease, I moved within a flow of self-referencing knowing that had acquired a life and momentum of its own. Eternities of time passed as morning moved into early afternoon. Then, in a sudden and unexpected rush, the seeking of the past six months and the concentration of the past three days finally burned a hole through the "ego-I." In an instant of grace the years of accumulated questions and yearnings opened into a joyful, sacred, and crystalline space of Knowing. Within a single, exhilarating moment everything became transparently self-evident—throughout the entire range of my experience, all was in its proper place and "made sense." This knowing was direct, transconceptual, self-evident, and unmistakably clear. Accompanying this inner experience was a subtle radiance that bathed all that I could see with a soft light—the furniture, plants, and walls were all infused with a golden luster and glow.

For the next several hours I stood virtually rooted in one place, physically stunned and mentally shocked to the deepest core of my being. Everywhere I looked, I saw an infusing radiance of immense intelligence, creativity, and love. I saw, and directly experienced, that everything, including "empty space," is visibly alive. Space was not simply the absence of form but the formless expression of infinite possibility. I also saw that the entire fabric of material reality is arising in a flow of continuous creation, that a reflective capacity is present throughout the universe, that an organizing geometry of elegant symmetry and simplicity infuses the universe, and that our cosmos exists within an ocean of boundless compassion. From mid-afternoon until early evening, with utter simplicity and breathtaking directness, every question about human evolution that I had ever imagined was effortlessly answered. Again and again, I was overwhelmed by the miracle of "ordinary reality"—by the immensity and depth of Life in which we are immersed, by the aesthetic and functional structure of existence, by the infinitely deep and compassionate Knowing that permeates the cosmos, and by the visible presence of Life-energy in the flow of continuous creation. This experience left me feeling un-shakably confident in the deep integrity of creation, profoundly grateful, inexhaustibly happy—and finally home.

In the days following this experience transparent insights coa-lesced into symbolic patterns representing the major stages of human evolution, both personal and civilizational. These symbolic patterns became living seeds of insight with a life of their own that coalesced into specific concepts and ideas. Although I realized these concepts would never convey more than a faint echo of the original experience, during the next few weeks I wrote several hundred pages describing the theory of "dimensional evolution" that lies at the heart of this book.

In the years following this experience I have done extensive re-search to find the flesh of meaningful language to place on these transparent dimensional bones. Although this book is a blend of intu-itive insights and many years of wide-ranging research, my primary objective has been to communicate the essence of the originating experience as faithfully as possible.

Because Knowing is uniquely personal, this book is no more than an aligning system or guiding pattern for inquiry that may point oth-ers toward the truth of their own experience. In that spirit I share this book—and the description of its origins—in the hope that it will serve the path of discovery for others.

$\mathcal{N}$OTES

Introduction: The Challenge of Planetary Civilization

1. See poll by the Gallup Organization of Princeton, N.J., "World Poll Finds Concern About Earth's Health," reported in the *San Francisco Chronicle,* June 10, 1992.

2. Carl Sagan, *The Dragons of Eden* (New York: Random House, 1977), p. 7.

3. Dennet's views are described by Bruce Bower in his article "Consciousness Raising," *Science News,* Vol. 142, Oct. 10, 1992, p. 233. See also Daniel Dennet's book, *Consciousness Explained* (Canada: Little Brown, 1991). Dennet is a materialist and asserts that "the mind is somehow nothing but a physical phenomenon. In short, the mind is the brain."

4. Ken Wilber, *Up from Eden* (New York: Anchor Press/Doubleday, 1981), p. 7. The psychiatrist and experienced meditator Roger Walsh gives this description of the Eastern paradigm in an article describing the worldview of Wilber: "Consciousness creates matter and matter evolves through successive biological, mental and consciousness (spiritual) levels back to self-recognition." See: Roger Walsh, "The World View of Ken Wilber," *Association for Humanistic Psychology Newsletter* (May 1982), p. 5.

5. Various expressions of this integrative view can be found in the works of Georg Wilhelm Friedrich Hegel, Henri Bergson, and Sri Aurobindo. For further

discussion see, for example: Michael Murphy, *The Future of the Body* (Los Angeles: Tarcher, 1992), pp. 186–88.

6. The strengths and weaknesses as well as the integration of Eastern and Western views of reality are discussed at greater length in my book *Voluntary Simplicity*, 1st ed. (New York: William Morrow, 1981), Chap. 10.

7. The designation of modern humans as *Homo sapiens sapiens* is widespread; see, for example: Joseph Campbell, *Historical Atlas of World Mythology, Vol. I: The Way of the Animal Powers, Part 1: Mythologies of the Primitive Hunters and Gatherers* (New York: Harper & Row, Perennial Library, 1988), p. 22; Richard Leakey, *The Making of Mankind* (New York: E. P. Dutton, 1981), p. 18; Mary Maxwell, *Human Evolution: A Philosophical Anthropology* (New York: Columbia University Press, 1984), p. 294; John Pfeiffer, *The Creative Explosion: An Inquiry into the Origins of Art and Religion* (Ithaca, N.Y.: Cornell University Press, 1982), p. 13.

8. The term *double-wisdom* is now used in popular language to describe the core potential of modern humans; see, for example: Pfeiffer, *The Creative Explosion*, p. 13, as well as *Newsweek* (Nov. 10, 1986), p. 62; and (Oct. 16, 1989), p. 71.

9. Arnold Toynbee, *Civilization on Trial* (New York: Oxford University Press, 1948), p. 55.

10. Ibid., p. 213.

11. Johannes Kepler quoted in Carl Sagan, *Cosmos* (New York: Book Club Associates, 1980), p. 56. Paul Dirac, one of the modern theorists who developed the field of quantum mechanics, expressed similar sentiments when he wrote that "God is a mathematician of a very high order, and He used very advanced mathematics in constructing the universe." P. Dirac, "The Evolution of the Physicists' Picture of Nature," *Scientific American*, May 1963.

12. A cosmology of seven or more dimensions is not without precedent. For example, in physics, string theorists are working with models of ten dimensions. The seven-dimensional model presented here has the advantage of greater simplicity and a pattern of symmetry that is congruent with self-referencing and self-organizing living systems.

Chapter 1: Contracted Consciousness and the Archaic Era

1. Carl Sagan and Ann Druyan, *Shadows of Forgotten Ancestors* (New York: Random House, 1992). Also see the adapted article, "How Much Are We Like the Chimps? What They Tell Us About Ourselves," *Parade* (June 7, 1992).

2. See, for example: Donald R. Griffin, *The Question of Animal Awareness: Evolutionary Continuity of Mental Experience* (Los Altos, Calif.: William Kaufmann, 1981). Also see: the more recent article by Griffin, "Animal Thinking," *Scientific American* (Nov. 1991), where he states, "The versatility with which animals cope with the challenges they face often suggests they are indeed thinking about what they are doing" (p. 144). Finally, see: Michael Winkelman, "The

Evolution of Consciousness: An Essay Review of *Up From Eden* (Wilber, 1981)," *Anthropology of Consciousness*, Oct.–Dec. 1990.

3. Joseph Campbell, *Historical Atlas of World Mythology, Vol. I: The Way of the Animal Powers: Part I: Mythologies of the Primitive Hunters and Gatherers* (New York: Harper & Row, Perennial Library, 1988), pp. 22–23. For a further discussion of *Homo habilis* as the ancestor of *Homo erectus*, see: *World Atlas of Archaeology* (New York: Portland House, 1985), pp. 308–09.

4. Adrienne L. Zihlman, "Woman the Gatherer: The Role of Women in Early Hominid Evolution," in *Gender and Anthropology*, ed. Sandra Morgen (Washington, D.C.: American Anthropological Association, 1989).

5. Richard Leakey, *The Making of Mankind* (New York: E. P. Dutton, 1981), p. 89.

6. Ibid., p. 94.

7. Campbell, *Mythologies of the Primitive Hunter-Gatherers*, pp. 22–23.

8. John Pfeiffer, *The Creative Explosion* (Ithaca, N.Y.: Cornell University Press, 1982), p. 11.

9. These two different views are well developed in the following two articles: Allan Wilson and Rebecca Cann, "The Recent African Genesis of Humans," *Scientific American* (Apr. 1982); and Alan Thorne and Milford Wolpoff, "The Multiregional Evolution of Humans," *Scientific American* (Apr. 1992).

10. Richard E. Leakey and Roger Lewin, *Origins* (New York: E. P. Dutton, Inc., 1977), p. 117.

11. Robert Wenke, *Patterns in Prehistory: Humankind's First Three Million Years*, 2nd ed. (New York: Oxford University Press, 1984), p. 114; Victor Barnow, *Anthropology* (Homewood, Ill.: The Dorsey Press, 1979), p. 95. For an alternative view, see: Marvin Harris, *Our Kind* (New York: Harper & Row, 1989), p. 87. Harris suggests these Neanderthal burials were accidental rather than deliberate.

12. Campbell, *Mythologies of the Primitive Hunter-Gatherers*, p. 25.

13. Oswald Spengler thought that recognition of death was the stimulus for cultural awakening. See: Oswald Spengler, *The Decline of the West*, Vol. I (New York: Knopf, 1926).

14. Randall White, *Dark Caves, Bright Visions* (New York: W. W. Norton & Co., 1986), p. 18.

15. Ibid., p. 19.

Chapter 2: Surface Consciousness and the Era of Awakening Hunter-Gatherers

1. John Pfeiffer, *The Creative Explosion* (Ithaca, N.Y.: Cornell University Press, 1982), p. 41.

2. See, for example, Sherwood Washburn, "The Evolution of Man," *Scientific American* (Sept. 1978). Washburn states that *"our ancestors lived in a world that seemed to them small and flat* and that they could assess only in very personal terms" (emphasis added; p. 194).

3. Henri Frankfort et al., *The Intellectual Adventure of Ancient Man* (Chicago: University of Chicago Press, 1946; Phoenix Edition, 1977), p. 4.

4. Ibid., p. 6.

5. Ibid., p. 21.

6. For background on the subtle topic of time, see, for example: Marie-Louise von Franz, *Time: Rhythm and Repose* (New York: Thames and Hudson, 1978); Joseph Campbell (ed.), *Man and Time* (New York: Princeton University Press: Bollingen Series, 1957); and J. T. Fraser (ed.), *The Voices of Time* (New York: George Braziller, 1966).

7. Malcolm Margolin, *The Ohlone Way: Indian Life in the San Francisco–Monterey Bay Area* (Berkeley, Calif.: Heyday Books, 1978), p. 91.

8. Richard Leakey and Roger Lewin, *Origins* (New York: E. P. Dutton, Inc., 1977), p. 154.

9. Mary Maxwell, *Human Evolution* (New York: Columbia University Press, 1984), pp. 308–09.

10. Yearly gatherings among an extended clan indicate an awareness of seasons and cycles; however, this awareness was apparently not sufficiently developed at this time to enable people to anticipate annual salmon runs, for example.

11. Joseph Campbell, *The Masks of God: Vol. 3, Occidental Mythology* (New York: Viking Press, 1964), p. 7.

12. Ibid., p. 202.

13. Joseph Campbell, *Transformation of Myth Through Time* (New York: Harper & Row, 1990), p. 12; Marija Gimbutas, *The Goddesses and Gods of Old Europe* (Berkeley: University of California Press, 1982).

14. Margolin, *The Ohlone Way*, p. 141.

15. Ibid., p. 5.

16. Frankfort, *Intellectual Adventure*, p. 7.

17. Theodora Kroeber, *Ishi in Two Worlds: A Biography of the Last Wild Indian in North America* (Berkeley: University of California Press, 1967), p. 23.

18. Roger N. Walsh, *The Spirit of Shamanism* (Los Angeles: Jeremy P. Tarcher, Inc., 1990), p. 15.

19. Heinrich Zimmer, *Myths and Symbols in Indian Art and Civilization*, ed. Joseph Campbell (Princeton University Press: Bollingen Series, 1972), p. 151.

20. Margolin, *The Ohlone Way*, p. 153.

21. See, for example: Joseph Campbell, *Historical Atlas of World Mythology, Vol II: The Way of the Seeded Earth, Part 1: The Sacrifice* (New York: Harper & Row, 1988).

22. Pfeiffer, *The Creative Explosion*, p. 64.

23. Ibid., p. 146.

24. Randall White, *Dark Caves, Bright Visions* (New York: W. W. Norton & Co., 1986), see p. 32 for time scale for faceless figurines. *World Atlas of Archaeology* (New York: Portland House, 1985), see p. 172 for figurines with eyes.

25. *The World Atlas of Archaeology*, p. 172.

26. Richard Leakey, *The Making of Mankind* (New York: E. P. Dutton, 1981), p. 184.

27. Robert Wenke, *Patterns in Prehistory*, 2nd ed. (New York: Oxford University Press, 1984), p. 173.

28. Joseph Campbell, *The Masks of God*, Vol. 3, *Occidental Mythology* (New York: Viking Press, 1964), pp. 505–06.

29. For the less contemporary view, that these two aspects of the feminine archetype may have developed separately see, for example: H. R. Hays, *In the Beginning: Early Man and His Gods* (New York: G. P. Putnam's Sons, 1963), p. 51. Also see: Annemarie de Waal Malefijt, *Religion and Culture* (London: Macmillan Company, 1968), p. 139.

30. Some anthropologists see the period marked by the emergence of agriculture and settled villages prior to the rise of city-states as a distinctly separate stage of development. Although this is plausible when viewed in terms of physical forms and activities, when viewed in terms of perceptual evolution, this seems to be a transitional time between two major perceptual paradigms.

31. Carl Sauer, *Agricultural Origins and Dispersals* (New York: American Geographical Society, 1952), reedited and republished as *Seeds, Spades, Hearths, and Herds* (Cambridge, Mass.: MIT Press, 1969). See also Campbell, *The Way of the Seeded Earth, Part 1: The Sacrifice*, p. 12.

32. See, for example, Riane Eisler, *The Chalice and the Blade* (San Francisco: Harper & Row, 1987); Elinor Gadon, *The Once and Future Goddess* (San Francisco: Harper & Row, 1989); and Ken Wilber, *Up from Eden* (New York: Anchor Press/Doubleday, 1981).

Chapter 3: Depth Consciousness and the Era of Agrarian-Based Civilizations

1. Richard Leakey and Roger Lewin, *Origins* (New York: E. P. Dutton, 1977), p. 114.

2. Kenneth Cameron, *Humanity and Society: A World History* (Bloomington, Ind.: Indiana University Press, 1973), p. 83.

3. Richard Leakey, *The Making of Mankind* (New York: E. P. Dutton, 1981), p. 207.

4. Joseph Campbell, *Historical Atlas of World Mythology, Vol. II: The Way of the Seeded Earth, Part 1: The Sacrifice* (New York: Harper & Row, 1988), pp. 12–17.

5. Richard Critchfield, *Villages* (New York: Anchor Books/Doubleday, 1983), p. 210.

6. Carol Tavris, *The Mismeasure of Woman* (New York: Simon & Schuster, 1992), p. 77.

7. Joseph Campbell, *Mythic Images of Man*, unpublished background material prepared for the report *Changing Images of Man*, Center for the Study of Social Policy, SRI International, Menlo Park, Calif., June 1973, pp. 14–15.

8. Joseph Campbell, *The Masks of God: Vol. 3, Occidental Mythology* (New York: Viking Press, 1964), pp. 505–506.

9. Joseph Campbell, *The Masks of God: Vol. 1, Primitive Mythology* (New York: Viking Press, 1959), p. 146.

10. Campbell, Ibid., p. 147. Also, see, for example, Evan Hadingham, *Early Man and the Cosmos* (Norman: University of Oklahoma Press, 1984). He explains, "The order perceived in the heavens provided a model that gave form and meaning to the actions of people on Earth. Whether their needs and decisions revolved around the right time to plant corn or the proper place to raise . . . a pyramid to honor a dead lord, the cosmic order provided them with guidance and justification" (p. 245).

11. Campbell, *The Masks of God: Vol. 3, Occidental Mythology*, pp. 505–06.

12. Campbell, *The Masks of God: Vol. 1, Primitive Mythology*, p. 149.

13. Joseph Campbell, *Historical Atlas of World Mythology, Vol. I: The Way of the Animal Powers: Part 1: Mythologies of the Primitive Hunters and Gatherers* (New York: Harper & Row, 1988), p. 10.

14. Samuel Kramer, *The Sumerians: Their History, Culture, and Character* (Chicago: University of Chicago Press, 1963), p. 113.

15. Frankfort et al., *The Intellectual Adventure of Ancient Man* (Chicago: University of Chicago Press, 1946), p. 137.

16. Frankfort, Ibid., p. 138.

17. *World Atlas of Archaeology* (New York: Portland House, 1985): "The first agricultural 'work' and the progressive mastery of the environment by the domestication of animals and plants coincides with a human spirituality now expanded to include both an 'above' and a 'below,' the order of the divinity and that of ordinary humanity" (p. 172).

18. See: Hadingham, *Early Man and the Cosmos*, p. 245.

19. See, for example: Robert Redfield, *The Primitive World and Its Transformations* (Ithaca, N.Y.: Cornell University Press, 1953).

20. Campbell, *The Masks of God: Vol. 3, Occidental Mythology*, pp. 248–49.

21. Kramer, *The Sumerians*, p. 33.

22. Bernard Campbell, *Human Evolution*, 2nd ed. (Chicago: Aldine Publishing Co., 1974), p. 348.

23. Kramer, *The Sumerians*, p. 260.

24. Ibid., pp. 264–67.

25. Cameron, *Humanity and Society*, p. 48.

26. Frankfort, *The Intellectual Adventure of Ancient Man*, p. 364.

27. Redfield, *The Primitive World and Its Transformations*, p. 22.

28. Peter Farb, *Humankind* (Boston: Houghton Mifflin Co., 1978), p. 135.

29. Reported in a documentary on the *CBS Evening News*, New York, May 15, 1989.

30. Critchfield, *Villages*, pp. 341–45.

31. Ibid., pp. 225–26.

32. Kramer, *The Sumerians,* p. 74.

33. For a discussion of the Inanna myth see, for example: Kramer, *The Sumerians,* pp. 116 and 160–61. Also see: Elinor Gadon, *The Once and Future Goddess* (San Francisco: Harper & Row, 1989), p. 142.

34. Richard Tarnas, *The Passion of the Western Mind* (New York: Harmony Books, 1991), p. 442.

35. Farb, *Humankind,* p. 159.

36. See: Ofer Zur, "The Psychohistory of Warfare: The Co-Evolution of Culture, Psyche and Enemy," *Journal of Peace Research,* Vol. 24, No. 2 (1987), p. 128.

37. Andrew Bard Schmookler, *The Parable of the Tribes: The Problem of Power in Social Evolution* (Berkeley: University of California Press, 1984), p. 21.

38. See: Robert Bellah, "Religious Evolution," in *American Sociological Review,* Vol. 29 (1964), pp. 358–74; also, Victor Barnow, *Anthropology* (Homewood, Ill.: The Dorsey Press, 1979), pp. 334–35.

39. Campbell, *The Masks of God: Primitive Mythology,* pp. 141, 145, and 402.

40. Among the books that were most helpful in developing this chronology were: the works of Joseph Campbell, cited throughout; Milton Hessel, *Man's Journey Through Time* (New York: Simon & Schuster, 1974); and Crane Brinton et al., *A History of Civilization, Volume 1: Prehistory to 1715* (New York: Prentice-Hall, 1984).

Chapter 4: Dynamic Consciousness and the Scientific-Industrial Era

1. Ron Atkin, *Multidimensional Man* (New York: Penguin Books, 1981). Atkin states, "Three-dimensional space is only a banal slice of the multidimensional structures we really live in." For a similar theme, see: Lama Govinda, *Creative Meditation and Multi-Dimensional Consciousness* (Wheaton, Ill.: Theosophical Publishing House, 1976).

2. Govinda, *Creative Meditation,* pp. 256–58.

3. See, for example: Leonard Shlain, *Art and Physics* (New York: William Morrow, 1991), pp. 48–54; also: Edward Burns, Robert Lerner, and Standish Meacham, *Western Civilizations,* Vol. I, 9th ed. (New York: W. W. Norton & Co., 1980), p. 402.

4. Jean Gebser, *The Ever-Present Origin,* trans. Noel Barstad with Algis Mickumas (Athens, Ohio: Ohio University Press, 1985), p. 10. There is evidence that the capacity for seeing things in perspective was not completely absent before the Renaissance. A Cro-Magnon artist, living roughly eighteen thousand years ago, produced a striking drawing done with depth perspective. Discovered in a cave along the coast of southern France, this charcoal drawing shows a bison in three-quarter profile with its head partially turned toward the artist. See: "The Hand of Time," *Life,* Dec. 1991, p. 56.

5. Georg Feuerstein, *Structures of Consciousness: The Genius of Jean Gebser—An Introduction and Critique* (Lower Lake, Calif.: Integral Publishing, 1987), p. 114.

6. Shlain, *Art and Physics,* p. 161.

7. Ibid.

8. Campbell quoted in: I. H. Rima, *Development of Economic Analysis* (Homewood, Ill.: R. D. Irwin Co., 1967), p. 4.

9. See: Ernest Becker, *The Denial of Death* (New York: Free Press, 1973); and Ken Wilber, *Up from Eden* (New York: Anchor Press/Doubleday, 1981), pp. 98–101.

10. Joseph Campbell, *The Masks of God: Vol. 3, Occidental Mythology* (New York: Viking Press, 1964), p. 504.

11. Quoted in Wilber, *Up from Eden,* p. 251.

12. On the other hand, this epoch elevated the rational intellect and gave citizens a healthy distrust of purely ecstatic experiences, thereby protecting humanity from the fascistic, shadow side of the ascent experience. See: Morris Berman, *Coming to Our Senses* (New York: Simon & Schuster, 1989), p. 303.

13. Evelyn Underhill, *Mysticism* (New York: Meridian Books, 1955), p. 30.

14. Kenneth Cameron, *Humanity and Society* (Bloomington, Ind.: Indiana University Press, 1973), p. 244.

15. Ibid., p. 290.

16. Berman, *Coming to Our Senses,* p. 131. Berman notes another interesting example suggesting the growth of reflective consciousness. From roughly 1500 onward the manufacture and distribution of mirrors increased exponentially—a fact he associates with the rise of individualism characteristic of the European Renaissance. "We find a sharp simultaneous increase in self-consciousness and in the quantity and technical quality of mirror production" (p. 48).

17. Ibid., p. 131.

18. Richard Tarnas, *The Passion of the Western Mind* (New York: Harmony Books, 1991), p. 282.

Chapter 5: Reflective Consciousness and the Era of Communication and Reconciliation

1. See, for example: Donella Meadows et al., *Beyond the Limits* (Post Mills, Vt.: Chelsea Green Publishing Co., 1992).

2. See, for example: Joseph V. Montville, "Psychoanalytic Enlightenment and the Greening of Diplomacy," *Journal of the American Psychoanalytic Association,* Vol. 37, No. 2 (1989). Also: Roger Walsh, *Staying Alive: The Psychology of Human Survival* (Boulder, Colo.: Shambhala/New Science Library, 1984).

3. Stephen Levine, *Who Dies?, An Investigation of Conscious Living and Conscious Dying* (New York: Anchor Press, 1982), pp. 180–81.

4. Stephen Levine, "The Great Addiction: A Case of Mistaken Identity," in *The Quest* (Winter 1991), p. 27.

5. Even trees, for example, seem to have a capacity for recognizing "self and other" in the way their roots grow. See: "Root Words," *Science News,* Vol. 139 (Mar. 23, 1991), p. 188.

6. Freeman Dyson, *Infinite in All Directions* (New York: Harper & Row, 1988), p. 297.

7. Roberto Assagioli discusses the disidentification process at length in his book *Psychosynthesis* (New York: Viking Compass Books, 1965).

8. The contemporary evolution of the masculine archetype is described by Sam Keen, *Fire in the Belly: On Being a Man* (New York: Bantam Publishers, 1991).

9. Quoted in Frank White, *The Overview Effect* (Boston: Houghton Mifflin Co., 1987), p. 38.

10. Donald Michael, *On Learning to Plan—And Planning to Learn* (San Francisco: Jossey-Bass Publishers, 1973).

11. George Gallup, Jr., "50 Years of American Opinion," *San Francisco Chronicle,* Oct. 21, 1985.

12. Ibid.

13. See the book by Meadows et al., *Beyond the Limits.*

14. Robert McNamara, former president of the World Bank, defined "absolute poverty" as "a condition of life so characterized by malnutrition, illiteracy, disease, high infant mortality and low life expectancy as to be beneath any reasonable definition of human decency."

15. For various definitions, see Duane Elgin, *Voluntary Simplicity,* 1st ed. (New York: William Morrow, 1981), p. 29.

16. Arnold Toynbee, *A Study of History,* abridgement of Vols I–VI by D. C. Somervell (New York: Oxford University Press, 1947), p. 198.

17. Ibid., p. 208.

18. Buckminster Fuller describes this process as "ephemeralization." However, unlike Toynbee, Fuller's emphasis was on designing material systems to do more with less rather than the coevolution of matter and consciousness. See, for example: Buckminster Fuller, *Critical Path* (New York: St. Martin's Press, 1981), p. 234.

19. Matthew Fox, *Creation Spirituality* (San Francisco: HarperSan Francisco, 1991), pp. 90–91.

20. Quoted in Stephen B. Oates, *Let the Trumpets Sound: The Life of Martin Luther King, Jr.* (New York: New American Library, 1982), p. 226.

21. Joseph N. Pelton, "The Globalization of Universal Telecommunications Services," in *Universal Telephone Service: Ready for the 21st Century?* (Queenstown, Md.: The Aspen Institute, 1991), p. 146.

Chapter 6: Oceanic Consciousness and the Bonding and Building Era

1. Teilhard de Chardin, *The Future of Man* (New York: Harper & Row, 1964), p. 57.

2. Bill Mastin, Urban Ecology Inc., P.O. Box 10144, Berkeley, Calif. 94709.

3. See: Robert Nisbet, *The Quest for Community: A Study in the Ethics of Order and Freedom* (San Francisco: ICS Press, 1990; originally published in 1953).

4. Stephen B. Oates, *Let the Trumpets Sound* (New York: New American Library, 1982), p. 79.

5. Malcom Muggeridge, *Something Beautiful for God: Mother Teresa of Calcutta* (New York: Harper & Row, 1971), pp. 65 and 69.

Chapter 7: Flow Consciousness and the Surpassing Era

1. See, for example: Garma C. C. Chang, *The Buddhist Teaching of Totality* (University Park: The Pennsylvania State University Press, 1971), p. 39 (and footnote 28 on p. 55).

2. It is important to differentiate the cosmic scale flow consciousness described here from the far more restricted definition of flow experience described by Mihaly Csikszentmihalyi in his book *Flow: The Psychology of Optimal Experience* (New York: Harper & Row, 1990).

3. A. K. Coomaraswamy, *Buddha and the Gospel of Buddhism* (New York: Harper Torchbooks, 1964), p. 95 (originally published in 1916).

4. See: the important insights of the Tibetan Dzogchen tradition and its process view of reality; in particular, Longchenpa, *Kindly Bent to Ease Us, Part Three: Wonderment,* trans. and annot. Herbert Guenther (Emeryville, Calif.: Dharma Publishing, 1976). Guenther writes that all entities "are a process and that apart from process there is no being. Being thus becomes synonymous with the experience of its dynamic process" (p. 77).

5. Lama Govinda, *Creative Meditation and Multi-Dimensional Consciousness* (Wheaton, Ill.: Theosophical Publishing Press, 1976), p. 287.

6. Quoted in J. M. Cohen and J. I. Phipps, *The Common Experience* (New York: St. Martin's Press, 1979), p. 140.

7. Michael Murphy and John Brodie, "I Experience a Kind of Clarity," *Intellectual Digest,* Jan. 1973, pp. 19–20; quoted in Michael Murphy and Rhea White, *The Psychic Side of Sports* (Menlo Park, Calif.: Addison-Wesley Publishing Co., 1978).

8. William Furlong, "The Fun in Fun," *Psychology Today,* Vol. 10., No. 1 (June 1976), p. 36; quoted in Murphy and White, *The Psychic Side of Sports.*

9. Tom Horowitz and Susan Kimmelman, with H. H. Lui, *Tai Chi Ch'uan: The Technique of Power* (Chicago: Chicago Review Press, 1976), p. 180.

10. George Sheehan, "Basics of Jogging," *Runner's World,* Vol. 12 (Aug. 1977), p. 36. Quoted in Murphy and White, *The Psychic Side of Sports.*

11. Steve McKinney, "How I Broke the World's Speed Ski Record," *Ski Magazine,* Vol. 39, No. 7 (Spring 1975), p. 77; quoted in Murphy and White, *The Psychic Side of Sports.*

12. Csikszentmihalyi, *Flow: The Psychology of Optimal Experience,* p. 65.

13. I particularly want to acknowledge Louise Leadbetter for her example of joyful work, technical mastery, and enthusiasm for life.

14. For more on this theme, see Peter Russell, *The Global Brain: Speculations on the Evolutionary Leap to Planetary Consciousness* (Los Angeles: J. P. Tarcher, 1983).

15. John Welwood, ed., *Ordinary Magic: Everyday Life as a Spiritual Path* (Boston: Shambhala, 1992), p. 6.

16. I have lost the original reference for this beautiful quotation, although I'm confident of its accuracy.

17. Ken Wilber, personal communication, Tiburon, California, 1983.

18. Although it is an esoteric topic at present, one of the pitfalls that I think we will have to work through in the seventh stage is learning to moderate our will-to-power in the area of conscious cocreation (a process now described roughly as psychokinesis). I assume that in the era of flow consciousness the process of continuous creation will be widely recognized, and in addition there will exist highly sophisticated biofeedback and consciousness feedback devices that can greatly accelerate the pace of experiential learning about the nature of our energetic connection with the ever-manifesting cosmos. Therefore I expect that some persons will seek to direct the flow of creation to their unique advantage in this epoch. To achieve our species-maturity, we will have to learn a subtle level of ethicality regarding how we consciously engage the flow of continuous creation. For further thoughts on this general theme, see my article, "The Ethics of Psi," *New Age,* Mar. 1978.

Chapter 8: Integral Awareness and the Initial Maturity of Planetary Civilization

1. Huston Smith, *The Religions of Man* (New York: Harper & Row, 1958).

2. Sogyal Rinpoche, *The Tibetan Book of Living and Dying* (San Francisco: HarperSanFrancisco, 1992), p. 165.

3. The stages of enlightenment that are depicted in the classic "Oxherding Pictures" can be found, for example, in Katsuki Sekida, *Zen Training* (New York: Weatherhill, 1975), p. 230. Also see: Philip Kapleau, *The Three Pillars of Zen* (New York: Harper & Row, 1966), p. 311.

4. Arthur M. Young, *The Reflexive Universe* (San Francisco: Robert Briggs Assoc. and Delacorte Press, 1976), p. xxi.

5. The geophysicist Louise B. Young makes the following comment in her book *The Unfinished Universe* (New York: Simon & Schuster, 1986): "Today geochemists and cosmologists are finding characteristics of self-organization in very large units of matter . . . the earth, the stars, the galaxies. So the phenomenon of organism must not be limited by size or level of complexity. Each self-organized unit possesses the innate tendency to preserve and extend its own existence" (p. 42).

6. Teilhard de Chardin, *The Future of Man* (New York: Harper & Row, 1964), p. 78.

7. Teilhard de Chardin, *The Phenomenon of Man* (New York: Harper & Row, 1959), p. 261.

8. Alex Grey, "Universal Mind Lattice," (painted in 1981, acrylic on canvas), reproduced in *Sacred Mirrors* (Rochester, Vt.: Inner Traditions International, 1990). The journal *ReVision*, Vol. 5, No. 2 (Fall 1982), described this as showing the larger "self" as a toruslike energy cell, "a fountain of consciousness within an infinite, omnidirectional network of similar cells."

9. Teilhard, *The Future of Man*, p. 186.

10. For a discussion of the development of extraterrestrial civilizations, see for example: Carl Sagan and I. S. Shklovskii, *Intelligent Life in the Universe* (San Francisco: Holden-Day, Inc., 1966); Magoroh Maruyama and Arthur Harkins (eds.), *Cultures Beyond the Earth* (New York: Vintage Books, 1975); Edward Regis, Jr. (ed.), *Extraterrestrials: Science and Alien Intelligence* (New York: Cambridge University Press, 1985); Frank White, *The Overview Effect: Space Exploration and Human Evolution* (Boston: Houghton Mifflin Co., 1987).

11. A breathtaking scenario for this is given in Olaf Stapledon's classic book *Star Maker* (New York: Dover Publications, 1937).

12. Mihail Nimay, *Book of Mirdad* (Baltimore: Penguin Books, 1971).

13. *Corpus Hermeticum XII*, in Frances A. Yates, *Giordano Bruno and the Hermetic Tradition* (Chicago: University of Chicago Press, 1964); quoted in Larry Dossey, *Recovering the Soul* (New York: Bantam Books, 1989), p. 215.

Chapter 9: The Changing Dynamics of Human Evolution

1. Peter Russell, *A White Hole in Time* (San Francisco: HarperSanFrancisco, 1992), p. 204.

2. Ibid., p. 224.

3. Teilhard de Chardin, *The Future of Man* (New York: Harper & Row, 1964), p. 185.

4. Ken Wilber, *Up from Eden* (New York: Anchor Press/Doubleday, 1981), p. 17.

5. Ibid., p. 325.

6. Alan Watts, *The Spirit of Zen* (New York: Grove Press, Inc., 1958), p. 101.

7. Arnold Toynbee, *Civilization on Trial* (New York: Oxford University Press, 1948), pp. 215–16.

8. John Lippman, "Global TV," *This World, San Francisco Chronicle/Examiner*, Dec. 6, 1992, p. 11.

9. David Remnick, "A Voice of Resistance in Lithuania's Second City," *Washington Post*, Jan. 25, 1991.

10. Kevin Kelly, "Deep Evolution: The Emergence of Postdarwinism," *Whole Earth Review* (Fall 1992), p. 15.

11. For statistics on population growth, see, for example, Peter Farb, *Humankind* (Boston: Houghton Mifflin Co., 1978), p. 94, 166, and 174.

12. T. S. Eliot, *Four Quartets* (New York: Harcourt & Brace, 1943).

13. See, for example: Morris Berman, *Coming to Our Senses* (New York: Simon & Schuster, 1989), pp. 180–81, who has an interesting discussion of how a society can either accelerate or arrest the development of innate human potentials for moral reasoning.

14. Arnold Toynbee, *A Study of History*, abridgement of Vols. I–VI by D. C. Somerwell (New York: Oxford University Press, 1947), p. 555.

15. A different view of evolution is provided by Teilhard de Chardin, who had faith that humanity's success was not merely "a probability but a certainty." See: *The Future of Man*, pp. 246–47.

16. See the calculations and reasoning of Carl Sagan and I. S. Shklovskii, *Intelligent Life in the Universe* (San Francisco: Holden-Day, Inc., 1966), pp. 409–18.

17. Arnold Toynbee, *A Study of History*, rev. and abridged by Arnold Toynbee and Jane Caplan (New York: Weathervane Books, 1972), p. 141.

18. Toynbee, *A Study of History*, abridgement of Vols. I–VI, p. 278.

19. Louise B. Young, "Easter Island: Scary Parable," *World Monitor* (Aug. 1991).

20. *Summa Theologica*, II-II, Question 66, Article 7, in *Aquinas, Selected Political Writings*, ed. A. P. d'Entreves, trans. J. G. Dawson (Oxford: Basil Blackwell, 1948), p. 171; quoted in William Aiken and Hugh La Follette (eds.), *World Hunger and Moral Obligation* (Englewood Cliffs, N.J.: Prentice-Hall, 1977), p. 30. Also see: Aquinas quoted in Matthew Fox, *Creation Spirituality* (San Francisco: HarperSanFrancisco, 1991), p. 44.

21. See, for example, the fascinating novel describing the "uplifting" of other species: David Brin, *Startide Rising* (New York: Bantam Books, 1983).

22. Ken Wilber gives an excellent summation of this difficulty in his chapter on "The Pre/Trans Fallacy," in *Eye to Eye* (New York: Anchor Press/Doubleday, 1983).

23. Lewis Thomas, *The Fragile Species: Notes of an Earth Watcher* (New York: Macmillan, 1992).

24. With respect to climate change, the United Nations–sponsored report *Our Common Future*, Gro Harlem Brundtland (chair), New York: Oxford Univ. Press, 1987, states that if present trends continue, greenhouse gases will double from preindustrial levels, "possibly as early as the 2030s" (p. 175). Although there is still much uncertainty as to the ultimate impact of global warming, it seems likely that it will destabilize previous climate patterns. For example, see: Robert Gilman in his overview article, "What's Wrong with the Climate," *In Context* (Summer 1989), No. 22. He states that, "in the immediate future, the more pressing concern is not the *average* weather but its *variability*" (p. 15). Also see: Dean Abrahamson (ed.), *The Challenge of Global Warming* (Washington, D.C.: Island Press/Natural Resources Defense Council, 1989). With re-

spect to population growth, see: the report *Our Common Future,* where the "medium range" projections for 2025 indicate a population of 8.2 billion persons (p. 101). These projections are now generally considered to be conservative. With respect to the depletion of relatively inexpensive oil reserves, the report states that "oil production will level off by the early decades of the next century and then gradually fall during a period of reduced supplies and higher prices" (p. 174). Also see: Norman Myers (ed.), *Gaia: An Atlas of Planetary Management* (New York: Doubleday/Anchor, 1984), who concludes, "If we continue consuming oil at present rates, known reserves will be depleted in about 30 years. . . . Oil, in short, may run out faster in terms of what we can afford than of what is physically available" (p. 113). Also see: John Gever et al., *Beyond Oil* (Cambridge, Mass.: Ballinger Publishing, 1986), where the authors conclude that in the United States "there are only ten or twenty years of per capita economic growth remaining before declining oil and gas production begins to drag the economy downhill" (p. 248). Although, worldwide, there is enough coal and natural gas to last for centuries, the greenhouse effect makes use of these nonrenewable resources very costly in terms of disruption of the global climate.

25. With respect to the pace of change at which various technologies will converge to create a universal telecommunications system for the developed nations see, for example: Joseph Pelton, "The Globalization of Universal Telecommunications Services," in *Universal Telephone Service,* Queenstown, Md.: The Aspen Institute, 1991. He states that "the universal global telecommunications network will serve as the main . . . telecommunications conduit for economic, social, cultural, and political exchange among the peoples of the planet Earth in the 21st century. . . . *This network may start to come into place around the second decade of the 21st century"* (p. 171, emphasis added). Pelton concludes, "The creation of a truly interconnected planet that provides economic, technical, cultural and social services with ease and grace—not to mention political enlightenment—could be the unique accomplishment of humankind in the 21st century" (p. 175). Also see Fig. 4, p. 154, where he estimates that access to fiber optics in developed nations will reach 90 percent by 2015, even without aggressive deployment.

26. I am grateful to Zach Lapid for suggesting several of these examples.

27. Toynbee, *A Study of History,* rev. ed. with Jane Caplan.

Chapter 10: The Perennial Wisdom and Human Evolution

1. See, for example: Aldous Huxley, *The Perennial Philosophy* (New York: Harper & Brothers Publishers, 1945); Ken Wilber, *The Spectrum of Consciousness* (Wheaton, Ill.: Theosophical Publishing House, 1977); Barbara C. Sproul, *Primal Myths* (San Francisco: Harper & Row, 1979); Robert S. Ellwood, Jr., *Words of the World's Religions* (Englewood Cliffs, N.J.: Prentice-Hall, 1977); S. E. Frost, Jr., *The Sacred Writings of the World's Great Religions* (New York: McGraw-Hill, 1943).

2. Quoted in Timothy Ferris, *Galaxies* (New York: Stewart, Tabori & Chang, 1982), p. 87.

3. Arnold Toynbee, *A Study of History,* abridgement of Vols. I–VI by D. C. Somervell (New York: Oxford University Press, 1947), p. 495.

4. Teilhard de Chardin, *The Phenomenon of Man* (New York: Harper Torch-books, 1965), p. 44.

5. David Bohm, *Wholeness and the Implicate Order* (London: Routledge & Kegan Paul, 1980), p. 175.

6. Quoted in D. T. Suzuki, *Zen and Japanese Culture* (Princeton, N.J.: Princeton University Press, 1970), p. 353.

7. Francis H. Cook, *Hua-yen Buddhism: the Jewel Net of Indra* (University Park: The Pennsylvania State University Press, 1977), p. 122.

8. *Chandogya Upanishad,* VI.9.4, *The Thirteen Principal Upanishads,* trans. Robert E. Hume, (New York: Oxford University Press, 1921, rep. 1975), p. 246.

9. Gospel of Thomas, *Nag Hammadi Library,* gen. ed. James M. Robinson (San Francisco: Harper & Row, 1977), p. 129–30.

10. Ibid., p. 118.

11. Quoted in Wilber, *Spectrum of Consciousness,* p. 301.

12. Quoted in Evelyn Underhill, *Mysticism,* (New York: Meridian Books, 1955), p. 101.

13. Ibid., p. 99.

14. Lex Hixon, *Coming Home* (New York: Anchor Books, 1978), p. 112.

15. Quoted in Wilber, *Spectrum of Consciousness,* p. 300.

16. Ibid., p. 299.

17. Quoted in Huxley, *The Perennial Philosophy,* p. 5.

18. Quoted in Thomas Berry, *The Dream of the Earth* (San Francisco: Sierra Club Books, 1988), p. 219.

19. Quoted in Andrew Greeley and William McCready, "Are We a Nation of Mystics?" in *The New York Times Magazine,* Jan. 26, 1975. Elsewhere Greeley states that "as much as one-fifth of the population has frequent mystical experiences." See: Andrew Greeley, *Ecstasy as a Way of Knowing* (Englewood Cliffs, N.J.: Prentice-Hall, Inc., 1974), p. 57.

20. John Mack, *Changing Models of Psychotherapy: From Psychological Conflict to Human Empowerment,* a paper published by the Center for Psychological Studies in the Nuclear Age, Harvard Medical School, Cambridge, Mass., June 1990, p. 6.

21. Greeley and McCready, "Are We a Nation of Mystics?"

22. Reported in *Brain/Mind Bulletin* 12:7 (Mar. 1987), p. 1; and Andrew Greeley, "The Impossible: It's Happening," *Noetic Sciences Review* (Spring 1987), pp. 7–9. A regional poll conducted in the San Francisco Bay Area gives more conservative but still striking results. It found that 27 percent said they had experienced being "very close to a powerful spiritual force that seemed to lift people out of themselves." Reported in *San Francisco Chronicle,* Apr. 24, 1990.

23. Greeley, "The Impossible: It's Happening."

24. Richard Bucke, *Cosmic Consciousness* (New York: E. P. Dutton & Co., 1969; originally published in 1901), p. 66.

25. Ibid., p. 76.

26. Quoted in Bucke, p. 78.

27. J. M. Cohen and J. F. Phipps, *The Common Experience* (New York: St. Martin's Press, 1979), p. 108.

28. Arnold Toynbee, *A Study of History*, rev. and abridged by Arnold Toynbee and Jane Caplan (New York: Weathervane Books, 1972), p. 498.

29. Ibid., p. 319.

30. Arnold Toynbee, *An Historian's Approach to Religion* (New York: Oxford University Press, 1956), p. 275.

31. Arnold Toynbee, *Civilization on Trial* (New York: Oxford University Press, 1948), p. 236.

32. Toynbee, *A Study of History*, abridgement of Vols. I–VI, p. 531.

33. Lewis Mumford, *The Transformations of Man* (New York: Collier Books, 1956), p. 173.

34. Ibid., p. 174.

35. Ibid., p. 176.

36. Joseph Campbell with Bill Moyers, *The Power of Myth* (New York: Doubleday, 1988), p. 53.

37. Joseph Campbell, *Historical Atlas of World Mythology, Vol I: The Way of the Animal Powers, Part 1: Mythologies of the Primitive Hunters and Gatherers* (New York: Harper & Row, 1988), p. 8.

38. Huston Smith, *The Religions of Man* (New York: Harper & Row, 1958), p. 311.

Chapter 11: Continuous Creation of the Cosmos

1. In my article "The Living Cosmos," *ReVision* (Summer 1988), I discuss the distinction between viewing the Big Bang as a mechanical explosion or a process of organic growth. Continuous-creation cosmology suggests that a seven-dimensional "seed" of self-organizing "cosmic-genetic material" may have emerged some fifteen billion years ago with all of the instructions necessary for growing a whole cosmic system. This "minicosmic factory" could have grown into our universe by continuously transforming ambient, hyperdimensional Life-energy into manifest matter-energy and space-time. In other words, the cosmos may have developed by continuously feeding upon or consuming the Life-energy of the Meta-universe and transforming it into material reality. If so, the development of our cosmos would be more accurately characterized as explosive organic growth than as a mechanical explosion.

2. Norbert Wiener, *The Human Use of Human Beings* (New York: Avon Books, 1954).

3. Guy Murchie, *Music of the Spheres* (Cambridge, Mass.: The Riverside Press, 1961), p. 451.

4. Max Born, *The Restless Universe* (New York: Harper & Brothers, 1936), p. 277.

5. Harold Puthoff, "Why Atoms Don't Collapse," *New Scientist,* July, 1987. Also see his article "Quantum Fluctuations of Empty Space: A New Rosetta Stone of Physics?," *Frontier Perspectives,* Vol. 2, No. 2 (Fall/Winter 1991), published by the Center for Frontier Sciences, Temple University, Philadelphia, Pa.

6. I am grateful to Bill Keepin for suggesting this analogy to me.

7. Peter S. Stevens, *Patterns in Nature* (Boston: Little, Brown & Co., 1974), pp. 4–5. The invisible architecture of space is suggestive of Rupert Sheldrake's theory of "morphic resonance." These fields may provide the energetic structure to guide the flow-through of Life-energy in the process of continuous creation.

8. John Wheeler, in *University: A Princeton Quarterly,* Vol. 53 (Summer 1973), p. 29; also quoted in Renee Weber, "The Good, the True, the Beautiful: Are They Attributes of the Universe?" *Main Currents in Modern Thought* (1975), p. 139.

9. David Bohm, *Wholeness and the Implicate Order* (London: Routledge & Kegan Paul, 1980), p. 191.

10. Fritjof Capra, "Modern Physics and Eastern Mysticism," quoted in Roger Walsh and Frances Vaughan, *Beyond Ego* (Los Angeles: J. P. Tarcher, Inc., 1980), p. 68.

11. Bohm, *Wholeness and the Implicate Order,* p. 11.

12. Erwin Schroedinger, *My View of the World,* p. 21, quoted in Ken Wilber, *Spectrum of Consciousness* (Wheaton, Ill.: Theosophical Publishing House, 1977), p. 59.

13. This cosmology assumes that while simultaneity does not exist within a four-dimensional, relativistic context, it can be a property of higher, more embracing dimensions. For a helpful discussion of the impossibility of simultaneity within four dimensions, see: Milic Capek, "Time in Relativity Theory," in J. T. Fraser (ed.), *The Voices of Time* (New York: George Braziller, 1966), pp. 444–47.

14. Matthew Fox, *Meditations with Meister Eckhart* (Santa Fe, N.M.: Bear & Co., 1983), p. 24. It is useful to distinguish two major kinds of "creation cosmology"—*original* creation and *continuous* creation. *Original* creation refers to the miracle that there is something here rather than nothing. *Continuous* creation refers to the miracle that once our cosmos came into existence, it has been upheld by the flow-through of immense amounts of Life-energy. Although the theory of dimensional evolution is compatible with both original creation and continuous creation, it is most strongly linked to the theory of continuous creation.

15. Matthew Fox, *Creation Spirituality* (San Francisco: HarperSanFrancisco, 1991), pp. 8 and 56.

16. D. T. Suzuki, *Zen and Japanese Culture* (Princeton, N.J.: Princeton University Press, 1970), p. 364.

17. Ibid., p. 257.

18. Alan Watts, *The Middle Way: Journal of the Buddhist Society* (London) (Feb. 1973), p. 156.

19. Joseph Campbell with Bill Moyers, *The Power of Myth* (New York: Doubleday, 1988), p. 217.

20. Quoted in Evelyn Underhill, *Mysticism* (New York: Meridian Books, 1955), p. 28.

21. Ibid., p. 29.

22. Quoted in Henri Frankfort et al., *The Intellectual Adventure of Ancient Man,* (Chicago: Univ. of Chicago Press, 1946), p. 381.

23. Underhill, *Mysticism,* p. 101.

24. Lama Govinda, *Creative Meditation and Multi-Dimensional Consciousness* (Wheaton, Ill.: Theosophical Publishing House, 1976), p. 207.

25. Ibid., p. 9.

26. Namkhai Norbu, *The Crystal and the Way of Light: Sutra, Tantra and Dzogchen,* comp. and ed. John Shane (New York: Routledge & Kegan Paul, 1986), p. 64.

27. See, for example: D. B. Macdonald, "Continuous Recreation and Atomic Time in Muslim Scholastic Theology," *Isis,* Vol. 9 (1927), pp. 326–44; also, Majid Fakhry, *Islamic Occasionalism and Its Critique by Averroes and Aquinas* (London: 1958). The Islamic view of occasionalism is more inclusive than the Western philosophy by the same name developed by the Cartesian school (which saw mind and body as absolutely separate; therefore bodily motion was dependent on the cooperation of God).

28. Samuel Umen, *The World of the Mystic* (New York: Philosophical Library, 1988), p. 178.

29. Lao-tzu, *Tao Te Ching,* trans. Gia-Fu Feng and Jane English (New York: Vintage Books, 1972).

30. Alan Watts, *The Spirit of Zen* (New York: Grove Press, Inc., 1958), p. 36.

31. David Maybury-Lewis, *Millennium: Tribal Wisdom and the Modern World* (New York: Viking, 1992), pp. 197–202.

32. Huston Smith, *The Religions of Man* (New York: Harper & Row, 1958), p. 73.

33. Heinrich Zimmer, *Myths and Symbols in Indian Art and Civilization,* ed. Joseph Campbell (Princeton, N.J.: Princeton University Press, Bollinger Series, 1972), p. 131.

34. Ibid., p. 131.

35. Ibid., p. 152.

36. Sri Nisargadatta Majaraj, *I Am That,* Part I, trans. Maurice Frydman (Bombay, India: Chetana, 1973), p. 289.

37. Quoted in Erich Neumann, *The Origins and History of Consciousness* (Princeton, N.J.: Bollingen Series, 1970), p. 5.

38. Quoted in Joseph Epes Brown, "Modes of Contemplation Through Action: North American Indians," *Main Currents in Modern Thought* (Nov.–Dec. 1973), p. 194.

39. Quoted in Fox, *Creation Spirituality*, p. 28.

Chapter 12: Coevolution and the Meta-universe

1. Richard Tarnas, *The Passion of the Western Mind* (New York: Harmony Books, 1991), p. 381.

2. Quoted in Renee Weber, "The Good, the True, and the Beautiful: Are They Attributes of the Universe?" in *Main Currents in Modern Thought* (1975), p. 139.

3. Michael Murphy, *The Future of the Body: Explorations into the Further Evolution of Human Nature* (Los Angeles: J. P. Tarcher, 1992), p. 193.

4. Stephen Mitchell (trans.), *Tao Te Ching: A New English Version* (New York: Harper & Row, 1988), Chap. 25.

5. John Welwood, "On Psychological Space," *Journal of Transpersonal Psychology*, Vol. 9., No. 2 (1977), p. 106.

6. See, for example, the Duke of Argyll, *The Unity of Nature* (New York: John Alden Publisher, 1884), p. 18; and David Heagle, *Do the Dead Still Live?* (Philadelphia: The Judson Press, 1920), pp. 43–44.

7. Quoted in Garma C. C. Chang, *The Buddhist Teaching of Totality: The Philosophy of Hwa Yen Buddhism* (University Park: The Pennsylvania State University Press, 1971), p. 111.

8. With respect to near-death research see, for example: Kenneth Ring, *Life at Death* (New York: Morrow/Quill, 1982); Melvin Morse and Paul Perry, *Closer to the Light* (New York: Villard Books, 1990); and Raymond Moody, *Life After Life* (Atlanta: Mockingbird Books, 1975).
There is an intriguing convergence of views between physicists and sages regarding the nature of light. David Bohm has described matter as "condensed or frozen light" and has said that light is the fundamental activity in which our existence is grounded. (See Renee Weber, *Dialogues with Scientists and Sages* (New York: Routledge & Kegan Paul, 1986, p. 45.) From the Gospel of Thomas, we find Jesus making this remarkable statement about the role of light in describing his origins. When asked by a disciple to describe where he came from, he said: "We came from the light, the place where the light came into being on its own accord and established itself." (James Robinson, ed. *Nag Hammadi Library*, 1st edition, San Francisco: Harper & Row, 1977, p. 123.) Also from Gnostic sources (quoting the words of Jesus as given by the disciple James), we find: "Search ever and cease not till ye find the mysteries of the Light, which will lead you into the Light-kingdom." (J. M. Cohen and J. F. Phipps, *The Common Experience*. New York: St. Martin's Press, 1979, p. 155.) If, as physicists indicate, we already live in a universe of light, then it seems quite plausible for mystics to suggest that we both come from and are evolving into more subtle ecologies of light.

9. Quoted in "The Gospel of Thomas," James Robinson, ed. *Nag Hammadi Library,* 1st ed. (San Francisco: Harper & Row, 1977), p. 124.

10. See, for example: Tsele Natsok Rangdrol, *The Mirror of Mindfulness: The Cycle of the Four Bardos,* trans. E. Kunsang (Boston: Shambhala Press, 1989).

11. Robert Bly (trans.), *The Kabir Book* (Boston: Beacon Press, 1977), p. 24.

12. Lama Govinda, *Creative Meditation and Multi-Dimensional Consciousness* (Wheaton, Ill.: Theosophical Publishing House, 1976), p. 200.

13. Murphy, *The Future of the Body,* pp. 225–27.

Chapter 13: Sacred Geometry and Stages of Growth

1. For an overview of Pythagorean thought, see: Richard Tarnas, *The Passion of the Western Mind* (New York: Harmony Books, 1991), pp. 10–11, 23, 46–47.

2. Crane Brinton et al., *A History of Civilization* (New York: Prentice-Hall, 1984), p. 58.

3. See, for example: Harold Puthoff and Russell Targ, "A Perceptual Channel for Information Transfer Over Kilometer Distances: Historical Perspective and Recent Research," in *Proceedings of the IEEE,* Vol. 64, No. 3 (Mar. 1976). Also see: Russell Targ and Harold Puthoff, *Mindreach: Scientists Look at Psychic Ability* (New York: Delacorte Press, 1977).

Appendix I: Correlations with Psychological Theories and Spiritual Traditions

1. See: Ken Wilber, *The Spectrum of Consciousness* (Wheaton, Ill.: Theosophical Publishing House, 1977); *The Atman Project: A Transpersonal View of Human Development* (Wheaton, Ill.: Theosophical Publishing House, 1980); *Up from Eden* (New York: Anchor Press/Doubleday, 1981); and *Transformations of Consciousness* (Boston: Shambhala, 1986).

2. The most useful and approachable overview of Gebser's work is found in the book by Georg Feuerstein, *Structures of Consciousness: The Genius of Jean Gebser—An Introduction and Critique* (Lower Lake, Calif.: Integral Publishing, 1987). Also see Gebser's book, *The Ever-Present Origin,* trans. Noel Barstad with Algis Mickumas (Athens, Ohio: Ohio University Press, 1985). Finally, a brief introduction to his thinking can be found in the booklet by Georg Feuerstein, *Jean Gebser: What Color Is Your Consciousness?* (San Francisco: Robert Briggs Associates, 1989).

3. See: Abraham Maslow, *Toward a Psychology of Being* (New York: Van Nostrand Reinhold, 1968).

4. See: Satprem, *Sri Aurobindo, or The Adventure of Consciousness* (Pondicherry, India: Sri Aurobindo Society, 1970); Sri Aurobindo, *The Life Divine* (Pondicherry, India: Sri Aurobindo Ashram, 1970). Also see: Ken Wilber et al., *The Transformations of Consciousness,* p. 6.

5. For the Theravada tradition, see, for example: Joseph Goldstein, *The Experience of Insight: A Natural Unfolding* (Santa Cruz, Calif.: Unity Press, 1976);

and Chogyam Trungpa (ed.), *Garuda IV: The Foundations of Mindfulness* (Berkeley, Calif.: Shambhala, 1976). With respect to the Mahayana tradition see, for example: D. T. Suzuki, *Outlines of Mahayana Buddhism* (New York: Schocken Books, 1963), and Robert Thurman (trans.), *The Holy Teachings of Vimalakirti: A Mahayana Scripture* (University Park: Pennsylvania State University Press, 1976). With respect to Tantra see, for example: Herbert V. Guenther and Chögyam Trungpa, *The Dawn of Tantra* (Berkeley, Calif.: Shambhala, 1975). With respect to Dzogchen teaching see, for example: Sogyal Rinpoche, *The Tibetan Book of Living and Dying* (San Francisco: HarperSanFrancisco, 1992); Tsele Natsok Rangdrol, *The Mirror of Mindfulness*, trans. E. Kunsang (Boston: Shambhala Press, 1989) and Namkhai Norbu, *The Crystal and the Way of Light: Sutra, Tantra and Dzogchen*, ed. John Shane (New York: Routledge & Kegan Paul, 1986).

6. Mihaly Csikszentmihalyi, *Flow: The Psychology of Optimal Experience* (New York: Harper & Row, 1990), see pp. 221–22 and the note on p. 278.

7. Michael Murphy, *The Future of the Body*, pp. 187–88.

8. Rangdrol, *Mirror of Mindfulness*, p. 55.

9. Wilber, *Up from Eden*, pp. 300–01.

10. Ibid., pp. 179–81.

11. Also see Feuerstein, *Structures of Consciousness*, where he contrasts and compares his view of Gebser's stages in history with those of Ken Wilber.

Appendix II: Meditative Origins of Dimensional Cosmology

1. This research was published as the report *Changing Images of Man*, SRI International, Menlo Park, Calif., May 1974; and subsequently republished under the same title by Pergamon Press in 1982 with Oliver Markley and Willis Harman as the editors.

SELECTED BIBLIOGRAPHY

Abel, Ernest L. *Ancient Views on the Origins of Life*. N.J.: Associated University Presses, 1973.

Abrahamson, Dean (ed.) *The Challenge of Global Warming*. Washington, D.C.: Island Press/Natural Resources Defense Council, 1989.

Aiken, William, and Hugh La Follette (eds.) *World Hunger and Moral Obligation*. Englewood Cliffs, N.J.: Prentice-Hall, 1977.

Argyll, The Duke of. *The Unity of Nature*. New York: John Alden Publisher, 1884.

Asimov, Isaac, and Frank White. *The March of the Millennia*. New York: Walker and Co., 1991.

Assagioli, Roberto. *Psychosynthesis*. New York: Viking Compass Books, 1965.

Atkin, Ron. *Multidimensional Man*. New York: Penguin Books, 1981.

Aurobindo, Sri. *The Life Divine*. Pondicherry, India: Sri Aurobindo Ashram, 1970.

Barber, Benjamin. *Strong Democracy: Participatory Politics for a New Age*. Berkeley: University of California Press, 1984.

Barnet, Richard. *The Lean Years: Politics in the Age of Scarcity*. New York: Simon & Schuster, 1980.

Barnow, Victor. *Anthropology.* Homewood, Ill.: The Dorsey Press, 1979.

Becker, Ernest. *The Denial of Death.* New York: Free Press, 1973.

Bellah, Robert. "Religious Evolution," *American Sociological Review,* 29 (1964), 358–74.

Bellah, Robert et al. *Habits of the Heart.* San Francisco: Harper & Row, 1985.

————. *The Good Society.* New York: Alfred A. Knopf, 1991.

Berman, Morris. *Coming to Our Senses.* New York: Simon & Schuster, 1989.

Berry, Thomas. *The Dream of the Earth.* San Francisco: Sierra Club Books, 1988.

Bly, Robert (trans.) *The Kabir Book.* Boston: Beacon Press, 1977.

Bohm, David. *Wholeness and the Implicate Order.* London: Routledge & Kegan Paul, 1980.

Born, Max. *The Restless Universe.* New York: Harper & Brothers, 1936.

Boulding, Elise. *Building a Global Civic Culture.* New York: Teachers College, Columbia University, 1988.

Boulding, Kenneth. *The Meaning of the Twentieth Century.* New York: Harper & Row, 1964.

Brin, David. *Startide Rising.* New York: Bantam Books, 1983.

Brinton, Crane et al. *A History of Civilization, Volume I: Prehistory to 1715,* 6th ed. New York: Prentice-Hall, 1984.

Brown, Lester. *Building a Sustainable Society.* New York: W. W. Norton, 1981.

————. *State of the World 1992.* New York: W. W. Norton, 1992.

Brundtland, Gro Harlem (chair). *Our Common Future.* A Report of the U.N.-sponsored World Commission on Environment and Development. New York: Oxford University Press, 1987.

Bucke, Richard. *Cosmic Consciousness.* New York: E. P. Dutton & Co., 1969; originally published in 1901.

Burns, Edward, Robert Lerner, and Standish Meacham. *Western Civilizations: Their History and Their Culture,* Vol. I, 9th ed. New York: W. W. Norton & Co., 1980.

Calvin, William H. *The Ascent of Mind.* New York: Bantam Books, 1990.

Cameron, Kenneth. *Humanity and Society: A World History.* Bloomington, Ind.: Indiana University Press, 1973.

Campbell, Bernard. *Human Evolution,* 2nd ed. Chicago: Aldine Publishing Co., 1974.

Campbell, Joseph. *The Masks of God: Vol. 1, Primitive Mythology.* New York: Viking Press, 1959.

————. *The Masks of God: Vol. 2, Oriental Mythology.* New York: Viking Press, 1962.

————. *The Masks of God: Vol. 3, Occidental Mythology.* New York: Viking Press, 1964.

―――. *Historical Atlas of World Mythology, Vol I: The Way of the Animal Powers, Part 1: Mythologies of the Primitive Hunters and Gatherers.* New York: Harper & Row, Perennial Library, 1988.

―――. *Historical Atlas of World Mythology, Vol II: The Way of the Seeded Earth, Part 1: The Sacrifice.* New York: Harper & Row, 1988.

―――. *Transformation of Myth Through Time.* New York: Harper & Row, 1990.

―――(ed.) *Man and Time.* New York: Princeton University Press, Bollingen Series, 1957.

Campbell, Joseph, with Bill Moyers. *The Power of Myth.* New York: Doubleday, 1988.

Capra, Fritjof. *The Tao of Physics.* Boulder, Colo.: Shambhala, 1975.

―――. *The Turning Point.* New York: Simon & Schuster, 1982.

Capra, Fritjof, and Charlene Spretnak. *Green Politics.* New York: E. P. Dutton, 1984.

Chang, Garma C. C. *The Buddhist Teaching of Totality: The Philosophy of Hwa Yen Buddhism.* University Park, Pa.: The Pennsylvania State University Press, 1971.

Cohen, J. M., and J. F. Phipps. *The Common Experience.* New York: St. Martin's Press, 1979.

Cook, Francis H. *Hua-yen Buddhism: the Jewel Net of Indra.* University Park, Pa.: The Pennsylvania State University Press, 1977.

Cook, Theodore Andrea. *The Curves of Life.* New York: Dover Publications, 1979; originally published in England in 1914.

Coomaraswamy, A. K. *Buddha and the Gospel of Buddhism.* New York: Harper Torchbooks, 1964; originally published in 1916.

Copleston, Frederick, S. J. *A History of Philosophy, Vols. VII–IX.* New York: Doubleday/Image Book, 1985.

Critchfield, Richard. *Villages.* New York: Anchor Books/Doubleday, 1983.

Csikszentmihalyi, Mihaly. *Flow: The Psychology of Optimal Experience.* New York: Harper & Row, 1990.

Da Free John. *The Enlightenment of the Whole Body.* Clear Lake, Calif.: Dawn Horse Press, 1978.

―――. *The Bodily Location of Happiness.* Clear Lake, Calif.: Dawn Horse Press, 1981.

Daly, Herman, and John Cobb, Jr. *For the Common Good.* Boston: Beacon Press, 1989.

Dammann, Erik. *The Future in Our Hands.* New York: Pergamon Press, 1979.

Darwin, Charles. *The Origin of Species.* New York: New American Library, 1958; first published in 1859.

Davies, Paul. *God and the New Physics.* New York: Simon & Schuster/Touchstone Books, 1983.

Deikman, Arthur. *The Observing Self: Mysticism and Psychiatry.* Boston: Beacon Press, 1982.

Devall, Bill, and George Sessions. *Deep Ecology.* Salt Lake City: Gibbs Smith, 1985.

de Waal Malefijt, Annemarie. *Religion and Culture.* London: Macmillan Company, 1968.

Diamond, Jared. "The Great Leap Forward," *Discover,* May 1989.

Dobzhansky, Theodosius. *Mankind Evolving.* New Haven: Yale University Press, 1962.

Donceel, J. F. *Philosophical Anthropology.* New York: Sheed and Ward, 1967.

Dossey, Larry. *Recovering the Soul: A Scientific and Spiritual Search.* New York: Bantam Books, 1989.

Dubos, René. *So Human an Animal.* New York: Charles Scribner's Sons, 1968.

Dyson, Freeman. *Infinite in All Directions.* New York: Harper & Row, 1988.

Easwaran, Eknath. *Gandhi the Man.* Petaluma, Calif.: Nilgiri Press, 1978.

———. *The Compassionate Universe: The Power of the Individual to Heal the Environment.* Petaluma, Calif.: Nilgiri Press, 1989.

Eddington, Arthur S. *The Nature of the Physical World.* New York: Macmillan, 1928.

Einstein, Alfred. *Relativity.* New York: Crown Publishers, 1961.

Eiseley, Loren. *The Immense Journey.* New York: Vintage Books, 1957.

Eisler, Riane. *The Chalice and the Blade.* San Francisco: Harper & Row, 1987.

Elgin, Duane. *Voluntary Simplicity.* New York: William Morrow, 1981 (rev. ed., 1993).

———. "The Living Cosmos: A Theory of Continuous Creation," *ReVision,* Vol. 11, No. 1 (Summer 1988).

Eliade, M. *The Myth of Eternal Return.* New York: Pantheon, 1954.

Eliot, T. S. *Four Quartets.* New York: Harcourt & Brace, 1943.

Ellwood, Robert, Jr. *Words of the World's Religions.* Englewood Cliffs, N.J.: Prentice-Hall, 1977.

———. *Mysticism and Religion.* Englewood Cliffs, N.J.: Prentice-Hall, Inc., 1980.

Elvee, R. (ed.) *Mind in Nature.* New York: Harper & Row, 1982.

Eppsteiner, Fred (ed.) *The Path of Compassion: Writings on Socially Engaged Buddhism.* Berkeley: Parallax Press, 1988.

Farb, Peter. *Man's Rise to Civilization: The Cultural Ascent of the Indians of North America,* 2nd ed. rev. New York: E. P. Dutton, 1978.

———. *Humankind.* Boston: Houghton Mifflin Co., 1978.

Fellows, Ward J. *Religions East and West.* New York: Holt, Rinehart and Winston, 1979.

Ferencz, Benjamin B., and Ken Keyes, Jr. *Planethood*. Coos Bay, Ore.: Love Line Books, 1991.

Ferguson, Marilyn. *The Aquarian Conspiracy*. Los Angeles: J. P. Tarcher, 1980.

Ferris, Timothy. *Galaxies*. New York: Stewart, Tabori & Chang, 1982.

Feuerstein, Georg. *Structures of Consciousness: The Genius of Jean Gebser— An Introduction and Critique*. Clear Lake, Calif.: Integral Publishing, 1987.

————. *Jean Gebser: What Color Is Your Consciousness?* San Francisco: Robert Briggs Associates/Broadside Editions, 1989.

Fox, Matthew. *Creation Spirituality*. San Francisco: HarperSanFrancisco, 1991.

Fox, Matthew (ed.) *Meditations with Meister Eckhart*. Santa Fe, N.M.: Bear & Co., 1983.

Fox, Matthew, and Brian Swimme. *Manifesto for a Global Civilization*. Santa Fe, N.M.: Bear & Co., 1982.

Frankfort, Henri, et al. *The Intellectual Adventure of Ancient Man*. Chicago: University of Chicago Press, 1946.

Frankl, Victor. *Man's Search for Meaning*. New York: Washington Square, 1963.

Fraser, J. T. (ed.) *The Voices of Time*. New York: George Braziller, 1966.

Freud, Sigmund. *Civilization and Its Discontents*, trans. James Strachey. New York: W. W. Norton & Co., 1961.

Fried, Morton. *The Evolution of Political Society*. New York: Random House, 1967.

Fromm, Erich. *The Revolution of Hope*. New York: Harper & Row, 1968.

Frost, S. E., Jr. *The Sacred Writings of the World's Great Religions*. New York: McGraw-Hill, 1943.

Fuller, Buckminster. *Critical Path*. New York: St. Martin's Press, 1981.

Gadon, Elinor. *The Once and Future Goddess*. San Francisco: Harper & Row, 1989.

Gandhi, Mahatma. *All Men Are Brothers*, ed. Krishna Kripalani. India: Navajivan Publishing House, 1960.

Gebser, Jean. *The Ever-Present Origin*, trans. Noel Barstad with Algis Mickumas. Athens, Ohio: Ohio University Press, 1985.

Gever, John et al. *Beyond Oil*. Cambridge, Mass.: Ballinger Publishing, 1986.

Ghose, Sisirkumar. *Mystics and Society*. New York: Asia Publishing House, 1968.

Gilman, Robert. "The Eco-Village Challenge," *In Context* (a quarterly journal), Bainbridge Island, Wash. (Summer 1991).

Gimbutas, Marija. *The Goddesses and Gods of Old Europe*. Berkeley: University of California Press, 1982.

Glenn, Jerome. *Future Mind: Artificial Intelligence.* Washington, D.C.: Acropolis Books, 1989.

Goldstein, Joseph. *The Experience of Insight: A Natural Unfolding.* Santa Cruz, Calif.: Unity Press, 1976.

Gore, Al. *Earth in the Balance: Ecology and the Human Spirit.* Boston: Houghton Mifflin Co., 1992.

Govinda, Lama. *The Psychological Attitude of Early Buddhist Philosophy.* New York: Samuel Weiser, 1974.

———. *Creative Meditation and Multi-Dimensional Consciousness.* Wheaton Ill.: Theosophical Publishing House, 1976.

Gowlett, John A. J. *Ascent to Civilization: The Archaeology of Early Man.* New York: Alfred A. Knopf, 1984.

Greeley, Andrew. *Ecstasy as a Way of Knowing.* Englewood Cliffs, N.J.: Prentice-Hall, Inc., 1974.

Grey, Alex. *Sacred Mirrors.* Rochester, Vt.: Inner Traditions International, 1990.

Griffin, David R. *The Reenchantment of Science.* New York: SUNY Press, 1988.

Griffin, David R., and Huston Smith. *Primordial Truth and Postmodern Theology.* New York: SUNY Press, 1989.

Griffin, Donald R. *The Question of Animal Awareness.* Los Altos, Calif.: William Kaufmann, Inc., 1981.

Grof, Stanislav. *Realms of the Human Unconsciousness.* New York: E. P. Dutton & Co., 1976.

——— (ed.) *Human Survival and Consciousness Evolution.* New York: SUNY Press, 1988.

Guenther, Herbert V. "Fact and Fiction in the Experience of Being," *Crystal Mirror,* No. 2. Berkeley: Dharma Publishing (Summer 1972).

Guenther, Herbert V., and Chögyam Trungpa. *The Dawn of Tantra.* Berkeley: Shambhala, 1975.

Guenther, Herbert V., and Leslie S. Kawamura (trans.) *Mind in Buddhist Psychology.* Berkeley, Calif.: Dharma Publishing, 1975.

Hadingham, Evan. *Early Man and the Cosmos.* Norman University of Oklahoma Press, 1984.

Hanh, Thich Nhat. *Being Peace.* Berkeley: Parallax Press, 1987.

———. *Interbeing.* Berkeley: Parallax Press, 1987.

Harman, Willis. *An Incomplete Guide to the Future.* Stanford, Calif.: Stanford Alumni Association, 1976.

Harman, Willis, and John Hormann. *Creative Work: The Constructive Role of Business in a Transforming Society.* Indianapolis: Knowledge Systems, 1990.

Harris, Marvin. *Our Kind.* New York: Harper & Row, 1989.

Hays, H. R. *In the Beginning: Early Man and His Gods.* New York: G. P. Putnam's Sons, 1963.

Heagle, David. *Do the Dead Still Live?* Philadelphia: The Judson Press, 1920.

Heilbroner, Robert. *An Inquiry into the Human Prospect.* New York: W. W. Norton & Co., 1974.

Henderson, Hazel. *The Politics of the Solar Age.* New York: Doubleday/ Anchor, 1981.

Herbert, Nick. *Quantum Reality.* New York: Doubleday, 1987.

Hessel, Milton. *Man's Journey Through Time.* New York: Wanderer Books, 1974.

Hixon, Lex. *Coming Home.* Garden City, N.J.: Anchor Books, 1978.

Hoffman, Edward. *Visions of Innocence: Spiritual and Inspirational Experiences of Childhood.* Boston: Shambhala, 1992.

Hoover, Thomas. *Zen Culture.* New York: Random House, 1977.

Horowitz, Tom, and Susan Kimmelman, with H. H. Lui. *Tai chi Ch'uan: The Technique of Power.* Chicago: Chicago Review Press, 1976.

Hubbard, Barbara Marx. *The Evolutionary Journey.* San Francisco: Evolutionary Press, 1982.

Hume, Robert (trans.) *Chandogya Upanishad, VI.9.4, The Thirteen Principal Upanishads.* New York: Oxford University Press, 1921; reprinted 1975.

Huxley, Aldous. *The Perennial Philosophy.* New York: Harper & Brothers Publishers, 1945.

James, William. *Varieties of Religious Experience.* New York: Collier, 1961.

Jantsch, Erich. *Design for Evolution.* New York: George Braziller, 1975.

Jantsch, Erich, and Conrad Waddington (eds.) *Evolution and Consciousness: Human Systems in Transition.* Reading, Mass.: Addison-Wesley Publishing, 1976.

Jaynes, Julian. *The Origin of Consciousness in the Breakdown of the Bicameral Mind.* Boston: Houghton Mifflin, 1976.

Jeans, James. *The Mysterious Universe.* London: Cambridge University Press, 1931.

Johnson, Allen W., and Timothy Earl. *The Evolution of Human Societies: From Foraging Group to Agrarian State.* Stanford, Calif.: Stanford University Press, 1987.

Johnston, Charles, M. *The Creative Imperative.* Berkeley: Celestial Arts Press, 1986.

———. *Necessary Wisdom: Meeting the Challenge of a New Cultural Maturity.* Berkeley: Celestial Arts Press, 1991.

Kapleau, Phillip. *The Three Pillars of Zen.* New York: Harper & Row, 1966.

Keen, Sam. *Fire in the Belly: On Being a Man.* New York: Bantam Publishers, 1991.

Keniston, Kenneth. *The Uncommitted.* New York: Harcourt, Brace & World, 1965.

Keys, Donald. *The United Nations and Planetary Consciousness.* New York: Agni Press, 1977.

Kidder, Rushworth M. *Reinventing the Future: Global Goals for the 21st Century.* Cambridge, Mass.: The MIT Press, 1989.

Kohlberg, Lawrence. *The Psychology of Moral Development: The Nature and Validity of Moral Stages.* San Francisco: Harper & Row, 1984.

Kramer, Samuel. *The Sumerians: Their History, Culture, and Character.* Chicago: University of Chicago Press, 1963.

Krishnamurti, J. *Freedom from the Known.* ed. Mary Lutyens. New York: Harper & Row, 1969.

Kroeber, Theodora. *Ishi in Two Worlds: A Biography of the Last Wild Indian in North America.* Berkeley: University of California Press, 1967.

Kuhn, Thomas S. *The Structure of Scientific Revolutions,* 2nd ed. Chicaco: University of Chicago Press, 1970.

Kuznets, Simon. *Modern Economic Growth: Rate, Structure and Spread.* New Haven: Yale University Press, 1966.

Lao-tzu. *Tao Te Ching,* trans. Gia-Fu Feng and Jane English. New York: Vintage Books, 1972.

Laszlo, Ervin. *Evolution: The Grand Synthesis.* Boston: Shambhala/New Science Library, 1987.

Leakey, Richard. *The Making of Mankind.* New York: E. P. Dutton, 1981.

Leakey, Richard, and Roger Lewin. *Origins.* New York: E. P. Dutton, Inc., 1977.

Leonard, George. *The Transformation.* New York: Delta Books, 1973.

———. *The Silent Pulse.* New York: Dutton, 1978.

———. *Mastery.* New York: Dutton/New American Library, 1990.

Levine, Stephen. *Who Dies?: An Investigation of Conscious Living and Conscious Dying.* New York: Anchor Books, 1982.

Linssen, Robert. *Living Zen.* New York: Grove Press, Inc., 1958.

Lodge, Sir Oliver. *Man and the Universe.* New York: George Doran and Co., 1908.

Longchenpa. *Kindly Bent to Ease Us, Part Three: Wonderment.* trans. and annot. Herbert Guenther. Emeryville, Calif.: Dharma Publishing, 1976.

Lovelock, J. E. *Gaia: A New Look at Life on Earth.* London: Oxford University Press, 1979.

Lovins, Amory. *Soft Energy Paths.* New York: Harper & Row, 1977.

McDermott, Robert (ed.) *The Essential Aurobindo.* New York: Schocken Books, 1973.

McIntyre, Joan (ed.) *Mind in the Waters.* New York: Charles Scribner's Sons, 1974.

Mack, John. *Changing Models of Psychotherapy: From Psychological Conflict to Human Empowerment.* Center for Psychological Studies in the Nuclear Age, Harvard Medical School, Cambridge, Mass., June 1990.

McLuhan, T. C. *Touch the Earth: A Self-Portrait of Indian Existence.* New York: Promontory Press, 1971.

McNeil, Elton. *The Psychoses.* Englewood Cliffs, N.J.: Prentice-Hall, 1970.

Mair, Lucy. *Primitive Government.* Indiana University Press, 1977.

Majaraj, Sri Nisargadatta. *I Am That,* Part I. trans. Maurice Frydman. Bombay, India: Chetana, 1973.

Malville, J. McKim. *The Fermenting Universe.* New York: The Seabury Press, 1981.

Manjusrimitra. *Primordial Experience: An Introduction to Dzogchen Meditation,* trans. Namkhai Norbu and Kennard Limpan. Boston: Shambhala, 1987.

Margolin, Malcolm. *The Ohlone Way: Indian Life in the San Francisco–Monterey Bay Area.* Berkeley, Calif.: Heyday Books, 1978.

Marien, Michael (ed.) *Future Survey Annual.* Bethesda, Md.: World Future Society, 1979–1993. (A comprehensive source of abstracts on futures-oriented literature, published yearly since 1979.)

Markley, Oliver, and Willis Harman (eds.). *Changing Images of Man.* New York: Pergamon Press, 1982.

Marsella, Anthony J., et al. (eds.) *Culture and Self: Asian and Western Perspectives.* New York: Tavistock Publications, 1985.

Maruyama, Magoroh, and Arthur Harkins (eds.) *Cultures Beyond the Earth.* New York: Vintage Books, 1975.

Maslow, Abraham. *Toward a Psychology of Being.* New York: Van Nostrand Reinhold, 1968.

Masuda, Yoneji. *The Information Society.* Tokyo: Institute for the Information Society, 1980 (published in the United States by the World Future Society, Bethesda, Md., 1981).

Maxwell, Mary. *Human Evolution: A Philosophical Anthropology.* New York: Columbia University Press, 1984.

May, Rollo. *Psychology and the Human Dilemma.* Princeton, N.J.: D. Van Nostrand Co., 1966.

Maybury-Lewis, David. *Millennium: Tribal Wisdom and the Modern World.* New York: Viking, 1992.

Meadows, Donella et al. *The Limits to Growth.* New York: Universe Books, 1972.

———. *Beyond the Limits.* Post Mills, Vt.: Chelsea Green Publishing Co., 1992.

Mendlovitz, Saul (ed.) *On the Creation of a Just World Order.* New York: Free Press, 1975.

Merrill-Wolfe, Franklin. *Pathways Through to Space.* New York: Julian Press, 1973.

———. *The Philosophy of Consciousness Without an Object.* New York: Julian Press, 1973.

Mesarovic, Mihaljo, and Eduard Pestel. *Mankind at the Turning Point*. New York: Dutton, 1974.

Michael, Donald. *The Unprepared Society: Planning for a Precarious Future*. New York: Harper Colophon Books, 1968.

———. *On Learning to Plan and Planning to Learn*. San Francisco: Jossey-Bass Publishers, 1973.

Milbrath, Lester W. *Envisioning a Sustainable Society*. New York: SUNY Press, 1989.

Miller, Ronald S., et al. *As Above So Below: Paths to Spiritual Renewal in Daily Life*. Los Angeles: Jeremy P. Tarcher, Inc., 1992.

Mische, Patricia and Gerald. *Toward a Human World Order*. New York: Paulist Press, 1977.

Mitchell, Stephen (trans.) *Tao Te Ching: A New English Version*. New York: Harper & Row, 1988.

———. *The Gospel According to Jesus*. New York: HarperCollins, 1991.

Montville, Joseph V., "Psychoanalytic Enlightenment and the Greening of Diplomacy," *Journal of the American Psychoanalytic Association,* Vol. 37, No. 2 (1989).

Moody, Raymond. *Life After Life*. Atlanta: Mockingbird Books, 1975.

Morris, David, and Karl Hess. *Neighborhood Power*. Boston: Beacon Press, 1975.

Morse, Melvin, and Paul Perry. *Closer to the Light*. New York: Villard Books, 1990.

Muggeridge, Malcolm. *Something Beautiful for God: Mother Teresa of Calcutta*. New York: Harper & Row, 1971.

Mumford, Lewis. *The Transformations of Man*. New York: Collier Books, 1956.

Munitz, M. *Space, Time and Creation*, 2d ed. New York: Dover Publications, 1981.

Murchie, Guy. *The Music of the Spheres*. Cambridge, Mass.: The Riverside Press, 1961.

Murphy, Michael. *The Future of the Body: Explorations Into the Further Evolution of Human Nature*. Los Angeles: Jeremy P. Tarcher, 1992.

Murphy, Michael, and Rhea A. White. *The Psychic Side of Sports*. Menlo Park, Calif.: Addison-Wesley Publishing Co., 1978.

Myers, Norman (ed.) *Gaia: An Atlas of Planetary Management*. New York: Doubleday/Anchor, 1984.

———. *The Gaia Atlas of Future Worlds*. New York: Doubleday/Anchor Books, 1990.

Naisbitt, John. *Megatrends*. New York: Warner Books, 1982.

Neumann, Erich. *The Origins and History of Consciousness*. Princeton, N.J.: Bollingen Series, 1970.

Nimay, Mihail. *Book of Mirdad*. Baltimore: Penguin Books, 1971.

Nisbet, Robert. *The Quest for Community: A Study in the Ethics of Order and Freedom.* San Francisco: ICS Press, 1990; originally published in 1953.

Nisker, Wes. *Crazy Wisdom.* Berkeley: Ten Speed Press, 1990.

Norbu, Namkhai. *The Crystal and the Way of Light: Sutra, Tantra and Dzogchen,* comp. and ed. John Shane. New York: Routledge & Kegan Paul, 1986.

North, Robert C. *The World That Could Be.* New York: W. W. Norton, 1976.

Northrup, F. *The Meeting of East and West.* New York: Collier, 1968.

Novak, Michael. *A Theology for Radical Politics.* New York: Herder and Herder, 1969.

Oates, Joan. *Babylon,* rev. ed. London: Thames and Hudson, 1986.

Oates, Stephen B. *Let the Trumpets Sound: The Life of Martin Luther King, Jr.* New York: New American Library, 1982.

Ornstein, Robert, and Paul Ehrlich. *New World, New Mind: Moving Toward Conscious Evolution.* New York: Doubleday, 1989.

Osborne, Arther (ed.) *The Teachings of Ramana Maharishi.* London: Rider & Co., 1971.

Peacock, James L., and A. Thomas Kirsch. *The Human Direction: An Evolutionary Approach to Social and Cultural Anthropology.* New York: Appleton-Century-Crofts, 1970.

Peck, Scott. *The Road Less Traveled.* New York: Simon & Schuster, 1978.

Pelton, Joseph N. "The Globalization of Universal Telecommunications Services," *Universal Telephone Service: Ready for the 21st Century?* Queenstown, Md.: Aspen Inst., 1991.

Peratt, Anthony L. "Plasma Cosmology," *Sky & Telescope* (February, 1992).

Pfeiffer, John. *The Creative Explosion: An Inquiry into the Origins of Art and Religion.* Ithaca, N.Y.: Cornell University Press, 1982.

Polak, Fred. *The Image of the Future,* trans. Elise Boulding. San Francisco: Jossey-Bass, Inc., 1973.

Prosterman, Roy L. *Surviving to 3000: An Introduction to the Study of Lethal Conflict.* Belmont, Calif.: Duxbury Press, 1972.

Puthoff, Harold, and Russell Targ. "A Perceptual Channel for Information Transfer Over Kilometer Distances: Historical Perspective and Recent Research," *Proceedings of the IEEE,* Vol. 64, No. 3 (March 1976).

Puthoff, Hal. "Why Atoms Don't Collapse," *New Scientist* (July 1987).

Putnam, John. "The Search for Modern Humans," *National Geographic,* Vol. 174, No. 4 (October 1988).

Rader, Melvin. *The Enduring Questions: Main Problems of Philosophy.* New York: Henry Holt & Co., 1956.

Radhakrishnan, S. *Eastern Religions and Western Thought,* 2nd ed. London: Oxford University Press, 1940.

———. *East and West.* New York: Harper & Brothers, 1956.

Ram Dass. *Journey of Awakening: A Meditator's Guidebook*. New York: Bantam Books, 1978.

Ramana Maharishi, Sri. *The Teachings of Ramana Maharishi*, ed. Arthur Osborne. London: Rider & Co., 1962, 1971.

Rangdrol, Tsele Natsok. *The Mirror of Mindfulness: The Cycle of the Four Bardos*, trans. E. Kunsang. Boston: Shambhala Press, 1989.

Ray, Benjamin C. *African Religions*. Englewood Cliffs, N.J.: Prentice-Hall, 1976.

Redfield, Robert. *The Primitive World and Its Transformations*. Ithaca, N.Y.: Cornell University Press, 1953.

———. *The Little Community and Peasant Society and Culture*. Chicago: The University of Chicago Press, 1960.

Regis, Edward Jr. (ed.) *Extraterrestrials: Science and Alien Intelligence*. New York: Cambridge University Press, 1985.

Register, Richard. *Ecocity Berkeley: Building Cities for a Healthy Future*. Berkeley: North Atlantic Books, 1987.

Rima, I. H. *Development of Economic Analysis*. Homewood, Ill.: R. D. Irwin Co., 1967.

Ring, Kenneth. *Life at Death*. New York: Morrow/Quill, 1982.

Robbins, John. *Diet for a New America*. Walpole, N.H.: Stillpoint Publishing, 1987.

Robinson, James (ed.) *Nag Hammadi Library*, 3rd ed. San Francisco: Harper & Row, 1988.

Rogers, Carl. *Carl Rogers on Personal Power*. Great Britain: Constable, 1978.

Roszak, Theodore. *Person/Planet*. New York: Anchor Press/Doubleday, 1978.

———. *The Voice of the Earth*. New York: Simon & Schuster, 1992.

Rucker, R. *Geometry, Relativity, and the Fourth Dimension*. New York: Dover Publications, 1977.

Russell, Peter. *The Global Brain: Speculations on the Evolutionary Leap to Planetary Consciousness*. Los Angeles: J. P. Tarcher, Inc., 1983.

———. *The White Hole in Time*. San Francisco: HarperSanFrancisco, 1992.

Saddhatissa, H. *Buddhist Ethics*. New York: George Braziller, 1970.

Sagan, Carl. *The Dragons of Eden*. New York: Random House, 1977.

———. *Cosmos*. New York: Book Club Associates, 1980.

Sagan, Carl, and Ann Druyan. *Shadows of Forgotten Ancestors*. New York: Random House, 1992.

Sagan, Carl, and I. S. Shklovskii. *Intelligent Life in the Universe*. San Francisco: Holden-Day, Inc., 1966.

Sahtouris, Elisabeth. *Gaia: The Human Journey from Chaos to Cosmos*. New York: Simon & Schuster/Pocket Books, 1989.

Satprem. *Sri Aurobindo, or The Adventure of Consciousness*. Pondicherry, India: Sri Aurobindo Society, 1970.

Sauer, Carl. *Agricultural Origins and Dispersals.* New York: American Geographical Society, 1952. Republished as: *Seeds, Spades, Hearths, and Herds.* Cambridge, Mass.: MIT Press, 1969.

Schaef, Anne Wilson. *When Society Becomes an Addict.* San Francisco: Harper & Row, 1987.

Schell, Jonathan. *The Fate of the Earth.* New York: Alfred A. Knopf, 1982.

Schindler, Craig, and Gary Lapid. *The Great Turning.* Santa Fe, N.M.: Bear & Co., 1989.

Schmookler, Andrew Bard. *The Parable of the Tribes: The Problem of Power in Social Evolution.* Berkeley: University of California Press, 1984.

Schumacher, E. F. *A Guide for the Perplexed.* San Francisco: Harper & Row, 1977.

Schwenk, Theodor. *Sensitive Chaos: The Creation of Flowing Forms in Water and Air,* trans. Olive Wicher and Johanna Wrigley. London: Rudolf Steiner Press, 1965.

Sciama, D. W. *The Unity of the Universe.* New York: Doubleday, 1961.

Sekida, Katsuki. *Zen Training.* New York: Weatherhill, 1975.

Sheldrake, Rupert. *A New Science of Life: The Hypothesis of Formative Causation.* Los Angeles: J. P. Tarcher, 1981.

Shi, David. *The Simple Life.* New York: Oxford University Press, 1985.

Shlain, Leonard. *Art and Physics.* New York: William Morrow, 1991.

Shostak, Marjorie. *Nisa: The Life and Words of a !Kung Woman.* New York: Vintage Books, 1983.

Singh, J. *Great Ideas and Theories of Modern Cosmology.* New York: Dover Publications, 1961.

Sklar, Lawrence. *Space, Time and Spacetime.* Berkeley: University of California Press, 1976.

Slaton, Christa. *Televote: Expanding Citizen Participation in the Quantum Age.* New York: Praeger, 1992.

Smith, Huston. *The Religions of Mankind.* New York: Harper & Row, 1958.

Sogyal Rinpoche. *The Tibetan Book of Living and Dying.* San Francisco: HarperSanFrancisco, 1992.

Sorokin, Pitirim A. *The Ways and Power of Love.* Chicago: The Beacon Press, 1954.

Spengler, Oswald. *The Decline of the West,* Vol. I. New York: Knopf, 1926.

Spretnak, Charlene (ed.) *The Politics of Women's Spirituality.* New York: Anchor Books, 1982.

Sproul, Barbara C. *Primal Myths.* San Francisco: Harper & Row, 1979.

Stapledon, Olaf. *Star Maker.* New York: Dover Publications, 1937.

Stavrianos, L. S. *The Promise of the Coming Dark Age.* San Francisco: W. H. Freeman, 1976.

Stevens, Peter S. *Patterns in Nature.* Boston: Little, Brown and Co., 1974.

Stringer, Christopher. "The Emergence of Modern Humans," *Scientific American* (December, 1990).

Stromberg, Gustaf. *The Soul of the Universe*. North Hollywood, Calif.: Educational Research Institute, 1940 and 1965.

Suzuki, D. T. *Mysticism: Christian and Buddhist*. New York: Macmillan, 1957.

———. *Outlines of Mahayana Buddhism*. New York: Schocken Books, 1963.

———. *Zen and Japanese Culture*. Princeton, N.J.: Princeton University Press, 1970.

Swimme, Brian. *The Universe Is a Green Dragon: A Cosmic Creation Story*. Santa Fe, N.M.: Bear & Co., 1985.

Swimme, Brian, and Thomas Berry. *The Universe Story*. San Francisco: Harper, 1992.

Targ, Russell, and Harold Puthoff. *Mindreach: Scientists Look at Psychic Ability*. New York: Delacorte Press, 1977.

Tarnas, Richard. *The Passion of the Western Mind*. New York: Harmony Books, 1991.

Tarthang Tulku. *Time, Space and Knowledge*. Calif.: Dharma Publishing, 1977.

Tavris, Carol. *The Mismeasure of Woman*. New York: Simon & Schuster, 1992.

Taylor, E., & Wheeler, J. *Spacetime Physics*. San Francisco: W. H. Freeman, 1966.

Teilhard de Chardin. *The Phenomenon of Man*. New York: Harper Torchbooks, 1965.

———. *The Future of Man*. New York: Harper & Row, 1964.

Thera, Nyanaponika. *The Heart of Buddhist Meditation*. London: Rider, 1972.

Thomas, Lewis. *The Fragile Species: Notes of an Earth Watcher*. New York: Macmillan, 1992.

Thurman, Robert (trans.) *The Holy Teachings of Vimalakirti: A Mahayana Scripture*. University Park: Pennsylvania State University Press, 1976.

Toffler, Alvin. *The Third Wave*. New York: Bantam Books, 1981.

Tough, Allen. *Crucial Questions About the Future*. Lanham, Md.: University Press of America, 1991.

Toynbee, Arnold. *Civilization on Trial*. New York: Oxford University Press, 1948.

———. *A Study of History*. Abridgement of Vols. I–VI by D. C. Somervell. New York: Oxford University Press, 1947; abridgement of Vols. VII–X, 1957.

———. *An Historian's Approach to Religion*. New York: Oxford University Press, 1956.

———. *Surviving the Future*. New York: Oxford University Press, 1971.

———. *A Study of History*. rev. and abridged by Arnold Toynbee and Jane Caplan. New York: Weathervane Books, 1972.

Trungpa, Chögyam. *Cutting Through Spiritual Materialism.* Berkeley Calif.: Shambhala, 1973.

———. *The Myth of Freedom.* Berkeley, Calif.: Shambhala, 1976.

———. (ed.) *Garuda IV: The Foundations of Mindfulness.* Berkeley, Calif.: Shambhala, 1976.

Umen, Samuel. *The World of the Mystic.* New York: Philosophical Library, 1988.

Underhill, Evelyn. *Mysticism.* New York: Meridian Books, 1955.

Vallee, Jacques. *Dimensions.* New York: Contemporary Books, 1988.

VandenBroeck, Goldian (ed.) *Less Is More.* New York: Colophon Books, 1978.

Vaughan, Frances. *Awakening Intuition.* New York: Doubleday/Anchor, 1979.

von Franz, Marie-Louise. *Time: Rhythm and Repose.* New York: Thames and Hudson, 1978.

Wagar, Warren. *Building the City of Man: Outlines of a World Civilization.* New York: Grossman Publishers, 1971.

———. *A Short History of the Future.* Chicago: University of Chicago Press, 1989.

Walsh, Roger. *Staying Alive: The Psychology of Human Survival.* Boulder, Colo.: Shambhala/New Science Library, 1984.

———. *The Spirit of Shamanism.* Los Angeles: Jeremy P. Tarcher, Inc., 1990.

Walsh, Roger, and Deane Shapiro. *Beyond Health and Normality: Explorations of Exceptional Psychological Well-being.* New York: Van Nostrand Reinhold Co., 1983.

Walsh, Roger, and Frances Vaughan. *Beyond Ego: Transpersonal Dimensions in Psychology.* Los Angeles: J. P. Tarcher, Inc., 1980.

Ward, Barbara. *The Interplay of East and West.* New York: W. W. Norton & Co., 1962.

Watts, Alan. *The Spirit of Zen.* New York: Grove Press, Inc., 1958.

Weber, Renee. *Dialogues with Scientists and Sages.* New York: Routledge & Kegan Paul, 1986.

———. "The Good, the True, and the Beautiful: Are They Attributes of the Universe?" *Main Currents in Modern Thought.* New York: Center for Integrative Education, Retrospective Issue, 1975.

Wiener, Norbert. *The Human Use of Human Beings.* New York: Avon Books, 1954.

Welwood, John. "On Psychological Space," *Journal of Transpersonal Psychology,* Vol. 9., No. 2., 1977.

——— (ed.) *Ordinary Magic: Everyday Life as Spiritual Path.* Boston: Shambhala, 1992.

Wenke, Robert J. *Patterns in Prehistory: Humankind's First Three Million Years.* 2nd ed. New York: Oxford University Press, 1984.

Wesson, Robert. *Cosmos and Metacosmos*. La Salle, Ill.: Open Court, 1989.

White, Frank. *The Overview Effect: Space Exploration and Human Evolution*. Boston: Houghton Mifflin Co., 1987.

White, John (ed.) *The Highest State of Consciousness*. New York: Doubleday/Anchor Books, 1972.

———. *The Meeting of Science and Spirit*. New York: Paragon House, 1990.

White, Randall. *Dark Caves, Bright Visions*. New York: W. W. Norton & Co., 1986.

Whitehead, Alfred North. *Process and Reality*. Corrected ed. New York: Macmillan Publishing/Free Press, 1978.

Whitrow, G. J. *The Natural Philosophy of Time*. 2nd ed. Oxford, Eng.: Clarendon Press, 1980.

Wilber, Ken. *The Spectrum of Consciousness*. Wheaton, Ill.: Theosophical Publishing House, 1977.

———. *The Atman Project: A Transpersonal View of Human Development*. Wheaton, Ill.: Theosophical Publishing House, 1980.

———. *Up from Eden*. New York: Anchor Press/Doubleday, 1981.

———. *Eye to Eye*. New York: Anchor Press/Doubleday, 1983.

———. *Quantum Questions*. Boulder, Colo.: Shambhala, 1984.

Wilber, Ken, and Jack Engler and Daniel Brown. *Transformations of Consciousness: Conventional and Contemplative Perspectives on Development*. Boston: Shambhala, 1986.

Winkelman, Michael. "The Evolution of Consciousness: An Essay Review of *Up from Eden* (Wilber, 1981)," *Anthropology of Consciousness* (October–December 1990).

World Atlas of Archaeology. New York: Portland House, 1985.

Young, Arthur, M. *The Reflexive Universe*. San Francisco: Robert Briggs Assoc. and Delacorte Press, 1976.

Young, Louise B. (ed.) *The Mystery of Matter*. New York: Oxford University Press, 1965.

———. *The Unfinished Universe*. New York: Simon & Schuster, 1986.

———. "Easter Island: Scary Parable," *World Monitor* (August 1991).

Zihlman, Adrienne L. "Woman the Gatherer: The Role of Women in Early Hominid Evolution," in *Gender and Anthropology*, ed. Sandra Morgen. Washington, D.C.: American Anthropological Association, 1989.

Zimmer, Heinrich. *Myths and Symbols in Indian Art and Civilization*, ed. Joseph Campbell. Princeton, N.J.: Princeton University Press, Bollingen Series, 1972.

Zur, Ofer. "The Psychohistory of Warfare," *Journal of Peace Research*, Vol. 24, No. 2, 1987.

INDEX

Page numbers in *italics* refer to illustrations.